F

Andrew Root journalist in the county since 1973. He is currently a chief sub-editor with the Kent Messenger Group and is also the author of *A Mosaic History of Higham*, his home village. Mr Rootes is married to a probation officer and lives in Canterbury.

Andrew Rootes

Front Line County

Kent at War, 1939–45

Robert Hale Ltd

First published in Great Britain 1980
Reprinted 1982
First paperback edition 1988

Robert Hale Limited
Clerkenwell House
Clerkenwell Green
London EC1R 0HT

British Library Cataloguing in Publication Data
Rootes, Andrew
  Front line county: Kent at war, 1939–45.
  1. Kent. Bombing by Germany. Luftwaffe,
  1940–1945
  I. Title
  940.54'21

ISBN 0-7091-8321-6 (hardback)
ISBN 0-7090-3473-3 (paperback)

Printed in Great Britain by
St Edmundsbury Press Limited,
Bury St Edmunds, Suffolk. Bound by
Woolnough Bookbinders

Contents

Illustrations

Acknowledgements

I am indebted to Lieutenant-Colonel Norman Field, of Bilting, who was kind enough to talk to me on several occasions about the Auxiliary Units he once led in Kent.

My thanks are also due to the following publishers for permission to quote from their books: Headley Brothers for *Though the Streets Burn*, by Catherine Williamson; Pan Books for *Operation Sealion*, by Peter Fleming; Hutchinson Publishing Group Ltd for *Kentish Fire*, by Hubert S. Banner; Michael Joseph Ltd for *Enemy Coast Ahead*, by Guy Gibson; and Batsford Ltd for *Canterbury*, by William Townsend.

I am also grateful to the *Kent Messenger* Group, which not only allowed me to quote from various of its contemporary publications but also provided all the photographs in this book.

But my special thanks are reserved for Ros, who kept doing the washing-up when it was really my turn and somehow found time to check the manuscript for typing mistakes.

FOR ROS
WITH LOVE
AND FOR
MY PARENTS

Introduction

The future of too many new buildings in too many towns in Kent began when the bombs started falling. And that was nearly half a century ago. New generations have the luxury of taking for granted the shops and the houses that grew out of the ruins – ruins which told clearly of the havoc wreaked by enemy raids. But other legacies of war were not so visible.

Spitfire pilots who flew out of Manston and never came back; ARP wardens who were on duty in the wrong place at the wrong time; children killed by a flying bomb in the 'safety' of rural Kent. All these tragedies, and many others, scarred the lives of families, widows and parents in a way they could never forget.

The ordinary people caught in this war wanted nothing more, probably, than to live ordinary lives until the peace came. But nearly 3,000 of them never made it. In a way, the shops and houses that rose from the bomb-sites where buddleia once grew are memorials to their fate.

And perhaps they should also be reminders that despite the Dunkirk spirit, the quiet heroism and the humour in adversity that doubtless existed (at least, among some of the people, some of the time) this war, like all wars, was mostly about innocent people being caught in a conflict not of their making.

Whether they were in uniform or out, nearly half a century ago they shared six years that new generations know only from history books. This, at least, is part of that history. It is a story of war on the home front in a county that faced the enemy across a small stretch of water that was no barrier to shells or aircraft or flying bombs or V2s. But it was a big enough barrier when it mattered most, a barrier to invasion.

If it had not been, the history in this book would be very different.

Andrew Rootes
Canterbury 1988

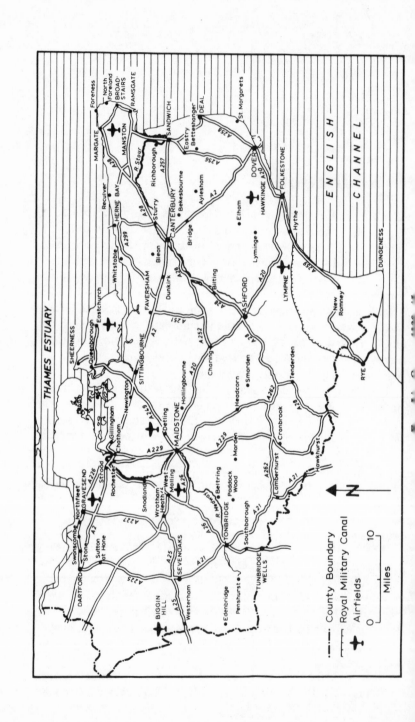

THAMES ESTUARY

ENGLISH CHANNEL

N

County Boundary
Royal Military Canal
Airfields

0   10
Miles

1. The Phoney Peace

In September 1935 a German couple moved into a bungalow in Broadstairs. The man described himself as a lawyer-novelist from Hamburg, and the pretty young girl with him he said was his niece. They rented the bungalow—'Havelock' in Stanley Road—from 11th September to 26th October. It would be a nice place in which to take a break by the sea on their motorcycle tour of England, they said. But the couple left the place on 24th October and never returned. The owner eventually called the police, who found that the man and his 'niece' were not what they seemed. There, in the clothing the man had left behind, was a sketch of the RAF airfield at Manston. The man was a German spy.

Dr Hermann Goertz was a finely built man in his forties, with two sabre-marks on his left cheek as the result of duelling. He had landed at Harwich on 29th August 1935 and had not been in England long before he was joined by Marianne Emig, a nineteen-year-old German girl who had arrived in England a few weeks earlier. He bought a powerful motorcycle and travelled round the country, with Marianne riding pillion, to wherever RAF airfields could be found. Dr Goertz would set up an easel nearby and pretend to be landscape-painting—although really he would be sketching the layout of the airfields and their defences.

They moved to Broadstairs from Mildenhall in Suffolk in September to begin their six-week stay in the bungalow, but shortly before the end of their tenancy there, they moved out. The owner of the bungalow, Mrs Florence Johnson, received a telegram from Dr Goertz in Dover saying they had gone to Germany for a few days; it asked her to take care of his 'combination' and photo. A postcard from Ostend the following day asked her to look after his 'bicycle combination'. Mrs Johnson went to check the inventory at the bungalow when the couple did not return at the end of the tenancy. She found the photo and camera but thought that the motorcycle had been stolen, because she could not find it, and called the police. The bungalow was searched by Special Branch officers, who found a pair of soiled white dungarees, which, it was realized, was what Dr Goertz meant by 'combination'. A small camera was found in one pocket of the dungarees; its developed film revealed pictures, about the size of stamps, of airfields and aircraft. They also found a sketch of nearby Manston airfield with various points explained by marginal notes. It was enough evidence for the police to issue a warrant for his arrest, should he ever return to Britain.

He did come back, but alone, landing at Harwich from the Hook of Holland on 8th November that year. He was arrested immediately and appeared in court at Margate later in the month. Dr Goertz, aged forty-five, was charged there with making a sketch-plan or note of Manston RAF station likely to be of use to an enemy, and with conspiring with Marianne Emig to commit offences against the Official Secrets Acts. When he was tried at the Old Bailey, he pleaded 'not guilty' and said he had come to England to get material for a novel. He was sentenced to four years in prison and taken to Maidstone jail, where he served his sentence; with remission, he returned to Germany a few months before war was declared.

But the spying career of Dr Goertz did not end there. He met several members of the IRA while in Maidstone prison, and in early May 1940 he dropped by parachute into Ireland in connection with a possible IRA-backed German invasion of the country. He was arrested in Dublin in November 1941 and interned for the rest of the war. Dr Goertz poisoned himself on 23rd May 1947, when told he was to be repatriated to Germany. The reason for his suicide is not known.

The period up to the outbreak of the war has been described as 'the phoney peace', because the troubled situation in Europe in the 1930s was such that many people thought war was inevitable long before it actually began. Hitler had come to power in 1933, and in April 1935 had re-introduced conscription and launched a re-armament programme. As early as the summer of 1935, therefore, the British government asked local authorities to prepare air-raid precaution plans. A total of 1,413 people in Britain had been killed by bombs from zeppelins and aircraft in the First World War and no one doubted that raids in a future war would be even more devastating. In October, Italy attacked Ethiopia.

The German anti-Jewish sentiment had found some supporters in

Kent. Five Blackshirts were fined a total of £14 by Margate magistrates in March 1936 for Jew-baiting in the town. The court heard that
on the night of 26th February a number of shop-windows had had the
word 'Jew' painted across them. All five men were present or past
members of the British Union of Fascists. The magistrates said: "It is
the sort of conduct which we are unaccustomed to in Margate, and we
have no intention of allowing it to grow."

The first steps towards tackling air-raid problems, particularly gas,
were taken in Kent at the beginning of March 1936. Sixty men and
forty women, all members of St John Ambulance Brigade units in
West Kent, spent all Sunday on an intensive training course in
anti-gas measures in the Corn Exchange at Maidstone. They were
qualifying as instructors and would in turn train hundreds of other
first-aiders.

March was also the month Hitler's forces began to occupy the
'demilitarized' Rhineland.

By the beginning of June 1936 the local authorities in Kent were
studying the circular on air-raid precautions issued by the county
council; some of the authorities were upset by the vagueness of the
circular, but one thing that did emerge was that Ramsgate was to
become the centre of an intensive anti-gas movement in East Kent at
the town's police station. All the authorities were asked to submit
their views on the proposals in the circular to the county council in
time for a conference on the subject in Maidstone on 13th July. This
meeting—held in the month in which the Spanish Civil War began—
took place in the Sessions House. 1936 was the year the Italians used
poison gas in their attacks in Ethiopia.

The town council in Margate approved an expenditure of £1,000 on
air-raid precautions in January 1937, although their decision did not
meet with the approval of everyone. Councillor F. Mellanby said:
"We have accepted the inevitability of war with as much fatalism as a
primitive people. If half the money spent on preparations for war had
been spent on preparations for peace, we should not be discussing
these measures now." Many people thought differently, however: in
February and March the British Empire Union carried out a recruit-
ing campaign for all the armed forces throughout Kent. The Observer
Corps, the plane-spotters who would pass information about enemy
raiders to the RAF and the ARP department, were meanwhile having
a supper at Ashford, at which Mr J. Day, the controller from Maidstone, said: "The next war—should it come—is bound to be in the air.

It is ghastly to think to what it might attain, but if the Air Force is to be equipped, as it looks as if it is going to be, then we may have little fear of being invaded." His words were, it turned out, prophetic.

The effects of the Spanish Civil War were being seen in Kent by that year. Sixty Basque children, aged from five to twelve, arrived in Tunbridge Wells at the beginning of June to seek refuge from the horrors of war. They were quartered at Rusthall Beacon, a large house near the Common, and were received by an army of willing helpers, including several interpreters. Two Spanish teachers and a mother travelled with the youngsters. It was, for many women in Kent reading of these evacuees, a taste of things to come.

Districts in Kent were continuing to work out their ARP plans, which—under the ARP Act introduced that year—they were formally required to submit for government approval.

Mr Geoffrey Lloyd, the Under-Secretary of State for the Home Office, came to Ashford Corn Exchange in March 1938 to talk about government policy and air-raid precautions. Many of the local authorities in Kent, he said, had shown admirable ingenuity and initiative. Deal had started early and had already held four air-raid exercises; Ramsgate had opened one of the earliest and best local anti-gas schools; Dover was fitting out caves as raid-shelters; Margate had changed some disused stables to a decontamination centre; and Gravesend had an excellent ARP school and had already trained five thousand members of the public in methods of gas-proofing refuge-rooms in their homes. The authorities in Ashford had done their part, he said, but the town needed four times as many volunteers as it had already. They had not yet received enough support from the people.

In March 1938 the German armies overran Austria and proclaimed it part of the German Reich.

Flight Lieutenant Eardley Wilmot, of the Home Office ARP Department, told an ARP meeting in Ashford at the beginning of April: "We are not making the people war-minded by telling them how to wear a respirator or how to gasproof a room any more than it can be said that steamship companies make their passengers wreck-minded by having lifeboat drill." And the Archbishop of Canterbury said in the *Canterbury Diocesan Gazette* for the month: "I have been requested and willingly consent to ask the clergy to encourage their parishioners to co-operate with the local authorities in such plans as may be put before them to make preparations for any possibility of an attack from the air. Even if there is nothing more than a possibility, it is our duty to be ready for it."

People in the Medway towns got their first taste of what an air-raid might be like at the end of May 1938 when a massive exercise was carried out in the area. Aircraft from Manston 'bombed' and 'machine-gunned' towns in the Thames Estuary on Tuesday 31st May in the biggest ARP test yet held in this country. The raids took place between 2pm and 4pm and again between 10pm and midnight in the 400 square miles of the Nore Command, including the Medway area. 'Bombs' fell on Rochester bridge, Gillingham Park, the town halls of Chatham, Faversham and Sittingbourne, and the railway station at Sheerness. About two thousand volunteers from the Medway area took part in the test, and children were given a half-day holiday so that their schools could be used as first-aid centres. The hours of film-shows were altered so that audiences could be out by 10pm. Imaginary fires caused by 'bombs' at Sittingbourne and Milton were dealt with by the fire brigade. People there took cover in the daylight raid, and patrols walked the streets looking for 'casualties'. Sirens, placed in church towers at Gillingham, warned of the raiders.

Air-raid precautions had been discussed in some form or other at county level for three years by then, but many people in Kent were still not sure what they should do in the event of a bombing attack. The *Kentish Express* newspaper spoke to 118 people across the county in September 1938 about these precautions—and most people admitted they had little idea of what to do. A clerk from Rochester said: "I have not been given any instructions. I should certainly not stop in the town if war was declared. My wife and I are keen on camping, and we should live in a tent on Burnham Downs until things died down." A householder from Saltwood, near Folkestone, said: "I have received no instructions whatever. If a raid occurred, I should send all my household staff into the woods with the orders to scatter." A housewife from Chatham, whose husband had volunteered for ARP work, said: "I wasn't here during the last war—and I hope I'm not in the next." A family man from Godmersham, near Ashford, said: "We have had masks fitted, but that is all. No one is very interested round here." And a man from Gravesend said: "I don't think people worry about it."

They had plenty to worry about later that month when it looked for a while as though Britain might go to war over Czechoslovakia. The ARP services were mobilized on 25th September; cellars and basements were requisitioned for air-raid shelters; and the government hastily published plans for the evacuation of two million people from London on 29th September. A total of 38 million gas-masks were issued to men, women and children—although not to babies. But by 30th September the crisis was over. Chamberlain had given in to Hitler's claim on the Sudetenland in Czechoslovakia. The rest of that country was taken over by Germany in March 1939. In the same month, Britain promised to support Poland in the event of a German invasion. Military conscription was introduced in Britain in April 1939.

Kent was one of fifteen counties in southern England to take part in a test black-out over the Saturday night and Sunday morning of 8th–9th July 1939. Sirens sounded at intervals between 10pm and 10.20pm, and then the incidents arranged as an exercise by each local authority began. Families screened their windows; motorists drove with only their sidelights on; road beacons were covered with sacks, and traffic lights had hoods fitted to deflect the light downwards. The test lost something of its realism because bad weather caused the RAF to call off its part in the exercise. But all the other tests passed without a hitch—or almost. When the chief warden at Rolvenden was told that his post had been bombed and that he had received head injuries affecting his reason, his protests were ignored as delusions, and, in spite of his resistance, he was strapped to a stretcher and taken to the casualty station. All the lights were switched out at a dinner in Ramsgate just as Captain H. Balfour, the Under-Secretary of State for Air, rose to speak. A 'corpse' rang up Margate police station to report that his post had been blown up by a bomb, killing everyone inside. And another message said: "A bomb has fallen on the circus, killing an elephant. Send the ambulance." When a length of iron piping was thrown at a fire-engine as it was passing through Margate, although no one was injured, police were rushed to the scene in patrol cars, and it was thought at first that the IRA might be involved. The following month, on 9th–10th August, an even greater trial black-out was held in twenty-six counties, including London.

Some of the many Jewish refugees who fled Hitler's Europe in 1939 found themselves staying at Richborough Camp, near Sandwich. The Central Council for Jewish Refugees asked the British government for a transit camp where people could wait before emigrating. About a hundred craftsmen arrived at the camp in February 1939 to make it ready for people fleeing from Germany, Austria and Czechoslovakia. There were a thousand men in the camp by May, and 3,500 by the outbreak of war. Most of them were Jews, but several hundred were 'non-Aryan' Christians and wives brought over as domestic workers for British homes.

About 2,500 of the refugees volunteered for National Service shortly before war was declared, and in the last week of peace some of them could be found filling sandbags for the protection of Sandwich. Many of them became part of a special formation of the Royal Pioneer Corps for building and supply-work behind the lines, and the camp became a training depot for those alien Pioneer companies. Five companies of about three hundred men each were formed quickly and sent to France early in 1940. The several hundred civilian men left behind filled a variety of posts—such as cooks, tailors and carpenters —as part of the training-centre. The centre was moved in the summer of 1940 when the Admiralty took over the camp. By this time many of the aliens had been distributed throughout the infantry, artillery, tank and parachute regiments, the commandos, the RAF and the Navy. The camp was later used to build part of the Mulberry harbours for D-Day. High walls screened the workshops from the road then, and buses travelling nearby had their windows blacked out until after the Allied landings.

British negotiations with Russia broke down on 21st August, and the German Foreign Minister was invited to Moscow on the same day. On 22nd August the British government announced that it stood by its promise to Poland. The Nazi-Soviet pact was signed on 23rd August. The Emergency Powers (Defence) Act was passed on 24th August, and on the same day military reservists were called up and the ARP services warned to stand ready.

It was about that time that a mysterious figure disappeared from East Kent only shortly before police went to arrest him. He was Dr Albert Tester (his title was legal and not medical) who had been sent to Kent by the Germans years before the outbreak of war and was thought to be a Gestapo chief who would have had the power of life and death over people in Kent in the event of a successful German invasion. He lived for a while with his wife and five children in a clifftop mansion called 'Naldera', immediately below the North Foreland lighthouse, but his family returned to Germany during the summer of 1939. A few days before war began, the authorities decided to detain Dr Tester, but police who went to arrest him found the house deserted and in darkness. He is thought to have escaped by rowing out to a submarine one night in a boat from the foot of the North Foreland cliffs. Dr Tester was heard of again in Rumania in 1944, when he was surrounded by advancing Russians at a place called 'Castle Mintia'. He was shot and killed when his car swerved and plunged into a ditch after crashing through a road-barrier. A positive identification of the doctor was not made until more than a year after his death, when the Russians, at the request of Britain, exhumed his body; confirmation of his identity came from the dental charts of Ramsgate dentist Brigadier J. Morley Stebbings, who had treated Dr Tester when he lived at Broadstairs.

The country, meanwhile, was teetering on the brink of war. Hundreds of people in West Malling rushed into the streets a few days before war began when they mistook a 4am fire-siren for an air-raid warning. A holiday-maker from Maidstone set off for his week at the seaside with a placard on his car saying: "Half a mo', Hitler—let's have our holiday first." Hop-pickers at Beltring practised working with their gas-masks on. An appeal for donors at the Blood Transfusion Centre in Maidstone brought in five thousand offers. And priceless thirteenth- and fourteenth- century stained-glass windows were removed from Canterbury Cathedral as a precaution— necessary, as it turned out—against bomb damage. But another precaution taken at the cathedral landed the Dean, the Rev. Hewlett Johnson, in hot water: loaded lorries were allowed to drive through the Great West Door of the cathedral to drop thousands of tons of earth in the nave for sandbags. This, some people thought, was taking things too far.

German troops invaded Poland on 1st September. The black-out began on that day, and one Ramsgate store alone sold between 4,000 and 5,000 yards of black curtain-material in less than twenty-four hours. But more ominous than that was the evacuation from London and the Medway towns, which also began on 1 September. Thousands of children, teachers, mothers, invalids and blind people began moving to reception-areas in Kent. The evacuation from the Medway area lasted two days, and that from London three. One of the more unusual victims of evacuation was Billingsgate fish-market—which was decentralized and sent to different towns throughout the country. One section was moved to a garage in Maidstone, where local people were to be found staring at the strange sight of porters carrying boxes on their heads. 'Wide boys' were attracted to the scene, slipping the odd pound note inside a newspaper in return for their order. But the market moved on the following year when the Battle of Britain turned Maidstone into a high-risk area.

At 11am on Sunday 3rd September the British ultimatum to Germany expired. Chamberlain came on the radio at 11.15am and told the nation that his work for peace had failed. The ten-year-old daughter of the vicar at a village near Canterbury went into the church

in mid-service and walked up the aisle to break the news to her father.
The country was at war.

2. The Phoney War

The first air-raid warning sounded in Kent and other parts of the country within a few minutes of Chamberlain's broadcast. But the All Clear came shortly afterwards. The warning had been given because of an approaching unidentified aircraft, which was soon found to be a friendly civil plane flying in from France. A similar false alarm occurred the following morning.

It was not until the morning of Wednesday 6th September that the Germans seemed to be sending over their first attacking force, when the radar station near Southend found itself plotting about two hundred aircraft heading towards the Thames Estuary from the east. Bomber and Coastal Commands reported that they had no aircraft operating in that area—so Fighter Command labelled the force as hostile and issued a preliminary warning at 6.45am. By 6.50am the radar indicated that the aircraft were flying up the Thames for an apparent mass attack on London. The air-raid warning sirens sounded for the third time in the war. Fighters from different squadrons were sent to meet the raiders shortly after the anti-aircraft guns at Clacton said they were firing at enemy twin-engined aircraft. The enemy was sighted; the battle in the skies began, and the casualties started to mount. The only problem was that no enemy aircraft happened to be in the area at the time; a technical fault in the radar had led the RAF to intercept itself. The twin-engined aircraft fired at by the gunners were Blenheim fighters, one of which was shot down; and the 'enemy' planes attacked by one squadron were the Hurricanes of another, two of which were shot down. One of those Hurricane pilots was killed. The anti-aircraft guns at Chatham had also fired at the fighters in this combat, which became known as 'The Battle of Barking Creek'.

Millionaire Arthur Nash, aged seventy-four, of Park Road, Ramsgate, had meanwhile become one of the first people in the country to be prosecuted for breaking the black-out law. He appeared at the local court only a few days after the outbreak of war on two charges of "failing to obscure lights at his residence, in contravention of light restrictions". A hostile crowd gathered outside his house, which had unscreened upstairs windows, and threatened on one occasion to throw stones from the garden rockery at them. The chairman of the bench said: "Personally it is quite immaterial to me whether you wish to endanger your own life, but your carelessness in endangering other persons is nothing less than brutal. The bench are determined to see that the population are protected. If you are brought here on future similar charges we will take certain steps which you will not like." He was fined £15.

By mid-November more and more people were beginning to appear in police courts all over the county for allowing lights to show at windows and doors during black-out hours. A florist from Dover was fined 10 shillings for showing a light at his shop window; he said he had spent hours blacking out the window and must have accidentally touched an electric switch at his elbow. The licensee at the New Inn at Murston, Sittingbourne, was fined £3 and ordered to pay 10 shillings costs for failing to screen his windows effectively; the police said he had been warned twice. The licensee of the Nevill Arms Hotel at Tunbridge Wells, who was an ARP warden, was also ordered to pay four shillings costs for an offence under the regulations. And a special constable at Herne Bay borrowed a ladder from the fire-station to break a window in Mortimer Street and put out a light showing there; the manager of the Timothy White and Taylor shop concerned was fined £3. The police were, it seemed, prepared to go to all lengths to enforce these lighting restrictions. In at least one case in Kent the offending light was inaccessible—so the police officer concerned simply got a rifle and put out the light with his first shot.

The black-out was not only inconvenient—it could also be dangerous. Casualties from incidents in the dark continued to mount throughout the war. A man of seventy-four was killed while crossing the A20 at Hothfield, near Ashford, shortly before 9pm on 15th December when he was knocked down by one car and run over by another; the cars would have been driving with masked headlights. Another man, this time aged seventy-eight, was killed on 17th December at Folkestone when he was also knocked down by a car while crossing the road at night. It was, said the coroner at his inquest, another of those black-out fatalities.

The outbreak of war had failed to induce a spirit of patriotism in everyone. Fascists were believed to have been responsible for disfiguring the war memorial in the Butter Market at Canterbury. Someone had painted 'Stop This War' in blue paint on the memorial and had added the Fascist symbol on the pavement. This daubing, discovered on Saturday 11th November, was scrubbed off by the women's section of the British Legion in time for the ceremony of wreath laying the following day.

Several incidents marred the otherwise quiet start to the war in Kent. A pilot landing at Biggin Hill decapitated the driver of a motor-mower with the wing of his Hurricane—the pilot, taxi-ing to a halt, saw the mower still running with the headless driver sitting upright in the seat. On another night early in September the searchlight company at Maidstone reported a German aircraft overhead, and though no other searchlight units or radars picked up the plane, Maidstone was adamant that its sound-detectors could still 'hear' the aircraft. The anti-aircraft guns were alerted as a precaution, and a British fighter was sent up to investigate. The mystery was solved twenty-five minutes later: the new sensitive sound-detector being used by the searchlight company had picked up the electric motor of their refrigerator, the door of which had been left open.

So little had happened in Britain by mid-October since war began that something like an air-raid warning earned considerable space in the papers—even when no plane or gunfire was heard. Such events were to become so common during and after the following summer that they were hardly worth mentioning. But the alarm which sounded in Kent shortly before 2pm on Tuesday 17th October was the nearest yet the country had come to an actual air-raid. Some people who had not gone to work in the afternoon went into their own shelters or stayed indoors, but many stood at front gates or in gardens scanning the skies for any activity. Some people caught in the streets when the sirens sounded headed for public shelters, although others carried on as though nothing had happened. And most people in the villages seemed to be gossiping and looking upwards, quite unperturbed, at their garden gates. A large number of people at Ramsgate, however, made themselves comfortable in the underground tunnels being built there; they took cover when the warning sounded at 1.45pm and stayed there until the All Clear sounded at 3pm. No sound was heard of the enemy during that alert, but aircraft and anti-aircraft guns were ready at their stations—just in case.

Then things began to happen off the Kent coast. An enemy aircraft was fired at by anti-aircraft guns on 20th November, although it dropped no bombs, and no air-raid warning was given. But later that day a warning was given in East Kent when an unidentified aircraft appeared overhead. The All Clear was given seventy-five minutes later. The following day, 21st November, a grey and blue Dornier 17 twin-engined reconnaissance bomber, commonly known as 'the Flying Pencil' because of its slim fuselage, was shot down by fighters off Deal. And on 22nd November the anti-aircraft guns were in action again when an unidentified aircraft appeared over the Thames Estuary. One enemy plane was shot down into the sea by anti-aircraft guns, and another driven away by fighters as they approached the south-east coast that night. The increased activity in the air prompted the following public warning from Sir Auckland Geddes, regional commissioner for the South-Eastern Civil Defence Region: "If you hear anti-aircraft fire or see an air battle going on when the warning-sirens have not been sounded, there is risk of injury from falling fragments of anti-aircraft shells or machine-gun bullets, and you should take shelter. It is foolhardy and not heroic to stand in the streets to watch the combat."

An exercise in the Medway towns on Sunday 21st January 1940 proved, in theory at least, that help from ARP units outside the area would be rapidly forthcoming in the event of a severe raid on the towns. It was the first large-scale practice to show how effective mutual support could be between units from throughout Kent and London. An emergency call was sent out soon after 6am to say that Chatham and the Medway towns had been devastated by bombing. Hundreds of Civil Defence workers in London and all parts of Kent were called into immediate action, and long convoys of fire-engines, ambulances and other ARP vehicles could be seen heading towards the Medway area throughout the morning. It was imagined that enemy aircraft had attacked Chatham Dockyard and scattered bombs on Chatham, Rochester and Gillingham. Within four hours 390 vehicles of all types and fifteen hundred personnel had arrived at Chatham.

Those taking part in the exercise were served with steaming cups of tea and fresh currant-buns at the drill-shed at the dockyard. The men later gathered to hear a speech by Admiral Sir Edward Evans, who said: "This is the best answer to those people who have nothing better to do than to write to the newspapers saying that ARP is nothing more than throwing darts and smoking cigarettes. Such people, who are not helping us to win the war, but cheering up the enemy, will be the first to snuggle down in the trenches and be glad of the protection given by the Civil Defence personnel."

The *Nora*, a 350-ton Dutch vessel, was mined on Monday 29th January while she was at anchor about a mile from the shore at Deal. A huge hole was blown in her stern, and the cook was injured when the galley was wrecked. The captain and mate were given head-injuries in the wheel-house by flying splinters of glass. A seaman blown overboard by the blast managed to keep himself afloat for thirty minutes until he was picked up by a patrol vessel, which also took the rest of the crew off the *Nora*, which was slowly sinking at the stern. Salvage tugs took the damaged boat in tow after the disaster and managed to beach her about 50 yards south of Deal Pier. She was completely submerged for some time until the rising tide lifted her and continued to hurl her against the side of the pier, which collapsed after standing the buffeting for some time. Many unsuccessful attempts were made to float the *Nora*, but she stood high and dry on the sea-front for a long time in the early part of the war.

Enemy bombers had yet to make their mark on the county, and the most exciting spectacle in early 1940 continued to be the ARP exercises.

Then the phoney war came to an end. Germany invaded Denmark and Norway on 9th April. And the first bombs to be dropped on England during the war fell in the early hours of Friday 10th May at Petham and Chilham. Numerous incendiary and high-explosive bombs were dropped by a single raider at 4.10am in fields and in Denge Wood and Penny Pot Wood. (It was thought that the plane had been damaged near the Thames Estuary and had released its load in sight of the Channel to escape.) Houses were shaken by the explosions, and the noise was heard by hundreds of people up to nearly eight miles away. No one was hurt in the bombing—but it was a bad start to a day which was to bring even worse news. Before dawn on 10th May the Germans launched their attack on Belgium and Holland and pushed on rapidly, in the next few days, towards France. At 6pm on 10th May Winston Churchill became Prime Minister.

The following day, at 8am, a weekend round-up began of several hundred enemy aliens in the eastern coastal area of the United Kingdom, from the Moray Firth to the Isle of Wight. A total of 175 were detained in Kent by the police. Twenty-one of them came from Folkestone, including a doctor with a practice there. Twenty people from Tunbridge Wells were sent to internment camps, including two men who were removed from St Augustine's Church during a service; they were taken away so quietly that Canon Hennesey, who was officiating, did not realize what had happened until after the service. Police called at the homes of all male enemy aliens, and by 10am on 11th May all of them had been handed over to military escorts and were on their way to internment camps. All other male aliens aged between sixteen and sixty were told at the same time that they must report daily to the police, must not use any motor vehicle or bicycle and must not be out of doors between 8pm and 6am. The police were helped by the military, who stopped cars on the roads and examined the papers of all those in them. Those who did not have their National Registration books with them were detained for inquiries.

It looked as though an invasion of Britain might take place at any time, so Anthony Eden, the new Secretary of State for War, broadcast a radio appeal on 14th May for men to join a new force of Local Defence Volunteers. This now well-known organization had its name changed in August 1940, at Churchill's suggestion, to 'the Home Guard'. Men at Gillingham and Cranbrook were signing on even while Eden was speaking, and other eager volunteers in Folkestone were still queueing at midnight.

The real war was getting nearer all the time. By the weekend of 18th–19th May, with the Germans by then in France, the sounds of battle could be heard clearly by those in East Kent. The *Kentish Express* said on 24th May: "People in Kent, especially those in the south-eastern portion of the county, are living in a state of tenseness and excitement while fighting rages in France and Belgium and aircraft roar overhead. Gunfire and the bursting of bombs are heard unceasingly from the other side of the Channel, and anti-aircraft defences in this country. Since Saturday the sounds have been more intense, and some people claim to have heard machine-gun fire over the Channel."

The Germans were pressing onwards, and it seemed as though nothing could stop them. The British Expeditionary Force on the Continent was being pushed back to the coast. Only a miracle, it began to seem, would prevent more than 300,000 men from being cut off and made prisoner.

3. An inspiration to us all

The evacuation which became known simply as 'Dunkirk' began quietly enough for the Southern Railway, which was to play such a large part in the episode. The company's official record of the evacuation opens on 13th May 1940 with an entry saying that military traffic was flowing smoothly and steadily from England via the Dunkirk ferry. But the situation soon changed. By 17th May, when the British, French and Belgian armies were being pushed back to the coast, it was reported that all north-east French ports were closed; by 20th May the German armour reached the Channel coast at Abbeville, and the port of Le Havre was also closed. Under the cliffs of Dover an evacuation was being discussed.

The British Expeditionary Force was being forced back to the sea, where it was feared they might be trapped and made prisoner by the rapidly advancing Germans. These advances and withdrawals by the various armies were happening so quickly that a meeting was called in naval headquarters at Dover on Monday 20th May to discuss the situation. On the agenda was the "emergency evacuation across the Channel of very large forces". These headquarters were housed in deep galleries cut into the chalk of the east cliff below Dover Castle by French prisoners-of-war in the first years of the nineteenth century. The office used by Vice-Admiral Bertram Ramsay of Dover took up a single gallery which ended at an embrasure in the cliff face; other members of his staff, and the staff office itself, were housed in smaller rooms leading deep into the chalk. There was a large room beyond these used normally for conferences in connection with the operation of the base. It had held auxiliary electrical plant in the Great War and was known as 'the Dynamo Room'. At the conference under Admiral Ramsay, it was decided to set up a new body to organize the evacuation in this room—which gave its name to the evacuation of Dunkirk: 'Operation Dynamo'.

It was decided originally that the evacuation should be carried out from Calais, Boulogne and Dunkirk, and that ten thousand men could probably be evacuated from each port every twenty-four hours—but that was before Calais and Boulogne fell.

Some troops, meanwhile, were already being evacuated from other ports, in cross-Channel steamers. A number of these boats of the Southern Railway had been chartered by the Admiralty since the beginning of the war as either military transports or hospital-carriers. Among them were the *Maid of Kent, Brighton, Isle of Thanet, Isle of Guernsey, Dinard, Paris* and *Worthing*, used as hospital-carriers, and the *Normannia, Lorina, Biarritz, Canterbury, Maid of Orleans, Whitstable, Autocarrier* and *Hythe*, used as military transports. On the first black day for Southern, Thursday, 23rd May, the *Maid of Kent* and the *Brighton* were bombed and sunk in the harbour at Dieppe; both were loaded with wounded and clearly marked as hospital-ships. But these earlier evacuations from the various ports—which lifted 58,583 British and 814 Allied troops to safety—were not part of Operation Dynamo. That began on Sunday 26th May.

The British forces in Boulogne had surrendered the previous day, 25th May; Calais was already under heavy attack, and the surrender of British forces there came at 3pm on the Sunday, although the British government was not aware of the surrender until the following day. Then, at three minutes to seven on the evening of 26th May, the Admiralty ordered the commencement of Dynamo. It had, in fact, already begun: Admiral Ramsay at Dover had decided that the situation in France had deteriorated so badly that at 3pm that afternoon he had sent the first personnel-ships towards Dunkirk. The first of those ships was already loading there when the Dynamo message came through.

The evacuation of Dunkirk lasted until 9am on Tuesday 4th June, the morning on which the town surrendered. It was thought on the Sunday that 45,000 troops might be saved from the clutches of the Germans, but by the end of the evacuation a staggering 338,226 British and Allied troops had been landed in England. Kent was the disembarkation area for most of them.

Southern Railway was now called on to move the troops almost as quickly as they landed. Nearly two thousand locomotives and carriages were provided for this purpose, many of them coming from Southern itself but the rest of the pool of trains being made up with stock from the GWR, LMS and LNER. It was uncertain at which ports the men might arrive, so Southern Railway had to be ready to

cover seven. Two of them, Newhaven and Southampton, were outside the county, but the other five were all in Kent. During the
evacuation Sheerness had seventeen trains, Margate seventy-five
trains and twenty-one ambulance-trains, Ramsgate eighty-two,
Folkestone sixty-four, and Dover the biggest share, 327 trains.

Dover was, of course, bound to be the busiest port during the
evacuation. Although the harbour there is big, the actual quays at the
time were small, except for the eight berths for cross-Channel
steamers on the Admiralty Pier. At the height of Dunkirk there were
often sixteen and sometimes twenty ships at these eight berths,
moored in tiers of two and three deep and all handled by tugs. They
berthed, unloaded their troops, pulled out, refuelled and returned to
Dunkirk. There were between forty and fifty mooring-buoys in the
main harbour, and these were constantly occupied with ships taking
stores, repairing minor damage and occasionally resting. The oil-
tanker *War Sepoy* was berthed at one of them, and she was continually
supplying fuel to the destroyers, oil-burning cross-Channel steamers
and pleasure-boats, and to all the other craft which pulled up alongside her.

Men from Kent were among those who took across some of the 665
small craft, which included Gravesend shrimping-boats, cockle-
boats, dredgers, trawlers, paddle-steamers, such as the *Medway
Queen*, and even a mudhopper. An appeal at Gravesend Labour
Exchange for volunteers to man them was answered readily, and the
heads of some local factories gave their men permission to go. Many
members of Gravesend ARP volunteered, but only ten of the younger
men were allowed to go; some of the volunteers were only fifteen and
sixteen years old. Sometimes the wives and families of the volunteers
were not even aware they had been to Dunkirk until they returned
home tired and dirty.

A small vessels pool was set up at Sheerness, and during the
evacuation it sent out a considerable number of small craft, including
a hundred motorboats, ten lighters, seven Dutch skoots, one oil-
tanker and six paddle-steamers. The engines of weekend yachts were
made fit for the Channel trip there, and stores and accommodation for
a stream of officers and ratings were produced. The chief constructor
at Sheerness dockyard was building small rafts to carry men, while the
shipwrights were making ladders to help the small boats load up with
men at Dunkirk. Red tape went by the board.

Lifeboats from Kent also played their part in the operation.
Howard Primrose Knight, coxswain of the *Prudential*, the Ramsgate

lifeboat, and coxswain Edward Drake Parker, of *Lord Southborough*, the Margate lifeboat, were each awarded the Distinguished Service Medal in recognition of their "gallantry and determination when ferrying troops from the beaches of Dunkirk". A report on them says:

> "Coxswain Knight and his crew took the Ramsgate lifeboat across to Dunkirk on the afternoon of Thursday 30th May 1940 towing eight wherries manned by naval ratings and loaded with cans of fresh water for the troops. They were at work all the Thursday night, the Friday and Friday night and continued until all the wherries were destroyed. They helped to bring off 2,800 men, and when they reached Ramsgate again on Saturday morning they had been on service forty hours. Coxswain Parker and the Margate crew also set out on the Thursday afternoon and arrived at the beaches at midnight. They rescued first a party of French soldiers, who waded out to the lifeboat in the darkness, and by 8.30 next morning had brought off five to six hundred men."

The commander of a destroyer (HMS *Icarus*) wrote to the Lifeboat Institution: "The manner in which the Margate lifeboat crew brought off load after load of soldiers under continuous shelling, bombing and aerial machine-gun fire, will be an inspiration to us all as long as we live."

The Dover lifeboat volunteered to take part in the evacuation but was ordered to remain at Dover for service in the area. *Charles Cooper Henderson*, the Dungeness lifeboat, was found with four naval ratings on board, broken down in the small hours of 1st June off Margate, and was brought in by Margate lifeboatmen. All the lifeboats survived except the *Viscountess Wakefield* of Hythe; she left Dover on a trip and disappeared without trace. Fifteen other lifeboats from as far north as Great Yarmouth and as far west as Poole were based at Ramsgate for the evacuation.

All the boats taking part in Dynamo had to risk the constant shelling and bombing which was battering Dunkirk and its sea-approach, and the first job on arriving at Dover was to sort out the dead from the living. The new Customs shed at the Marine Station was used as a mortuary, the old Customs shed as a clothing store, many of the men arriving practically naked in tattered rags. Dogs which had attached themselves to the troops as they passed through Belgium and France poured off the vessels when they berthed, and a lorry came to Dover each day to take these stray animals away.

The troops were exhausted when they landed, and the whole of Kent was virtually ransacked to collect food and clothing for them, collection-centres being set up at Redhill, Tonbridge, Faversham and

Headcorn. The Mayor of Canterbury, Catherine Williamson, had a loudspeaker fixed to the fifteenth-century Guildhall and appealed through it for transport from Canterbury to Ramsgate to carry clothes and other provisions given by the Salvation Army. Volunteers throughout the county worked all hours to feed the troops, and nowhere was this more true than at Headcorn.

The small station there will never be as busy again as it was during that period. Train after train paused at the village to allow a total of 145,000 troops to get their first decent meal in days. A large barn near the station was turned into the catering headquarters, where the food was prepared entirely by the volunteers and carried across a field as each of the 207 trains pulled in for its eight-minute stop. The stationmaster, assistant stationmaster and two casual porters had their hands full. The military provided the food and forty soldiers to dish it out, helped by forty to fifty local women who worked in eight-hour shifts for nine days and nights cutting up 2,500 loaves each day. Nineteen stoves were on the go day and night to produce tea and coffee; one woman worked for twenty-four hours without a break; another said she had cut so many sandwiches she never wanted to eat anything again; beef was roasted on spits in open trenches next to the railway; a million sardines were supplied, along with huge stacks of bully beef and margarine; and often five thousand eggs were shelled at any one time. One evening five thousand meat pies, five thousand sausages and five thousand rolls were delivered—and were all eaten by early the following afternoon. Not enough cups could be produced, so drinks were handed into the trains in tin cans, and a cry of "sling them out", when time was up, brought a shower of cans clattering onto the platform; as the train pulled away, professional and amateur helpers collected the cans to wash them ready for the next train.

Every alternate train helped the flow of traffic by not stopping until it reached Paddock Wood, where the troops were treated similarly to those who stopped at Headcorn. And the story was much the same all over Kent. Hundreds of men who had only rags round their feet were given socks and boots; house-to-house collections of clothes were made; bakers worked overtime to supply the canteens where women volunteers were preparing food for the troops; more volunteers, many of them young girls, were at the harbour entrances handing out food and tea as early as 4am—and were still there late at night; postcards were given out so that the men could inform their families that they were safe; and many men were given food and drink by people who dipped into their own pockets to provide it.

Many stations in the county played a large part in ensuring that the troops had a smooth trip.

Tonbridge was another stop used as a feeding-area—a stop where staff worked eighteen hours a day and then helped with the volunteer catering. The wife of the stationmaster started a refreshment scheme: queues actually formed as waiting civilians put money into collecting boxes; £25 was raised on the first day, £125 on the second, and by the end of Dynamo more than £1,000 had been collected. All expenses were paid, and so much per week, for a while, was sent to wounded soldiers at Pembury Hospital. The stationmaster's wife was awarded the OBE for her work at that time. Two firms sent sixty thousand cigarettes for the troops; and one man gave two suits from his luggage to two soldiers he saw without clothes in a train.

Most of the trains stopped at Ashford for water, the majority coming from Dover and Folkestone, and some from Margate. From 31st May to 4th June single-line traffic only was on the move between Ashford and Hothfield, so that seventeen trains with 183 coaches could be berthed on the down line between those points. The signalmen worked twelve hours a day, and, somehow, the normal morning services to London ran almost on time—much to the amazement of season-ticket holders.

Special trains from Margate and Ramsgate stopped at Faversham, as did a few from Dover via Canterbury East. The feeding arrangements were handled by the military. Twenty minutes were allowed for each train to stop for food, but no train took more than thirteen minutes, though many trains carried more than seven hundred men.

Dover was the busiest station, with 327 trains moving 180,982 troops, but Ramsgate was by no means an idle second. No fewer than 42,783 men were carried inland on eighty-two special trains. On Sunday 2nd June there were twelve troop specials, one ambulance train and five civilian evacuation specials with four thousand children. Two of the four platforms at the station were used by the men from Dunkirk, another for ambulance trains and evacuees, while ordinary traffic had to make do with the fourth only. Forty local women carried out feeding arrangements, and some staff worked twenty-two hours at a time. A clothing-store was opened there, and socks were washed by women volunteers and passed on to the next train-load of men. Many of the men arrived naked except for a blanket around them, while others were covered in oil. One man left the clothing-store kitted out in a college blazer, striped city trousers and white plimsols. Four nurses were at the station, and twenty-four buses were used to ferry people from the harbour to the station.

Many buses were used in Margate to get troops to the station from the pier, where thirty vessels were berthed at one time on 2nd June. Eight empty trains waited in the station, and seventy-five special trains moved 38,000 troops during Dynamo. Normal services were hardly affected, although a bus service was introduced to link Margate with Ashford when there were disruptions. Dreamland amusement park was used as a clothing-store, and seven thousand men used it each day between 29th May and 1st June. There were also three civilian evacuation specials on 2nd June with 2,200 people dovetailed in with the military specials. One train was given over entirely to Polish airmen.

Nine boilers on the beach for making tea were among the sights which greeted troops landing at Folkestone. Here 35,000 men were moved in sixty-four special trains. A steep gradient of one in thirty connected the harbour to the main line, and three engines were required to help trains along that stretch. All those trains had to be slotted in with the large number from Dover. Between 16th and 26th May the harbour also had to cope with nine thousand refugees.

And still, meanwhile, more and more men were lifted from Dunkirk. The numbers rose, and on Tuesday 28th May seventeen large vessels arrived at Dover at once in the morning—included in the personnel were fifteen thousand French troops. The peak day of the evacuation was 31st May, when 68,014 troops were brought across the Channel. A total of 34,484 men were landed at Dover in those twenty-four hours from twenty-five destroyers, twelve transports, fourteen drifters, fourteen mine-sweepers, six paddle mine-sweepers, five trawlers, sixteen motor yachts and small vessels, twelve Dutch skoots, four hospital-ships and twenty-one various foreign vessels. On 4th June, the last day of the evacuation, there were sixty vessels in Dover at the same time.

Southern Railway was called on once more on 29th May when all its steamers of 1,000 tons or more were requisitioned by the government at noon. The steamers *Lorina* and *Normania* were sunk the following day, and the *Isle of Guernsey* was bombed and machine-gunned. The steamer *Canterbury* went out of service for a few days on 31st May, and the steamer *Paris* was sunk on 2nd June. By the time the evacuation was over, the crews of the cross-Channel boats had earned seven DSCs, two DSMs and six Mentions in Despatches.

A total of 620 special trains run by Southern Railway moved 319,056 of the troops from the start of the evacuation to the end of

Operation Dynamo. The first of those actually taking part in Dynamo left the Kent coast at 4am on 27th May and the last at 4pm on 4th June. Nearly seven thousand coaches were involved in the operation. All the trains ran without prior advice and on no pre-arranged paths; it was a triumph for improvisation.

Dunkirk may have been a miracle—but it was certainly not a victory. Through the retreat and on the beaches the British Army had lost 68,111 men killed, missing, wounded or taken prisoner. It also lost 2,472 guns, 63,879 motor vehicles, 20,548 motorcycles, 679 out of 704 tanks, and half a million tons of military stores and ammunition. A total of 243 ships were sunk during the evacuation, including six British destroyers, and the RAF lost 474 aircraft. Britain was almost defenceless—and across the Channel Hitler was planning his invasion of the Kent coast.

Plans to counter such an invasion included an order on 31st May that all signposts throughout the country be taken down, all milestones uprooted and the names of all streets, railway stations and villages obliterated. Signposts began re-appearing in towns after October 1942 and in rural areas after May 1943, but all emergency restrictions on the exhibition of place-names were not cancelled until October 1944.

In the early hours of Tuesday 25th June—the day the French armistice came into force, a small and amateurish party of British Commandos set out from Folkestone, Dover and Newhaven on its first cross-Channel raid. The hundred or so men slid out of the harbours in high-speed RAF launches manned by civilians. When they reached mid-Channel, they blackened their faces with grease-paint bought at short-notice from a theatrical costumier in Soho. They were armed with twenty tommy-guns, all that the Army could spare from its total depleted reserve of forty. One group ran down a sea-plane in the harbour at Boulogne before landing in the dunes near the town and surprising some Wehrmacht sentries. Others went ashore near Le Touquet and attacked a big building which looked like a garrison HQ; they killed two German soldiers there, although it did not occur to them to take their personal documents. These Commandos were cheered by every vessel they passed on the way into harbour; but one of the boats was not allowed into Folkestone harbour for several hours because no one on board could prove he was who he said he was. Thus ended the first British attack on Nazi-occupied Europe.

One of the stranger incidents in Kent during the war happened shortly after Dunkirk in the early hours of 6th June, when four torpedoes, thought to have been fired by enemy torpedo-boats, came ashore at intervals of between half a mile and a mile at Walmer, Prince of Wales Terrace, North Deal and Sandwich Bay. The ones that landed at Deal and Walmer slid up the beach and stopped on a bank of shingle; none of the four missiles exploded. Residents of Prince of Wales Terrace were woken in the early hours and not allowed to return to their homes until experts had made the weapons harmless. People going to work a little later that morning found the sea-front guarded by soldiers with fixed bayonets. Each of the black-nosed torpedoes was 18 feet long. It was said that the Germans were experimenting with a new type of torpedo.

Apart from that, the month of June had been relatively quiet as far as enemy action was concerned. A bomb destroyed Lenham Congregational Chapel at 4.30pm on 1st June, thirty minutes after a group of children had left it. Rubbish, tiles and bricks were strewn over a wide area but no one was hurt. Slight damage was done at Upnor on 19th June, and four craters were made in a field at Doddington on 22nd June. But the first recorded death by bombing in Kent did not occur until 3rd July, when a bomb at Bekesbourne killed one person, seriously injured two and slightly hurt another.

A single raider flying high above Ashford dropped several high-explosive bombs on Newtown on 17th July. One exploded when it hit an iron girder in a building at the railway works, injuring several workmen; others fell on the green at Newtown, and the flats along one side were wrecked, while a pair of houses on the other side was also hit. Three people were killed, one of them a baby. That raid also left one person seriously injured and ten others slightly hurt.

The most serious raid in the county so far occurred at 1.10am the following day when bombs fell in the Nelson Road area of Gillingham. One woman was blown out of bed and into a fireplace, although without injury, and a baby was buried in some debris but dug out unhurt. A part-time air-raid warden of eighteen, who was also a local Scout troop leader, lay for more than four hours after worming his way through a ruined house to cover the faces of a man and woman trapped in the wreckage. He protected them from the showers of dust which fell with every movement of the rescue-squad behind him. He chatted to the couple cheerfully for that time, and when they were finally rescued, he collapsed with exhaustion. He was later awarded the OBE Gallantry Medal and the Silver Cross of the Scouts for his heroism. Rescuers worked from 1.30am–6am during the night to free three people trapped altogether. Among the five people killed in that raid were a couple who had returned to their bed from their shelter. Four people were also seriously injured in the attack and twenty-two slightly hurt, including twelve children.

By the middle of July a curfew had been imposed under the Defence Regulations on people living in certain parts of Kent, prohibiting their being outside between half an hour after sunset and half an hour before sunrise unless they had police permission. The order affected areas in the boroughs of Gillingham, Queenborough, Margate, Ramsgate, Sandwich, Deal, Dover, Folkestone, Hythe, New Romney and Lydd, the urban districts of Sheerness, Whitstable, Herne Bay and Broadstairs, and the rural districts of Strood, Swale, Sheppey, Eastry, Dover and Romney Marsh.

The fourth and last recorded fatal bombing incident in July happened at Oare, near Faversham, on 19th July. A Home Guard member was killed when he left home to fetch his wife from a neighbour's house—just as the first bomb fell. A girl of fourteen was blown off her bicycle while riding home but was only slightly hurt. A woman was also slightly injured in this raid. The blast of one of the bombs was so strong that an eight-foot length of iron tramline lying in one of the gardens was lifted high in the air and blown 20 yards or so before bringing down telephone wires.

It was also in July that a German aircraft was brought down in a hop-garden at Collier Street, south of Maidstone. A farmer nearby did not hear the dogfight above him, or the plane crash, because of the noise of the tractor he was driving, so he knew nothing of the incident until the pilot came up to him, saluted and told him in perfect English what had happened. The farmer then took the pilot home, where his wife gave him a cup of tea. All three waited until the police came to take the pilot away.

4. He's coming! He's coming!

"IN ENGLAND THEY'RE FILLED WITH CURIOSITY
AND KEEP ASKING 'WHY DOESN'T HE COME?'
BE CALM. BE CALM. HE'S COMING! HE'S COMING!"

Hitler at a rally on 4th September 1940

There is little doubt that Hitler would have had a good chance of success had he launched an invasion of England immediately after Dunkirk, for the British Army had lost almost all its modern equipment in France. The 1st London Division was responsible for the defence of the coast from Sheppey to Rye—which would have been a key area in an invasion, but this division had only eleven 25-pounder field guns out of the seventy-two it ought to have had, plus four obsolete 18-pounders and eight 4·5-inch howitzers from the Great War. The division had no anti-tank guns at all, instead of the forty-eight it ought to have had; twenty-one Bren-gun carriers instead of ninety, and not a single Bren gun—when it should have had 590.

Hitler, however, was not yet ready to strike against Britain. He did not want to attack Britain and would much rather have had peace between the two nations so that he would be free to launch an assault on Russia in 1941. But he realized that peace might not be acceptable to Britain. So at the beginning of July the Germans began to plan an invasion.

Control of the English Channel was essential. A month of attacks on British convoys therefore began on 3rd July, together with air battles over the Channel, with the aim of securing control for Germany. That period is sometimes known as 'the Battle of the Channel'.

It was now only a question of time before the Battle of Britain began. On 16th July Hitler issued War Directive No 16, which said: "As England, in spite of her hopeless military position, has so far shown herself unwilling to come to any compromise, I have decided to begin preparations for, and if necessary to carry out, the invasion of England. This operation is dictated by the necessity of eliminating Great Britain as a base from which the war against Germany can be fought. If necessary, the island will be occupied." The landing operation, he said, must be a surprise crossing on a broad front from Ramsgate to the Isle of Wight. The preparations had to be ready by the middle of August. To make a landing in England possible, he added, the RAF had to be effectively beaten from the skies, the sea-routes cleared of mines, and guns brought up to dominate and protect the entire coastal front area. The invasion would be referred to, he said, by the codename 'Sealion'.

The German Army did not want a narrow front, arguing that it would be like sending its men into a sausage-machine, but this idea of a broad front of about 200 miles along the south coast was not supported by the German Navy, which said it could not hope to protect a crossing over such a wide area. So the final plan for Operation Sealion was for an invasion along the coast from Folkestone to Brighton. The most favourable combination of moon and tide would fall between 19th and 26th September; D-Day was set for 21st September.

The number of troops which were to take part in the assault was reduced drastically over the planning period. The original number suggested in July was forty divisions; this was later whittled down to thirteen divisions, about 250,000 men. But the final figure of 60,300 men was the equivalent of only three divisions, to be made up of 6,700 men from each of the nine divisions which would be in the first wave. Four divisions of the 16th German Army were to embark at Rotterdam, Antwerp, Ostend, Dunkirk and Calais and to land in the Folkestone-St Leonards area; two divisions of the 9th German Army, embarking at Boulogne, were to land in the Bexhill-Eastbourne area; and three divisions of the 9th Army, sailing from Le Havre, were to land between Beachy Head and Brighton.

The attack on the Kent part of the coastline was to be carried out by men from the 17th and 35th Divisions of the XIII Corps of the 16th Army, who were to land between Folkestone and Dungeness. They were to be helped on D-Day by the 7th Flieger (Paratroop) Division, which was to drop onto the high ground round Folkestone in the Lympne and Lyminge area. Once it had captured that ground, it was to have secured crossings over the Royal Military Canal for the benefit of the seaborne troops in that area, while establishing a road-block on the Canterbury-to-Folkestone road at the same time. It was planned, provisionally, to drop other airborne troops on the downs above Brighton.

All the troops were to expand a bridgehead so that in 16th Army's sector they held a line running from Canterbury along the River Stour to Ashford, and passing through Tenterden and Hawkhurst to Etchingham; the bridgehead line in the 9th Army sector was to run from the high ground 29 kilometres north and west of Bexhill, and through Uckfield to the high ground west and south-west of Lewes. Within twenty days they were to have broken out of the bridgehead and captured the country up to a line which ran from Gravesend through Reigate, Guildford and Petersfield in Hampshire to reach the sea at Portsmouth. During this second phase the 16th Army would be responsible for the country north of a line running from Etchingham to Reigate in Surrey, while the 9th Army fought in the area south of that. By the beginning of October, according to the plans for Operation Sealion, nearly all Kent would have been captured by the Germans.

By the time Hitler issued War Directive No 16, he had already let six weeks of indecision slip by since Dunkirk—and he was still hoping to avoid an invasion. In a speech to the Reichstag on 19th July he made what he called his "final appeal to reason and common sense". It had never been his intention to destroy or even harm the British Empire, he said; the struggle between the two nations, if it continued, could end only with the annihilation of one of them: "Mr Churchill may believe this will be Germany; I know it will be Britain." Copies of this speech were scattered over England by high-flying aircraft—and were usually auctioned in aid of Red Cross funds. On the morning of 10th August, a hundredweight of these leaflets were dropped over the county by a German plane; they fell to the ground at Barming Mental Hospital.

On 21st July Hitler was telling his Commanders-in-Chief that an invasion would be the most effective way of bringing about the end of the war. He gave Operation Sealion top priority and stepped up the collecting of the necessary ships from Western Europe. The construction of all warships, except U-boats, was stopped, and dockyards and slipways were requisitioned. There was no time to build special invasion craft so river barges, motorboats, tugs and coasters were conscripted and converted. The Naval Staff in Germany estimated that it would need 1,722 barges, 471 tugs, 1,161 motor boats and 155 transports to meet the minimum demands of the Army.

The Battle of the Channel, meanwhile, was continuing in Germany's favour. The back of the 11,500-ton Admiralty tanker *War Sepoy* was broken on 18th July by a bomb which fell near her in Dover harbour. The *Sepoy*, which had been a valuable refuelling ship during Dunkirk, was later towed to the western entrance of the harbour and sunk as a blockship. All big-ship convoys in and out of London had been driven out of the Channel after 4th July, and all coastal convoys had been stopped after 25th July. On 27th July a surprise attack was carried out on Dover harbour by 120 aircraft, sinking the destroyer *Codrington* in the harbour and damaging two others. One of the damaged destroyers, the *Walpole*, was towed to Chatham the next day. The news of this attack, and that a battery of heavy coastal guns was being set up by the Germans near Calais, prompted the Admiralty to abandon Dover as a base for anti-invasion warships; the remaining destroyers were withdrawn to Sheerness and Harwich. Another ship was sunk off Portland on 29th July, and after that day there was a ban on the use of destroyers in the Channel during daylight. The daytime Channel was German.

There was a lull in the Channel battle from about the last week of July to the end of the first week in August because there were no more targets in the Channel for the Luftwaffe to attack or for the RAF to protect. This was bad news for the Germans, who were committed to seek and destroy the RAF—to clear them out of the skies in preparation for the invasion, so Me109s were sent to roam over the Channel and south-east England in large formations to draw up the British fighters in conditions favourable to the Germans. But the bait, generally, was not accepted; the British were using the lull to improve their defences. This state of affairs lasted until 8th August, when the Luftwaffe was presented with a target it wanted to attack and which it was worthwhile for the RAF to protect.

The target was convoy CW9, codenamed 'Peewit', which had sailed from the River Medway on the previous evening's tide. The twenty merchant-ships of the convoy were colliers heavily laden with part of the 40,000 tons of seaborne coal and coke required each week to keep industry going in the south. They were escorted by nine naval vessels, including two destroyers, with fully-manned anti-aircraft guns and balloons attached to the ships by cables. The convoy was spotted by German radar as it attempted to pass through the Straits of Dover and attacked by E-boats, the German torpedo-boats, in the half light of early morning. Three ships were sunk and two damaged. That attack was followed by three separate air-attacks during the day. Between

3am and 5.30pm all the raids between them had sunk seven merchant-ships, damaged eight (some of them beyond repair) and damaged six rescue-ships. Only four of the merchant-ships sailed into Swanage in Dorset virtually unscathed. Also on that day two Spitfires from Manston were shot down by Messerschmitts in the Dover area at 10.45am, and a Blenheim from Manston was shot down into the sea off Ramsgate; the crew of all the aircraft were killed.

On 6th August Field Marshal Goering, head of the Luftwaffe, summoned his senior commanders for a final review of the plans for Operation Sealion, The Luftwaffe's main task, he said, was to eliminate the RAF as a fighting force and to strangle Britain's supply-lines by destroying her ports and shipping. The initial blow of this great assault by the German Air Force was planned for 10th August; and Goering gave this day the codename 'Adlertag', 'Eagle Day'. In the event, it was postponed because of bad weather and re-set for 13th August.

Reports from German crews who had been on a big raid to Portsmouth on 11th August showed that British radar had given considerable warning of their approach, so on 12th August—the eve of Eagle Day—German aircraft left France with a clear plan: they were to put out of action all known radar stations between the Thames Estuary and Portland, and to take advantage of the likely radar black-out by attacking RAF fighter stations near the coast. Two of the five radar stations attacked that day were in Kent. One of them was on top of the cliffs at Dover, and its four 350-foot-tall masts could be seen clearly by the Germans on the other side of the Channel. This was a Chain Home Low station, which could detect aircraft coming towards England at sea level. The other radar (or Radio Direction Finding, as it was then known) was at the Chain Home station at Dunkirk, near Canterbury. This had a greater range than the station at Dover and could frequently spot planes 60–80 miles off the coast.

Twelve Spitfires from Biggin Hill saw the first action on Monday, 12th August, when they became involved in a dogfight with nine Messerschmitts over New Romney at 7.30 in the morning. One spitfire pilot had to bale out when his plane was hit and caught fire; he was picked up by a motor torpedo-boat, suffering from burns, and landed at Dover. Four other Spitfires were damaged, but they managed to destroy two enemy aircraft in the process.

Then the real business of the day began. Sixteen Me110s took off from the airfields at Calais at 8.40am to attack the four radar stations at Dover, Dunkirk, Rye and Pevensey. The first four planes pulled away from the formation and headed towards the tall masts at Dover; their bombs rocked the pylons and destroyed some of the huts there. The next four planes few north across Kent to attack Dunkirk, one of the planes dropping a bomb so close to the transmitter block that the whole concrete building moved several inches on its base; other huts there were also hit. Every building, except the transmitting and receiving block, was hit at Rye; and one bomb in the raid on Pevensey cut the electricity cable and put the whole station off the air.

Most of the bombs at Dunkirk had fallen within the station compound, but no vital damage was done, and the radar remained on the air. The other radar stations, however, had been silenced, and a 100-mile gap had been torn in the radar chain. They were out of action for only six hours, but it was time enough for German fighters to attack the airfields at Lympne and Hawkinge a little later that morning. Junkers bombers dropped 141 bombs on Lympne, causing considerable damage but not seriously affecting the operation of Fighter Command because the airfield had been used only in emergencies since June. The raid on Hawkinge was more important. An attack by Junkers there destroyed two hangars, the station workshops and four fighters on the ground. All services were restored within twenty-four hours, however.

A little later, at about 11am, six Spitfires from Manston arrived too late to prevent a dive-bombing attack on the convoys codenamed 'Agent' and 'Arena' off the North Foreland and the Thames Estuary; and they in turn were attacked by the escorting Messerschmitts. The Spitfires landed back at Manston to refuel as another attack took place on a convoy between Deal and Ramsgate. Twelve Hurricanes from Hawkinge and three from North Weald chased the bombers away—but a pilot from each squadron was killed when two planes from each squadron were shot down off the coast.

A Wren and a Naval officer had a narrow escape during an attack on Dover harbour, in which planes also fired at the barrage-ballons. The couple had just arrived at Princess Pier in a car when the dive-bombing began. They got out of the car quickly and took shelter under some goods trucks standing nearby. When the raid was over, they found they had been sheltering under an ammunition wagon.

A force of fifteen Junkers put the radar station at Ventnor on the Isle of Wight out of action at noon; it did not come back on the air until ten days later.

But the most serious raid on Kent took place at 12.50pm. Spitfires from Manston were on the point of taking off when Messerschmitts bombed and machine-gunned the airfield without warning. Eighteen Dorniers swept over at the same time and dropped a dense pattern of bombs. The airfield disappeared under a cloud of smoke and flames as 150 bombs hit workshops, hangars and a Blenheim twin-engined night-fighter. Few of the Spitfires managed to take off, and those that did found that the German planes were already streaking home after a raid which had lasted barely five minutes. The airfield was badly cratered—but it was back in operation in twenty-four hours. There were three small raids against coastal towns in Kent by about twenty Dorniers during the evening.

The radar stations and the airfields at Lympne, Hawkinge and Manston had been the main targets on 12th August, but civilians had also been killed in Kent by stray bombs during the day. The biggest death-toll occurred at Bekesbourne, near Canterbury, where six people died, one was seriously injured and another slightly injured. About two hundred high-explosive and incendiary bombs had dropped in the area at 5.30pm, wrecking two cottages and blocking the railway line. Other bombs had killed one person at Ramsgate, two people at Sarre in east Kent and one at Worth near Sandwich. But late in the morning, not long before noon, there occurred a new form of enemy action which was to plague the coastal towns of Kent for more than the next four years: the cross-Channel guns in France began shelling Folkestone and Dover, killing two people in Dover, seriously injuring three others and slightly hurting nine. Before the shelling ceased, at the end of September 1944, about 150 people had been killed by these missiles in Dover—which suffered far worse than any other town, Folkestone, Deal, Ramsgate and Hythe.

By the end of the day Air Chief Marshal Sir Hugh Dowding, the Commander in Chief of Fighter Command, had ordered one squadron south to its base at Debden in Essex, and five other squadrons in the north were told to be ready to move south at a moment's notice. He had figured that the minor raids on the convoys during the day had been attacks designed to cover the Luftwaffe's main aims. Dowding realized that the main assault on Britain was about to open. The Battle of Britain was about to begin.

5. Eagle Day arrives

Eight airfields in Kent became well-known because of their wartime use, but only four of them played a major part in the Battle of Britain. Those four were Biggin Hill, Manston, Hawkinge and Gravesend. The two airfields at Eastchurch and Detling were used by Coastal Command; Lympne was used only in emergencies; and the bombing of the partly-built airfield at West Malling by a Dornier on 10th August, and by other planes on subsequent days, meant that it was not possible for it to accept its first squadron of Spitfires until 30th October that year. The county itself was part of Number 11 Group of Fighter Command, which covered the south-east and London from its group HQ at Uxbridge.

The British aircraft which left their mark on this period were, of course, the Spitfire and the Hurricane. The Spitfire has become the better-known of these two fighters, but the Hurricane, which went into production a year before its counterpart, outnumbered the Spitfire during the battle, and it has been estimated that the Hurricane pilots were credited with four-fifths of all enemy aircraft destroyed from July to October 1940. Their rivals were the Messerschmitt 109, judged to be about equal in performance overall with the British pair—although it could be out-turned by both of them, and the twin-engined Messerschmitt 110, which was less manoeuvrable than the other three and was later relegated to a night-fighter role. The three types of German bomber most commonly overhead during that long, fine summer were the Heinkel, the Dornier and the Junkers.

This is a brief background to Adlerangriff, the German-named 'Battle of the Eagles'. It began on 13th August—and it began with a blunder.

Tuesday 13th August: A thick layer of cloud hung over south-east England, and Goering decided to postpone the main attack until the afternoon. But seventy-four Dornier bombers failed to get this cancellation and flew on towards Kent, unaware that their fighter escort had been grounded. Spitfires from Manston intercepted the raid before it reached Sheppey and continued to harass it as it split up over the island, one group of thirty-nine planes making for the naval base at Sheerness while the rest bombed the airfield at Eastchurch from 1,500 feet. This attack, which took place soon after 7am, destroyed five Blenheims of Coastal Command and one of several Spitfires which were there temporarily. The operations block was also destroyed; fourteen soldiers and airmen were killed, and twenty-six others seriously injured. There was widespread damage and disrupted communications, but the airfield was in operation again before the end of the day.

Other bombers were on their way to attack the airfield at Rochester shortly after 5pm that afternoon when they were spotted by Hurricanes operating from North Weald in Essex. They had failed to find their target anyway, so they turned back, scattering bombs on Ramsgate, Ashford, Canterbury and Lympne.

But what came next was the worst attack of the day; a carefully calculated and devastating raid on Detling airfield, near Maidstone. The attack was made by about forty Ju87s—the infamous Stuka divebombers, which swept over the airfield at 5.16pm, just as the messes were filling for the evening meal. Three of the messes were wrecked, as were all the hangars, and the station commander was killed when one bomb scored a direct hit on the operations block. Detling housed the Ansons of 500 (County of Kent) Squadron, which by the end of May had flown 272 patrols, covered 1,386 flying hours and had five combats with the enemy; by the time the smoke cleared over the airfield, twenty-two aircraft had been destroyed on the ground.

A WAAF who was there at the time said: "I looked out of my bedroom window . . . and saw a soldier running. We take very little notice of the noise of planes for they are about continuously, but to see a soldier run is unusual. Looking out further, I saw more soldiers running and realized there was a raid right on us—we had had no warning. I dashed down into our dug-out only just in time. The noise was terrific, and I was deaf for two days afterwards. When I came out, I shall never forget the sights which met my eyes."

Not only were the hangars, the workshops and the quarters laid flat, but the taxi-ways and hardstandings had been turned into a cratered mess. A total of sixty-seven service and civilian personnel had been killed in the raid, and work went on for hours to rescue the injured. The award of the Military Cross, rare in RAF history, went to Pilot Officer D. Elliott, who had helped rescue some injured people in the ruins of the operations room, even though he was injured himself. Military Medals were presented to Corporal B. Jackman, who had operated his twin Lewis guns until the gun-post was wrecked by a direct hit which severely injured him, and to WAAF Corporal J. Robins, who gave first-aid to those wounded when a shelter was hit, remaining with the injured until all of them had been evacuated to hospital. Lieutenant D. Curry RN, one of the sailors attached to Detling, was awarded the DSC for his outstanding coolness in the face of danger.

Elsewhere in Kent, two people had been killed by bombing at Whitstable, and two others at Sheppey. A total of forty-six German aircraft had been destroyed by the end of the day for the loss of only thirteen British fighters in air combat. It is true that a further forty-seven British planes were destroyed on the ground at six airfields—including the twenty-eight at Detling and Eastchurch, but only one of those was a fighter; and Detling, which was not even a Fighter Command airfield, was soon repaired.

Wednesday 14th August: Clouds kept the attacks down to about a third of what had been planned. A total of forty-two Hurricanes and Spitfires from Biggin Hill, Hawkinge and Manston took off at 11.50am and tangled with about 120 Messerschmitts, which were escorting eighty Stuka dive-bombers. The result was a dogfight of more than two hundred aircraft over Dover. Eight of the barrage-balloons at Dover were destroyed, and one group of Stukas bombed and sank the Goodwin lightship. Manston airfield was then attacked by Messerschmitt 110s. Three Blenheim bombers were destroyed, and four hangars went up in smoke, but two of the raiders were brought down by gunfire from the ground.

Thursday 15th August: The day began with another Luftwaffe muddle. Goering had decided that the huge number of raids planned for the day could not take place because heavy cloud had been forecast; but the weather had cleared up by mid-morning, and a more junior officer decided to launch the attack on his own initiative. His decision set in action the Luftwaffe's biggest assault of the whole battle. More than five hundred enemy bombers were escorted by 1,256 fighters in fighting that ranged from Devon to Scotland. The RAF lost thirty-four fighters in the air that day with another sixteen lost on the airfields attacked. But the Luftwaffe lost about seventy-five aircraft (a disputed figure sometimes given as fifty-five) and soon began to refer to that day as *'der schwarze Donnerstag'*—'Black Thursday'. It was a Thursday which began with raids on the airfields at Hawkinge and Lympne.

Eleven Hurricanes from Hawkinge and twelve Spitfires from Hornchurch across the Thames were patrolling an area ten miles west of Dover when about fifty Stukas appeared over Hawkinge shortly after 11.30am. Two of them were shot down by Hurricanes, the crews of both being killed; one crashed near Folkestone and the other struck high-tension wires on the outskirts of the town and smashed into some houses. Then two Spitfires were shot down, the pilot of one being picked up from the sea and taken to hospital while the other was shot down near Ashford and taken to Ashford Hospital. The pilots of two Hurricanes were unhurt when they were both shot down south of Folkestone.

The attack on Hawkinge airfield was made by enemy aircraft at 11.35am. There were no casualties, even though a direct hit by a 500-kilo bomb wrecked a hangar, and a 250-kilo bomb smashed one end of a barrack block. Four bombs which fell outside the airfield caused a lot more damage by cutting cables which carried power to the radar stations at Dover, Rye and Foreness (where there was a Chain Home Low station like that at Dover). They were not back in action until much later in the day. Other bombers had made a dive-bombing attack on Lympne airfield meanwhile. Their bombs scored a direct hit on the sick quarters, few buildings were left undamaged, and the airfield was out of action until the evening of 17th August, although some British fighters managed to touch down there before then. Manston's turn came soon after noon, when twelve Messerschmitts raked the airfield with cannon and machine-gun fire, causing sixteen casualties and destroying two Spitfires on the ground.

Just a few hours later a much more massive raid began shaping up over the Channel—and another two Kent targets were in its sights.

A total of eighty-eight Dornier bombers and more than 130 escorting Messerschmitts approached Deal at 3.30pm, while more than sixty Messerschmitts swept in over Kent on either side of Dover. And all that could be diverted to meet them were twelve Hurricanes from Croydon, twelve Hurricanes from North Weald and twelve Spitfires from Kenley in Surrey. The Germans claim that their pilots shot down eight British planes for the loss of only two. All the Dorniers flew on to Faversham and then split up, some attacking Eastchurch again—and some to attack Rochester.

Two aircraft factories were based at Rochester airfield, the most important of which was the Shorts factory. It had been built quickly in 1938 to produce the Stirling four-engined heavy bomber, which Bomber Command was counting on for its attacks against the industrial centres of Germany. The first seven Stirlings had just been completed when the eighteen Dorniers came in over the airfield and factory in an arrowhead formation from the south-east. Hundreds of 100-lb bombs were dropped all over this area before the bombers turned away to the north. Hundreds of men had been sheltering all round the factory, but the only casualties were two men in a small metal shelter inside the building—one was dead, the other injured.

The most important part of the factory was the finished parts store, where thousands of items for the Stirlings were kept. This wooden building was on fire. The damage elsewhere was not as great as might have been expected from the three hundred bombs which fell. Six nearly-complete aircraft had been damaged beyond repair, but seven complete fuselages, machine-tools and other parts of the factory were undamaged. The most disastrous loss was that of the finished parts, which would have to be made again. The result was that the production of the Stirling was set back for more than a year—and the RAF lost nearly two hundred of these planes because of this delay. It was decided to disperse much of the factory, and in little more than a fortnight after the raid machine-tools and thousands of other items had been moved in local lorries and RAF trailers to a large railway shed at Swindon and a factory building at South Marston. A total of 353 Stirlings were eventually built at those two places. But the link with Rochester was not severed: a total of 145 Stirlings were built in the city, their bodies made at Short's seaplane works on the Esplanade and taken to the airfield for assembly.

Another attack had been made, meanwhile, at 3.25pm at Hawkinge, although again there were no casualties or serious damage to the base. One of the raiders during the day, chased by three British fighters, dropped a shower of bombs on a small area at Lynsted, near Faversham. One of them scored a direct hit on the parish church, which was badly damaged; the Rev. L. Ehrmann, the vicar, turned a large room at the vicarage into a chapel. Other raids were carried out on Maidstone, Dover, Rye and Foreness radar. Formations of Dorniers flew over the Kent coast shortly before 6.30pm, while fifteen bomb-carrying Messerschmitts and eight fighter Messerschmitts swept in near Dungeness for an attack on Croydon airfield, where they killed sixty-eight people and injured 192. Some of the Dorniers bombed the partly-completed airfield at West Malling, which was not yet a regular fighter station; and with this last attack Black Thursday came to an end.

Friday 16th August: But West Malling was not left alone for long. About two dozen Dorniers attacked it again at 10.45am, dropping more than eighty bombs on and round it. They destroyed a two-seater Army Co-operation Lysander and put the airfield out of operation for four days.

A formation of 150 enemy aircraft crossed the Kent coast near Dover about noon and fanned out in several groups to the north and north-west. Some of them were about to deal the most devastating attack on a civilian target which the county had yet experienced. The victim was Northfleet. Thirty Spitfires from Manston, Kenley and Hornchurch and twenty-one Hurricanes from Biggin Hill and Hawkinge were sent up to meet these raiders. One Hawkinge pilot was killed when his plane crashed with a Dornier over Smarden in the head-on attacks which the Hurricanes made. Five Spitfires were shot down by Messerschmitts near Deal at about 12.45pm.

Among the various scattered raids carried out by the Dorniers meanwhile was the serious attack on Northfleet at about 12.30pm. The bombers swept across the town as the anti-aircraft guns put up a heavy barrage. The sky sounded full of planes, but little could be seen except for the black puffs of smoke as the anti-aircraft shells burst. About 106 high-explosive bombs, varying from 50 to 250 kilos, were dropped across Northfleet from Hall Road to the Bowaters factory, where slight damage was caused.

One man was running to a shelter with his baby son in his arms when he was hit in the face by a splinter—he did not dare to stop but ran to the shelter with blood streaming down his face. A shower of machine-gun bullets rattled on the road and against houses in one street. A car standing by the kerb was hit by more than fifty bullets and reduced to a burned-out shell by the fire they caused. A greengrocer who had just unhitched his horse from his cart when the bombs fell was knocked down by the blast, got up and was knocked down again by a piece of flying masonry—deciding he had had enough for one day, he hitched up his horse again and drove off home. A woman who was hurt when her Anderson shelter was split open made money for charity from her escape by charging a penny for people to inspect the shelter.

A bomb fell in front of a first-aid party being driven to its station. The car overturned when the driver swung the wheel round to avoid a crater which appeared in the centre of the road. One of the five people inside was injured, but the others went on to deal with casualties in the area.

The railway line was damaged, and the woodwork room at the Colyer Road school was burned out. The Rosherville Schools were also damaged, and homes were badly hit in Mitchell Avenue, Waterdales, Colyer Road, Vale Road, Preston Road, Detling Road and the London Road. A total of twenty-nine people were killed in the raid, eighteen seriously injured and nine slightly hurt. Civil Defence officials visited Northfleet to inspect the damage and learned lessons at the scene for the future.

Eight Messerschmitts swept over Manston airfield late in the afternoon and destroyed a Spitfire and a Blenheim on the ground by raking buildings and parked aircraft with machine-gun fire.

Sunday 18th August: Twelve Spitfires from Hornchurch were scrambled at 12.38pm to meet about three hundred enemy aircraft over Kent; and seventy more fighters from nine squadrons were taking off to meet this huge force within minutes. West Malling was bombed, but the raiders were concentrating on Biggin Hill and Kenley.

Nine Dorniers flew low over the airfield at Biggin Hill at 100 feet about 1pm and were met by Hurricanes from two squadrons; two bombers were shot down; two others were so badly damaged that they crashed in the Channel, and three force-landed in France. The pilot of one of the German planes that returned safely had been killed over Biggin Hill, and his plane was flown back to France by the flight engineer, who was awarded the Knight's Cross for his action but a week later was shot down over London and taken prisoner. The raid on the airfield was closely followed by another attack by Junkers, but both raids between them did little more than crater the landing-ground, although two people were killed and three wounded by the five hundred bombs which fell. Officers and men began to fill in the hundreds of craters that pockmarked the airfield, with picks, shovels, household brooms and even their bare hands. A bomb-disposal squad which arrived found to its disgust that some of the unexploded bombs were British ones which had been captured during the fall of France; some of them dated from the early 1920s. One of the Junkers in the raid was shot down near Tonbridge by the Kent air ace Flight

Lieutenant Stanford Tuck, who then had to bale out of his Spitfire because of the return fire from the bombers.

Twelve hedge-hopping Messerschmitts carried out a strafing raid on Manston at 3.30pm. They killed one groundcrewman, injured fifteen others and destroyed two Spitfires with cannon and machine-gun fire.

Five separate formations converged on Kent at about 5pm but were unable to reach their target of Croydon because of the strong opposition from Spitfires and Hurricanes from North Weald and Horn-church. They dropped their bombs over a wide area of Kent and Surrey instead. The sirens sounded late in the Medway Towns, and fifty-nine casualties were reported there—although no deaths; but bombing caused the death of one person at Kemsley, near Sitting-bourne, and killed three people at Sevenoaks. Two pilots from Hawkinge were killed when seven Hurricanes from the airfield were shot down during the day, four of them coming down near Canter-bury. Five Messerschmitts were shot down over Ashford by Hurri-canes from Rochford.

Monday 19th August: Fourteen soldiers and sailors at Dover were killed when a lone plane dropped ten bombs round the Castle. Two of them fell on a field at Edinburgh Hill, where the men were playing football. Huts at the Connaught Barracks were damaged in this attack, which came just after 3pm, and about twenty other people were injured. The dead sailors were from HMS *Burke* and *Brock*, and the soldiers from the Fifth Field Training Regiment and the Green Howards.

Tuesday 20th August: A total of twenty-seven Dorniers and an escort of about thirty Messerschmitts were reported flying up the Thames Estuary at 2.20pm—and more than forty fighters from six squadrons were scrambled to meet them within eight minutes. A Dornier was shot down by Hurricanes from Kenley over its target of Eastchurch, which had sent ten bombers to attack Boulogne Harbour only two days before. Six Spitfires from Rochford harried raiders as they withdrew along the North Kent coast; two Dorniers were shot down and crashed near Eastchurch; a Messerschmitt was shot down and crashed near Faversham, and a Blenheim from Manston was damaged in a raid on the airfield at about that time.

It was on that day that Winston Churchill, referring to the thousand or so young British pilots who were fighting the Battle of Britain, said:

"Never in the field of human conflict was so much owed by so many to so few."

Wednesday 21st August: Two lone Dorniers swooped out of the skies an hour after each other that afternoon and caused the first deaths in Canterbury with the bombs they dropped. The first attack came at 2.43pm when two bombs fell on allotments behind the Dover railway on the south-east of the city. The allotments were blotted out, and a large crater was made in an adjoining field—but the only casualty was a chaffinch. The more serious raid occurred at 3.40pm, when one bomb fell in a builder's yard and another on a row of cottages in Cossington Road. The bomb which hit the yard did little damage, but the bomb which fell on the homes caused a terrific explosion; a big crater filled with debris was about all that could be seen of eight cottages when the smoke and dust had settled. Five people were killed, one seriously injured and another five slightly hurt.

One woman who was in her garden at the time escaped with shock and bruises when she was blown over a wall and into a garage yard. Bedding was blown onto the roof of a tall building some way away, and people were thrown to the ground in nearby streets. One man, who crouched against a wall when he heard the bombs falling quite close to him, was not hurt, even though debris hit the wall near him, but when he stood up, he saw his crouching shape outlined on the wall by blast-dust.

Thursday 22nd August: Messerschmitts attacking the convoy *Totem* off the coast were in turn attacked by Spitfires from Biggin Hill and Hornchurch soon after 1pm. A Hornchurch pilot was shot down and killed off Deal; a Biggin Hill pilot who was shot down and crash-landed at Hawkinge escaped unhurt shortly before his plane blew up. More Messerschmitts carried out a raid on Manston at 6.50pm, dropping six heavy bombs on the airfield. The bombs hit hangars, radio-stores and squadron offices, but there were no casualties. A Spitfire pilot from Manston was shot down and killed by Messerschmitts near Dover half an hour later. Two people at Dover had been killed by shelling during the day, four seriously injured and seven slightly hurt.

6. The Critical Period

Bad weather had brought a comparative lull in the battle since 19th August, but the weather had improved, and on 24th August a new phase of the Battle of Britain began. It had always been the Luftwaffe's intention to gain mastery of the air, but it now pursued this aim with raids that were better planned and more intense. This period between 24th August and 6th September brought Fighter Command so near to destruction that it became known to them as 'the critical period'. Kent, as always, was at the forefront of the assault; Ramsgate in particular was to suffer on that day.

Saturday 24th August: A squadron of Defiants was being refuelled at Manston shortly before lunch that day when hurried warning was given of approaching enemy aircraft. They were almost immediately set upon by twenty Junkers bombers and their fighter support. The Defiants were raked by machine-guns and hit by bombs even while they were taxi-ing for take-off. Those planes which did get off the ground chased the raiders across the Channel—within five minutes they had lost their commanding officer and two other aircraft.

A devastating raid had meanwhile been carried out at Manston. The bombers had roared in low and had been fired at by the five Bofors guns which protected the airfield. By the time they had disappeared, they had left behind them seventeen casualties and three badly damaged aircraft. All that was left of one guardhouse was a bomb crater, 40 feet deep. All communications had been cut by a bomb which severed 248 telephone and teleprinter circuits at one blow, putting the airfield out of contact with its 11 Group headquarters. Contact was eventually established with a local Observer Post through the Maidstone centre, and one Observer volunteered to cycle to Manston and report on the situation. Post Office engineers were called in quickly and found themselves sitting next to unexploded bombs as they tried to sort out and reconnect the hundreds of cut wires. Great risks were also taken by firemen from Margate, who salvaged Browning machine-guns from the ruins of the blazing armoury.

But not everyone at Manston was covering himself with glory. Attacks on the airfield had been so frequent that most people preferred to sleep in the shelters there rather than spend the night in some of the barrack blocks which still stood. The latest raid had terrified so many men that one officer could not find enough airmen above ground to hold a pay-parade. A squadron leader had prevented another officer from going into a shelter to shoot the first man who refused to come out; and the chaplain disarmed an officer who was threatening to kill everyone in the mess. Some local civilians took the opportunity to loot the damaged buildings for RAF tools and spares.

The raid on Manston that Saturday had made the airfield virtually useless for anything but a forward base for refuelling. Living-quarters had been destroyed, and unexploded bombs which fell among the station buildings forced the evacuation of all administrative personnel except those needed for ground defences and servicing. No. 600 Squadron of Blenheims, which was based at Manston for night-bombing, had been moved to Hornchurch on 21st August; and now RAF ground staff were moved to billets in Westgate.

The first wave of aircraft which carried out this attack created so much smoke and chalk-dust that the target was obscured by the time the following planes arrived. These other planes decided instead to bomb the small flying-club field at Ramsgate—which had no military value—and in doing so caused the highest death-toll the town was to experience during the war. This German raid killed thirty-one people, seriously injured eleven and slightly wounded forty-seven more.

It is estimated that anything up to eleven thousand people used the tunnels in the town for shelter during the attack, and there is little doubt that this action kept the casualty figures down. About 250 high-explosive and incendiary bombs were dropped on the town and the club airfield, and the area was also machine-gunned. Damage was widespread; streets were blocked; gas and water mains were fractured, and there were seventeen unexploded bombs dotted over the borough.

Two Auxiliary Firemen were cycling to duty when the raid began. Bombs started falling all round them, one of which burst in a nearby field, blowing the two men across the road and into a hedge. One man was given a deep wound from a bomb splinter, and the other went to help him, even though he also had received two wounds from the bomb. A plane then machine-gunned the couple. The man with the slighter injuries was hit in the arm by three bullets, one of which cut an artery. He was now wounded five times and weak from the loss of blood, but he still dragged his heavily-built friend to a sheltered spot before going for help. He had to climb over piles of masonry, broken glass and telephone wires and stagger 350 yards before he reached a first-aid post. His friend died later in hospital, but the rescuer recovered after treatment and was awarded the George Medal by the King for his act of gallantry.

A grocery store in the centre of Ramsgate was wrecked by a bomb which fell through the roof. The manager and his staff had gone to the firm's underground shelter only a few minutes before. A man who was standing outside a shop on the other side of the road was blown through a plate-glass window and killed. The gas works was hit and put out of action, and two members of the staff were killed there while running for cover. Among the dead were a married couple and their three-year-old child who had left home after the All Clear had sounded and were near the centre of town when the alarm-sirens went again; they began to hurry back but were killed by a bomb before they reached home. The wife of a newsagent died because she stopped to serve a customer instead of running for shelter; the customer was seriously injured, but a newsboy helping in the shop was not hurt.

The Mayor of Ramsgate, Alderman A.B.C. Kempe, had a lucky escape during the attack. The council offices at the time were on the cliff overlooking the harbour, and staff there had made a habit of standing in the open to watch the air-battles rather than take cover. They were doing so when one youngster shouted out that the planes were dropping bombs. Everyone, including the Mayor, dashed for shelter. A bomb fell only 10 yards behind Alderman Kempe and blew him down a passage. He was not injured, but the offices were badly damaged, even though they were not directly hit. The borough surveyor and his staff of seven, however, were sheltering in the reinforced basement of another building when it collapsed on them: they dug their way out unhurt.

Camden Square was among those places in the town badly damaged in the bombing. The warden's concrete shelter there was split from side to side. Two sisters from across the road dragged the badly-injured warden from the wreckage; their own house was also wrecked in the raid. The Assembly Hall was also demolished, but a notice on its ruined walls said, "Cheer up, the best part of history is still to be written." Five pubs were also hit by bombs, although the landlord of one of them did not let that interfere with his business: he sold beer through gaps in his damaged walls immediately after the raid. A baker was about to deliver bread to a house when a bomb fell on it, also wrecking his van. He was all right, and so were the occupants, who had been sheltering in the cellar. The baker helped them out, brushed them down and then delivered the bread he still had safely in his basket. Among the dead was a woman of seventy-five whose husband arrived home just in time to take her in his arms and kiss her before she died. Six of the nine lifeboatmen who were sheltering in a cellar at the harbour were injured when a bomb fell outside the entrance. Their lifeboat station was also badly damaged and closed until 11th October, although the coxswain and two other members were still unfit for duty by then. The men had been standing by to rescue German airmen shot down in the sea.

The council had anticipated air-raids by spending £60,000 to kill two birds with one stone, cutting 3½ miles of passages through the chalk cliffs all over the town. Their first use was as air-raid shelters; but they had also been built in such a way that they could be used for a new drainage-system when the war was over. The Mayor said after the raid that those tunnels had saved ninety per cent of the population. It is estimated that anything up to eleven thousand people sheltered in the passages, and there is no doubt that the death toll would have been higher without them. One bomb fell on an electric cable and plunged the tunnels into darkness, but hurricane-lamps soon appeared, and order was restored. People who had lost their homes in the raid decided to live in the tunnels instead: they put up their bunks there, screened them off and cooked Sunday joints on small oil-stoves. Some of them could be seen at the tunnel entrances the following day, sunning themselves in deckchairs and reading newspaper accounts of the bombing they had recently experienced. The passages were made so homely that it became difficult to get people out to fire-watch. The tunnels were later closed during the day by the council.

The town was without gas for twelve days because the gas-works had been hit. A small baker's shop at the back of the works was wrecked by the blast: its ceilings were down; the windows were missing, and the doors had gone, but the following day the baker could be found sitting in the bakehouse watching his ovens. He had opened up the bakehouse that morning to cook any meat brought to him, and in those ovens were more than a hundred Sunday roasts, ranging from sixpence-worth of meat to joints for whole families.

A rest-centre was set up in the old Constitutional Club after the raid and members of the WVS helped the homeless there. They cooked three hundred meals on six primus stoves in twelve days for people made homeless by the bombs, and 140 of those people were accommodated in the centre on one night alone. Supplies of clothing were sent by the British and Canadian Red Cross and the Friends of America. Casualty lists were posted in public places. Prince Bernhard of the Netherlands visited the town with members of the American Red Cross on 25th August, and this was followed by a visit to Ramsgate and Manston airfield by Winston Churchill on 28th August.

Monday 26th August: Forty Heinkels and twelve Dorniers, escorted by eighty Messerschmitts, crossed the coast north of Dover at about 11.30am. The main force flew west, but some of the Messerschmitts strafed small towns and villages in East Kent and shot up the barrage-balloons at Dover. Some Heinkels turned south and dropped bombs on Folkestone, killing two people, seriously injuring four and slightly hurting nineteen others. The bombs wrecked eight five-storey tene-ment houses in Marine Terrace, trapping a woman who had sheltered in the larder of one of them. PC W. Spain braved falling debris and the risk of collapsing walls to make his way to her and comfort her until the rescue squad arrived. He was later awarded the George Medal for this act.

Forty Hurricanes and thirty Spitfires were sent to intercept the bombers and became involved in dog-fights which raged from Canter-bury to Maidstone. Defiants from Hornchurch attacked Dorniers near Herne Bay and lost three aircraft in the process.

Tuesday 27th August: This time it was Gillingham's turn to suffer its worst raid of the war. Shortly before midnight the town was attacked by German bombers who scored a direct hit on the bus depot; the resulting fire destroyed nearly half the Maidstone and District fleet based there. Their bombs also killed twenty people, seriously injured twenty-two and slightly hurt eighteen others.

The main block of the depot was quickly well alight, and the heat from the fire was so great that houses on the other side of the road began to smoulder. Depot staff, servicemen and civilians immediately tried to save the buses which were parked away from the burning area, but rescue-work was hampered because the steering-wheels were padlocked as a precaution against an attack by parachute troops—and only two of the staff had keys. The bricks on the floor got red-hot and made the tyres of the buses expand to three times their normal size, when they would explode and move a bus about three feet from where it had been standing. Rescuers also had to brave exploding petrol-tanks and girders which bent under the heat and trapped some of the buses.

One bus which could not be started was bumped out by putting another bus behind it. A sailor who helped out had never driven anything in his life before, but he eventually managed to get a bus moving, bouncing it off several of the others in the process, and drove it away from the blaze. But on reaching the end of the road he found he was unable to stop it—so he deliberately drove it into a telephone kiosk and went back for another. The fire brigade was soon on the scene, even though their own station had been hit at the same time. It was their first big job of the war. They used twenty-one hoses to tackle the blaze, three of which were cut when they were run over by some of the buses being rescued.

An ambulance was being repaired in the garage at the time of the raid, and one man decided he was not going to let a fortnight's work on her be wasted. He went in the blazing building to retrieve it, but the heat was too much for him; he collapsed at the wheel and had to be dragged out. A roll-call revealed that three staff who had been in the messroom at the time of the bombing were missing. Firemen damped down the flames to make a passage to the room. The missing men were found dead in the tangled wreckage.

Fire-fighting went on until 4am in the morning; and at 5am the workers' buses left on their routes as usual—or almost. Fifty buses had been destroyed in the attack, but seventy had been saved. These had to be searched for the following morning because their rescuers had driven them off and left them anywhere. Depot staff were getting drivers to collect replacement buses from all over south-east England even before the fire was out. Service the day after the raid was more or less normal—but with a motley collection of buses which even included the open-top vehicles used on Hastings promenade during the summer. One of the few things to survive at the smouldering depot was a notice saying 'No smoking'. Buses were dispersed every night after the attack in case of similar raids. And a few weeks after the bombing, staff who had helped save the buses were given a bonus—of £5.

It was not the first time buses had been damaged, anyway. They often returned to the depot with broken windows of plastered with chalk from the blast of an explosion. The run between Maidstone and

Chatham, via Rochester airfield, was thought to be the worst: one old bus was sprinkled wth shrapnel so often that it was known as 'the Pepperpot'.

The bombs during the raid on Gillingham also caused a lot of damage elsewhere in the town. A high-explosive bomb which fell on Gillingham Co-operative store severely damaged the shop and scattered bags of sugar, bottles of hair-cream and food tins all over the street and nearby houses. A newsagent, a sub-post office and a butcher's shop were also hit. Gas and water mains were fractured. Incendiary bombs fell everywhere, including one on a theatre where the audience was enjoying a show. A member of staff saw it and went to move it, with the help of the manager and stage-manager, but it fell through the roof and onto the ceiling before they could get to it. The stage-manager went into the loft to tackle it but was overcome by fumes and had to be rescued by the manager. The bomb was put out, meanwhile, and the first the audience knew of the incident was when they were asked to leave.

Wednesday 28th August: An enemy formation of twenty-three Dorniers and sixty Messerschmitts was attacked by Hurricanes from Gravesend and Kenley as it made its way to Eastchurch. The raiders managed to drop more than a hundred bombs on the airfield shortly after 9am. They destroyed several light bombers on the ground but without putting the airfield out of action.

Thursday 29th August: A dozen Messerschmitts caught twelve Hurricanes from Gravesend by surprise over Kent and shot down two, both pilots baling out unhurt, one near Hawkinge.

Friday 30th August: That Friday turned out to be a black day for Biggin Hill, even though it began for that airfield with the rout of a raiding formation. The air over the county was constantly busy in the morning as numerous raids were intercepted above Kent. No less than forty-eight Observer Posts in Kent and Surrey reported combats overhead at one stage.

One Hurricane pilot who had been attacked by enemy planes shortly after 11am was found dead in his burned-out plane at Rochester. Spitfires from Hornchurch were on patrol over Gravesend when they were attacked at 11.25am, and one of their pilots was shot down and wounded. But the raiders did not have everything their own way. Three Hurricanes from Kenley became separated from the rest of their squadron and had just passed south of Maidstone at about 17,000 feet when they saw a massive formation of Messerschmitts about 500 feet above and in front of them. The three immediately attacked, and one of them was shot down wounded near Redhill. But another of the three, a squadron leader, shot down four of the Messerschmitts south-east of Maidstone within a few minutes shortly before noon.

This huge force of 150 bombers and a similar number of fighters as escort had fanned out over Kent and was flying towards the ring of airfields round London. The Observer Corps and radar gave ample warning of their approach, and the controller at Biggin Hill was able to get his squadrons up in time to meet the raiders. This attack on the enemy planes was so successful that only some of the bombers got through, and most of their bombs fell outside the airfield—although they did cause a lot of damage in the villages of Biggin Hill and Keston.

The next enemy assault was mounted soon after 1pm, and waves of bombers and Messerschmitts crossed the south Kent coast at twenty-minute intervals from 1.30pm onwards. A lucky hit in the morning had put seven Kent and coastal radar stations off the air so that only five fighter squadrons could be directed onto the raiders. It was during that assault that bombers attacked Lympne airfield shortly after 3pm. Four bombs exploded, and five male civilians were killed. But the most serious group of raids of the day began to approach the coast at 4pm. During the next two hours about 740 aircraft flew in over Kent and the Thames Estuary towards targets at Luton, Oxford, Slough, North Weald, Kenley and Biggin Hill. And this time the enemy planes took this last airfield by surprise. The time was 6pm; the warning came just as a stream of airmen was pouring out of the mess.

Ten Junkers swept in over the Biggin Hill airfield below 1,000 feet and dropped sixteen 500-kilo bombs. The men ran for the nearest shelter. There was not room for all of them—but it turned out that those left outside were the lucky ones. All that was left of the shelter after five minutes was a crater littered with bits of uniform and flesh. Anti-aircraft gunners firing at the raiders were joined by some of the off-duty control staff, who climbed onto the roof of the officers' mess and blazed away ineffectively with a Lewis gun. Six Spitfires from one squadron at the airfield managed to take off and claimed two 'probables'; but another squadron was already airborne too far away to defend its base.

By the time the bombers flew off, they had wrought havoc. The workshops, the NAAFI and some of the cookhouses were wrecked; all the water, electricity and gas mains were cut; one hangar was hit, and two aircraft were burned out; the sergeants' mess, the WAAF quarters and the airmen's barracks were uninhabitable. The death-toll was thirty-nine, with twenty-six injured. WAAFs in the women's trench remained calm during the bombing, even when the entrance blew in and a hot blast bowled them over. Another bomb fell even closer and caused the concrete walls of the shelter to cave in, smothering those inside with stones and chalky earth. They lay in the dark, waiting to be dug out. Pilots leapt from their cockpits to help airmen reach the women. Only one was dead. One officer had camouflaged his Morris Minor on the morning of the raid and had left it under a tree outside a hangar to let the paint dry. He found that not only had his car gone after the bombing, but so had the tree. The man eventually found the Morris on its back in the hangar—the hole in the hangar roof showing how it had got there.

Hornchurch took over temporary control of the Biggin Hill sector as men worked all night to restore communications with 11 Group headquarters. A temporary link was made, and the operations room was back on the air by the following morning.

Saturday 31st August: Three Hurricane pilots from a squadron of the Royal Canadian Air Force were shot down wounded near Dover at about 8am by Messerschmitts which shot down every barrage-balloon over the town. But the first real assault on Kent came soon after 9am when two groups of enemy aircraft flew in over the county. The first group, which consisted of about twenty Dorniers and a fighter escort, dropped eighty bombs on Eastchurch airfield; the raiders caused some damage but nothing that seriously affected the operation of the base. The other group, made up of Me109s and Me110s, carried out a series of strafing runs on Detling airfield, though without finding the parked aircraft they were after.

Two waves of Dorniers and Heinkels, escorted by Messerschmitts, were later sent to attack the airfields at Biggin Hill and Croydon. Twelve Hurricanes from Croydon were only just taking off as the first bombs from twelve low-flying Dorniers fell on the east side of their airfield at about 1pm. The squadron left the eruption of smoke and debris behind them and as they climbed could see the distant black smoke from the other attack on Biggin Hill. The Hurricanes caught up with the Messerschmitts which were escorting the bombers at

9,000 feet over Tunbridge Wells. Squadron Leader Peter Townsend was aiming at an Me109 when he was hit by a burst from an Me110. He baled out, landed in brambles at Hawkhurst and was taken to Croydon hospital, where his left big toe was amputated after a piece of shell was removed from his foot; his parachute was put on display by the local police, where it raised £3 for the local Spitfire Fund. That attack on Biggin Hill had meanwhile been carried out by twenty or so Heinkels bombing from about 12,000 feet. They severed all the telephone lines which had been so laboriously repaired since the previous day's raid, destroyed two of the remaining three hangars and hit messes, living-quarters and the important sector operations room.

Enemy aircraft carried out a series of low-level raids in the afternoon on the radar stations at Foreness, Dunkirk, Rye, Beachy Head and Pevensey. All were damaged but back on the air by the end of the day. Biggin Hill was attacked again at about 5.30pm when Junkers and Messerschmitts dropped about thirty bombs on the airfield. Other bombs during the day had killed two people at Deal, one person on Sheppey, one at Whitstable and one at Hollingbourne. Hounds of the East Kent Hunt fared luckier in their bombing ordeal this month: their kennels suffered a direct hit, and the dogs were blown far and wide by the explosion, but they were all recovered unhurt during the next two days.

Sunday 1st September: Radar stations in Kent reported the first signs of an enemy raid forming over France at 10.20am, and at 10.55am about 120 bombers and fighters flew in over Dover along a front that was five miles long. They split into two groups, which each split again fifteen minutes later as the first squadrons from 11 Group struck. But the British fighters were seldom able to break through the escorting Messerschmitts and reach the bombers. The targets of this phase were the airfields at Biggin Hill, Detling, Eastchurch and the London docks.

The next phase began at about 1.40pm when 170 Dorniers and Messerschmitts crossed the Kent coast. Shortly before 2pm they were spotted, flying at 15,000 feet near Biggin Hill, by a squadron of Hurricanes from Croydon. The squadron was attacked continuously by Messerschmitts while climbing 5,000 feet to attack the formation. One Hurricane pilot hit a straggling Dornier, whose rear gunner baled out while the pilot attempted a forced landing near the railway at Lydd. This British pilot found his oil-pressure dropping, so he landed at Lympne. But while his aircraft was being serviced, the airfield was bombed, and his aircraft was hit, killing one groundcrewman and seriously wounding another. Another Dornier was shot down between Hamstreet and Hythe, and a third south of Tunbridge Wells.

The morale of the Germans at this period, thinking that the RAF was close to defeat, may be gauged by an incident which took place in the Medway Towns that day. A German pilot, under armed escort, was looking out of the window when his train stopped at Chatham. A waitress ran out of the buffet and rattled a Mayor of Chatham's Spitfire Fund collecting-box under the prisoner's nose. The pilot asked the guard for his wallet, smiled and put a 5 mark note into the box before his train pulled out.

The final phase of the attacks began about 5.30pm when seven enemy formations, composed mostly of fighters, swept in over the Kent coast. While they carried out strafing attacks over the county, a small group of Dorniers bombed Biggin Hill for the third time that day.

These bombers destroyed the sector operations room with a direct hit, cratered runways again and severed all communications lines. Two WAAF telephone-operators stayed at their switchboard throughout the raid and survived flying debris when a 250-kilo bomb brought down the heavy concrete ceiling round them. Each of them was awarded the Military Medal for devotion to duty. Post Office engineers were again at work reconnecting cables, working in craters filled with water and escaping gas and in constant danger from further bombs. They restored the main cables, then, shortly after 6pm, had to patch lines to a makeshift operations room in a local village shop. They had rigged up basic communications within an hour and provided the temporary centre with an adequate switchboard by working through the night. These men also repaired the main cable again during the night, when it was cut once more, and reconnected a number of local observer posts which had lost their telephone lines.

One person had been killed during the day when a plane crashed at Elham, and two died when a bomb fell at Gravesend.

Monday 2nd September: The day began at 7am when a formation of about forty Dorniers and a hundred or so Messerschmitts assembled behind Calais. The Dorniers split up over the Maidstone area and attacked Biggin Hill, Eastchurch, Rochford and North Weald. Nine more bombers swept in low to carry out another raid on Biggin Hill while nine Spitfires were tangling with Dorniers and Messerschmitts at 13,000 feet over Maidstone. A bomb on the town killed two people that day. Dog-fights over Maidstone were so common during the height of the battle that pupils at Maidstone Grammar School had to comb their football pitch before each game to clear it of splinters from fallen bombs and anti-aircraft shells.

The next raid approached Dover about noon, and more than seventy Hurricanes and Spitfires intercepted 250 German fighters and bombers over Kent. Two Messerschmitts were destroyed in combat over Ashford. One Hurricane pilot was shot down and killed at 1.12pm in one of these combats—he was the brother of another Hurricane pilot who had been killed the previous day when his parachute failed to open after he had had to bale out.

Another raid of more than 250 enemy aircraft crossed the coast near Dover shortly after 5pm. About seventy Hurricanes and fifteen Spitfires from ten squadrons ran into about 160 Messerschmitt fighters near Ashford, and one of the biggest dog-fights of the day developed. Twelve Hurricanes were drawn into a trap over Dover when they followed a group of withdrawing Messerschmitts. One pilot was shot down unhurt and force-landed north of Dover as a result of this move before the fight was broken off when the Dover barrage began firing.

Bombers had meanwhile attacked seven airfields, including those at Eastchurch, Detling and Biggin Hill. The airfield at Detling was attacked by about forty Dorniers. They dropped a hundred high-explosive bombs but caused little damage. But that Monday was a black day for Eastchurch. One of the bombs dropped by the Dorniers hit the bomb-dump and exploded 350 bombs, virtually demolishing every building within 400 yards and destroying five aircraft on the ground. At least two civilians were killed, and others were wounded. The attack wrecked hangars, caused large craters and cut drainage-mains, power-cables and most of the communication-lines. Most personnel were moved that day to Eastchurch village, while some airmen were evacuated to Leysdown. A total of three aircraft were destroyed on the ground at Detling and six at Eastchurch as a result of the enemy raids.

Tuesday 3rd September: One of four Messerschmitts shot down the previous morning had been claimed by Pilot Officer Richard Hillary, who had by now shot down three Messerschmitts in five days. On that day, at about the same time, he was shot down into the sea near the North Foreland and hideously disfigured by burns when his Spitfire burst into flames. He was rescued by Margate lifeboat. Hillary was later to become famous as the author of *The Last Enemy*, a book about the air-fighting. He eventually recovered from his burns and returned to combat. He was killed in a training flight accident in 1943, at the age of twenty-four.

Wednesday 4th September: The airfields at Lympne and Eastchurch were attacked with bombs and gunfire in the morning, but the biggest raid of the day was not mounted until noon, when about seventy Heinkels and Dorniers, with an escort of more than two hundred Messerschmitts, approached the Kent coast between Dover and Hastings and split up to attack Canterbury, Faversham, Eastchurch, Reigate and Redhill. One of the midday raids slightly damaged the Short Brothers factory at Rochester.

The Kent raids, generally, were tackled successfully by nine squadrons of Hurricanes and Spitfires which turned some of the enemy formations away before their fighter escorts could interfere. Two Hurricane pilots were killed at 9.30am in the morning raids; one was shot down east of Folkestone, while the other baled out after being shot down near Folkestone and was killed by enemy fighters while descending.

One German pilot who had to bale out during an air battle that day ripped his parachute as he jumped but landed safely on a haystack near the road from Sevenoaks to Westerham. A passing bus stopped sharply, and the driver and conductor armed themselves with spanners before tackling the man. The pilot, thinking the couple were in military uniforms, came to attention, gave a Nazi salute and said "Biggin Hill *ist kaputt.*" Bombs which had been meant for that airfield in one of the lunchtime raids had, in fact, fallen wide and destroyed only a line of telegraph poles. But the driver was so angry that he hit the pilot on the head with his heaviest spanner, knocking him out cold.

Thursday 5th September: Eight Hurricanes from Croydon attacked more than a hundred enemy aircraft north of Dungeness at about 10am. One Hurricane pilot hit a Messerschmitt. He drew alongside the damaged enemy plane twice, over-excited by the battle perhaps, and signalled the German pilot to land. The pilot merely shook his fist and opened fire. But the British pilot eventually shot him down into the sea 10 miles off Dungeness, where he was picked up unhurt. Heinkels and Junkers attacked the oil-storage farm at Thameshaven in the afternoon and set five of the tanks on fire.

It was on that day that an Me109, flown by Franz von Werra, was shot down at Marden at 3.25pm by a Spitfire. Werra became famous as 'the one that got away'—the only German prisoner-of-war captured in Britain who escaped back to Germany. He escaped twice in Britain but was quickly recaptured and taken to Canada, where he got away again from a moving train and made his way to the then neutral United States before returning home.

Friday 6th September: Two bombs which fell on Dartford killed twenty-four people shortly after midnight by destroying most of the women's block at the County Hospital and wrecking houses in the nearby Anne of Cleves Road. Two of the dead were members of staff, and six staff and nine patients were also injured in the raid. The block concerned was replaced during the war by a single-storey building. The hospital itself was damaged on fourteen other occasions.

A person was killed at Hollingbourne that day by a cannon shell. Other raiders appeared over Kent about 9am, and within the next thirty minutes or so had shot down twelve Hurricanes over the county.

7. By no means defeated

The most decisive day of the battle was, as we shall see, 15th September, though 7th September also has some claim to this distinction. The resources of Fighter Command were stretched almost to the limit by this time: only 840 of its one thousand pilots were trained and fit for action—and no one could tell how long they could keep the upper hand if the battle continued at its recent intense pitch. Fighter Command did not know it, but it was in for a respite. Another phase in the Battle of Britain was about to begin.

It was a phase which began with a mistake. Hitler had banned raids on London, but on the night of 24th August about ten German bombers dropped their loads on central London after losing their way to targets at Rochester and Thameshaven. They were the first bombs to fall on the centre of the city, and the following day Churchill ordered an immediate retaliation-raid on Berlin. There were four more raids on the German capital during the next week. Hitler demanded immediate reprisals and, on 7th September, the daylight bombing offensive was switched to London. The pressure, at last, was off the heavily attacked airfields in the south-east.

Saturday 7th September: It was a sunny day of good flying weather, but, unusually, there was no sign of enemy aircraft over England for hour after hour. Then the first few planes appeared on the radar screens at 3.54pm; the first Observer Corps report on the enemy formation, which reached the Maidstone centre at 4.16pm, told of hundreds of aircraft approaching the Kent coast between Deal and the North Foreland. And on and on they came. A total of 348 bombers and 617 fighters, ranged from 14,000 to 23,000 feet, were advancing towards the Thames Estuary along a 20-mile front. It was the biggest raid Fighter Command had ever faced.

Eleven British squadrons were ordered into the air at 4.17pm, and all remaining Spitfire and Hurricanes were brought to readiness six minutes later. All twenty-one squadrons based within 70 miles of London were in the air or under take-off orders by 4.30pm. British pilots breaking out of a layer of haze east of Sheppey at that time found themselves on the edge of a massive armada, towering above them for more than 1½ miles and covering 800 square miles.

The first wave of enemy aircraft flew straight to the London docks, while the second flew over central London and then back over the East End and the docks. By 5.45pm the German formations had turned south and east and were heading home. The fires raging in the East End acted as a beacon for the follow-up raids which continued from 8pm that night until 4.30am the following morning. The attack had been devastating. The death-toll was 306, with 1,337 more seriously injured in London itself and a further 142 killed in the suburbs.

The fighters of Fighter Command had meanwhile been engaging the enemy where they could and had inflicted a loss of forty-one aircraft on the Germans for its own loss of twenty-eight. At least eighteen of the British planes had been shot down over Kent and the Thames Estuary between five and six pm.

The British Chiefs of Staff had been meeting in London a few hours before that massive daylight assault, weighing up all the evidence from reconnaissance and secret intelligence. "A significant item of intelligence" they discussed was the landing of four German spies on the Kent coast on 3rd September. These spies—about whom we shall hear more later—had confessed after their quick arrests that they were sent to report on troop movements, news which seemed to clinch the theory that Hitler's plans for an invasion were so advanced that his armies might try to land at any time. The bombing of London strengthened that impression. So at 8pm that night the General Headquarters of the Home Forces issued the codeword 'Cromwell' to its Eastern and Southern Commands.

'Cromwell' was a warning to the troops that an invasion was imminent and probable within twelve hours, but it created much excitement and confusion when it reached the troops, including those in other parts of the country who had been given 'Cromwell' for information only. This confusion seems to have occurred because not everyone concerned knew exactly what it meant, most believing it to mean that an invasion was already taking place. The Home Guard was not given the message officially, but many units got to hear about it. Church bells—which were supposed to be rung only when enemy parachutists dropped—were sounded; country road-blocks were closed in many parts of the country; telephone-operators refused to accept non-official calls, and several road bridges were demolished in one sector of Eastern Command. The Germans, however, did not come. And that night the aircraft of Bomber Command were sent to attack the invasion barges and military dumps in the Channel ports, which were then pounded night after night by the bombers.

Six people were killed during the day when bombs wrecked an underground shelter on a farm at Hawkinge and demolished two houses. This was part of an attack carried out by Messerschmitts which swept over the airfield there at 1,500 feet and dropped bombs on the officers' mess.

Sunday 8th September: Two small groups of raiders, each consisting of about thirty Dorniers, crossed the coast west of Dungeness at 11.45am on their way to attack airfields and suburbs south of London. They were engaged by four squadrons of Hurricanes between Maidstone and Rochester, and several Dorniers were shot down before their fighter escort could interfere. During that day bombs killed four people in the Dartford rural area, one person at Malling and another at Dover.

Monday 9th September: Nearly half the bomber formations heading towards London in the afternoon were turned back by RAF fighters. Hardly any of the bombers succeeded in hitting their targets, and the others were so badly affected by interceptors and anti-aircraft fire that they scattered their bombs where they could. One such group of raiders was thwarted so successfully in its attempts to reach London that it dropped its bombs on Canterbury instead.

A number of German planes being driven back by Spitfires dropped fifty-five bombs of various sizes in three distinct lines across the city at about 5pm. The bombs fell in the north of the city, damaging property in the Whitstable Road, St Dunstan's Street, St Peter's Grove, St Stephen's Road, the Cathedral Precincts and even Thanington. The raid lasted only five minutes or so, but by the time the enemy aircraft left, they had killed nine people, seriously injured six and slightly hurt seven. Telephones in the Civil Defence control room were undamaged, however, and for the next ninety minutes everyone there worked feverishly to cope with the messages coming in asking for help of some sort. Every call for an ambulance or rescue-party was plotted on a map with a flag: within twenty minutes nearly all the flags available were pinned on the map, and there was only one ambulance to spare.

One of the bombs had scored a direct hit on the East Kent bus-garage in St Stephen's Road, where the bomb burst on a girder, burned out three buses, almost wrecked two and damaged another. The only casualty there was a man who was cut. Another bomb demolished a parish hall and killed three ARP wardens who were on duty. One woman was injured when the Methodist School shelter in St Peter's Grove was hit; she was hurt shielding her baby with her body.

One of the luckiest escapes was that of five people, including a child, who rushed to shelter in the scullery when they heard the bombs falling—the scullery, in which the five were left unhurt, was almost the only part of the house left intact. A man and his daughter were having tea in their front room when a bomb exploded in the garden, and the front of the house fell away from them; they were unhurt but startled. A man was killed at Thanington, and his wife injured in the raid; the couple had moved there recently from Dover because they thought it would be safer.

Four people were also killed that day by shelling at Dover.

Tuesday 10th September: About twelve Junkers crossed the coast singly between Dover and Southampton in the evening and dropped bombs on Portsmouth Dockyard and at Littlehampton, Farnborough and Bognor Regis. Bombs which fell on Kent killed three people at Whitstable and four at Sevenoaks.

Wednesday 11th September: Bomber formations, escorted by more than two hundred fighters, flew up the Thames Estuary towards London at about 3pm. Many of the Messerschmitts ran low on fuel and had to break off early, leaving some of the Heinkels without protection when more than sixty Hurricanes and Spitfires from six squadrons attacked them. Seven bombers were shot down and ten damaged as they struggled to reach the coast.

But it was the coastal town of Dover which suffered most in Kent that day. Dorniers attacked the town soon after 3pm and dropped more than twenty-six bombs across the borough. This raid was over quickly, but the town was also hit by ten shells in a shelling attack which went on until late in the afternoon. By the time the day was over, sixteen people had been killed, including nine service personnel, thirteen people seriously injured and thirty-six slightly hurt.

Most of the damage was done in an area which ran parallel to the sea-shore, crossing the Grand Hotel and Townall Street. Some people on the top floor of the hotel fell to the ground when it received a direct hit, but only two there were killed. One wing of the hotel had collapsed; the Sailors' Home was wrecked, and the 'Sussex Arms' pub and surrounding property in Townall Street were demolished. It was eleven days before some of the bodies were recovered. Seventy houses and shops were left in ruins, and seventy more were seriously damaged, along with gas and water mains. Councillor John Walker, a boat-proprietor who had strongly opposed government demands that some members of the town council should be ready to evacuate the area, took shelter under one of his boats on sea-front during the raid: he and his dog were killed there by a bomb which set fire to the boats.

Two people were also killed that day by a bomb which fell at Tunbridge Wells. At least twenty-one British fighters were shot down over the county and the Thames Estuary, all between 3.50pm and 6.23pm.

Thursday 12th September: No one in Tunbridge Wells seemed worried by a lone aircraft which circled the town at between 5,000 and 6,000 feet in the afternoon. He looked as though he might be on a re-connaissance flight. But all doubts were dispelled when the single raider drew off to a point outside Tunbridge Wells and made a turn, catching the town by surprise as it dropped its load of bombs shortly after 5pm. By the time the raid was over, Tunbridge Wells had suffered its highest death-toll of the war: eleven people killed, three seriously injured and fourteen slightly hurt.

The streets were crowded with shoppers when the first bomb fell on waste land behind the hospital. The next fell at one of the hospital entrances and wrecked the outpatients, casualty and dental departments there. Staff remained calm; nurses went about their work as normal, and none of the patients was wounded; but a boy delivering a paper to the hospital was seriously injured in the blast, and he died later in hospital. A house nearby collapsed when a bomb exploded close to it, and a maid who, getting ready for her evening out, had been having a bath, was trapped under the debris. She was protected from falling masonry by the angle of the roof as it fell to the ground. She had just dried herself when the bombs fell and was therefore 'scantily clad' when rescued by a party of soldiers. She escaped with minor injuries.

The bomb that did the most damage fell near the foundations of a building used by wholesale grocers and provisions merchants. Incendiary bombs which fell at the same time set fire to the wreckage under which several workers and the managing director were buried. It was there that most of the deaths occurred. Work at the building finished at 5pm normally, but five drivers had got in rather late that day and, after settling a query, were chatting at the loading-dock. The death-toll would not have been as high without that delay. The fire brigade, Auxiliary Fire Brigade, rescue-squads, demolition-squads and first-aid units had rushed to the scene. That bomb had been the last to fall on the town.

A young woman was walking along the pavement with a small boy only 30 yards from the Roman Catholic church when she heard the scream of bombs. She covered the boy with her body and sheltered close to the wall. A coat she was wearing was blown off her shoulders, but she was not scratched. Another woman who was carrying a shopping-basket found herself left holding only the handle after the explosion—the basket and the goods in it had disappeared.

Friday 13th September: Reports from reconnaissance aircraft showed that invasion barges were still being assembled in the Channel ports. So on the evening of 11th September Bomber and Coastal Commands raided the coast with every aircraft available. More than a hundred planes dropped about 80 tons of bombs on the docks at Calais, Dunkirk, Le Havre and Boulogne in only three hours. They destroyed up to a hundred of the barges. And on the nights of 12th and 13th September British planes attacked yet again and destroyed seventy landing-barges in the ports of Boulogne, Calais and Antwerp. When Hitler heard this news on 14th September, he postponed Operation Sealion to 27th September.

Bombs which fell at Maidstone that day killed four people and seriously injured seven others.

Saturday 14th September: Bad weather prevented any important targets being attacked that day, although random bombs killed forty-nine people in the Kingston and Wimbledon areas of London. Twelve high-explosive bombs which fell in the Swanscombe area at 4.24am wrecked three houses, killed five people and slightly injured another.

Eleven British fighters were shot down over Kent; two of the Hurricanes were hit by Spitfires, and it is believed that Spitfires were also responsible for three of the other Hurricane casualties. All the aircraft were shot down between 4pm to 4.30pm. The pilot of one of those believed to have been hit by a Spitfire was unhurt and force-landed at Gravesend; another was injured when he baled out near Tonbridge, and the third baled out unhurt near Maidstone. Both pilots in the planes definitely damaged by Spitfires were unhurt, one force-landing at West Malling and the other landing at his base.

Sunday 15th September: It was on that day, now celebrated each year at 'Battle of Britain Day', that the battle reached its climax. The first big raid which crossed the Kent coast in the morning was badly hit by RAF fighters, as was another a few hours later. Goering had sent over five fighters for every bomber, yet a third of these bombers were still shot down. The pressure had been taken off Fighter Command when the offensive was switched from their airfields to London on 7th September. Its pilots had used the lull wisely, and by the dawn of that day Fighter Command was stronger and better equipped than it had ever been. By nightfall they had shot down about sixty German planes (thirty-four of which were bombers) for the loss of only twenty-six fighters. They experienced the fiercest, most confused and most widespread fighting of the whole battle, but by the time it had ended, the invasion of Britain was no longer feasible.

The main bomber formation of a hundred Dorniers and a massive fighter escort was attacked by about twenty Spitfires as it crossed the coast at Dungeness at 11.35am. More and more British fighters joined in the fray as the formation headed towards London. The capital came in sight at 11.55am, just as no fewer than nine British squadrons suddenly appeared and smashed the formation of Dorniers in a tremendous assault. The German raiders were being attacked now by more than 160 Spitfires and Hurricanes, and they could do little more than drop their bombs at random before trying to escape as best they could over the Kent coast.

At least eight British fighters were shot down over Kent between 11.50am and 12.20pm. One Hurricane pilot was killed when his plane crashed into Staplehurst railway station, while another was killed when he was shot down at Mounds Farm, Lynsted; a third was killed when he was hit by an Me109 over Kent, and a fourth was missing, presumed killed, after combat over Longfield. A Hurricane pilot who was hit in the leg baled out at Sevenoaks; another baled out unhurt when he was shot down near Maidstone, and a third baled out slightly wounded after being hit over West Malling. A Spitfire pilot was killed when he was shot down near Gravesend and crashed with his aircraft.

The next raid approached London along a 10-mile front over North

Kent shortly after 2pm. It consisted of three waves of more than 150 Dorniers and Heinkels, together with another massive fighter escort. Orders to scramble were given to Fighter Command pilots between 1.50pm and 2.20pm, and 170 Hurricanes and Spitfires met the German bombers over Kent. The German escort held them off for more than ten minutes without any widespread disruption to the bomber formation, but another thirteen British squadrons then reached the scene. The enemy bombers, having met something like three hundred fighters over Kent and London, quickly unloaded their bombs over East London and flew south-east as fast as they could.

At least nine British fighters were shot down over Kent between 2pm and 3.10pm. One Hurricane pilot who was hit near Tonbridge was killed when his parachute failed to open after he baled out; another was unhurt when his plane was damaged by Me110s over Kent, and a third baled out unhurt at Hawkinge. Another Hurricane pilot baled out grievously wounded and burned at Dartford, while two others baled out unhurt, one at Dartford and the other over Marden after his plane collided with a Dornier. A Spitfire pilot was killed when he was shot down over the county. A Hurricane pilot baled out slightly wounded in the leg near Chatham, while another pilot also baled out slightly wounded near Appledore. The German planes brought down that day included a Heinkel shot down near Dartford, and Me109s near Maidstone, Margate, South Kent, Sheppey, two over Dungeness and another somewhere else in Kent.

A Spitfire pilot from Hawkinge dived towards two Me109s from 28,000 feet during the afternoon. He followed one of the planes down when they broke away and fired at it over Dungeness. He eased back on the stick and promptly blacked himself out. When he recovered consciousness, he was upside-down over Maidstone—30 miles away. The Spitfire, which becomes tail-heavy in a dive, had pulled out of its own accord.

Someone on the ground had an equally lucky escape when another fighter aircraft, this time German, crashed into a village at 1.52pm and caused the only recorded civilian death in Kent that day. The fighter crashed in flames on a building at Bilsington, near Ashford, killing one man, seriously injuring another and slightly hurting some-one else. The timber and brick building was burned out, and the force of the explosion scattered wreckage over a wide area. The roofs of several cottages in the area were damaged, and a small general shop about 40 yards away was partly wrecked. It was the widow who lived there who had a lucky escape. Pieces of machinery smashed through the shop window close to her, and part of the petrol tank flew past her head. When she dashed into her living-room, she found a wheel from the plane burning there, and the machine-gun ended up on her bed upstairs. The woman carried on with her business in spite of shattered windows and gaping holes in the wall. The pilot of the plane survived to be taken prisoner.

The weather was too poor for large-scale air fighting on 16th September, and more turbulent weather was expected. Hitler agreed with his Naval Staff the following day that the RAF was not yet beaten. In view of that fact, and because of the weather, he announced his decision to postpone the invasion 'until further notice' on the afternoon of 17th September. The War Diary of the Naval Staff records: "The enemy air force is still by no means defeated; on the contrary, it shows increasing activity." On 19th September Hitler ordered that no more shipping was to be assembled in the Channel ports, and he agreed that the barges and transports which had already been collected (about twelve per cent of which had been destroyed or damaged by the RAF) could be dispersed to safer areas. The invasion was postponed definitely on 12th October until the spring of 1941. In January 1941 Hitler ruled that all preparations should be stopped.

Operation Sealion was dead. The Battle of Britain was over.

8. Hide and Seek

In the early hours of Tuesday 3rd September 1940, exactly one year after war began, four incompetent German spies landed on the Kent coast between Hythe and Dungeness. They were all ill-trained, and their mission was a hopeless failure. All of them were captured within thirty-six hours, and before the year was out, three of them were hanged in Pentonville Prison.

This episode of espionage is tinged with moments of farce. Only one of the men could speak fluent English; they had all apparently got drunk the night before they landed, and the downfall of one of them was caused when he went into a pub in Lydd and asked for alcohol at 9.30 in the morning. Only one of the spies managed to send messages back to his controllers, and the three messages which survived to be used in evidence against him were all worthless from an operational point of view.

The four men were Charles van der Kieboom, aged twenty-six, and Sjord Pons, twenty-eight, both Dutchmen, Rudolf Waldberg, the only German in the party, and Carl Meier, twenty-four, a man of doubtful origin who claimed that he, too, was Dutch.

There could be little doubt that Kieboom was not English. Not only did he have a limited command of the language but, because of his Dutch father and Japanese mother, he suffered the additional hazard of looking oriental. When his country was mobilized to face Germany, he served with his friend Pons as a driver in a motor battalion for ambulance troops, leaving the Dutch Army on 30th June 1940. Pons spoke a little English but understood the language only if it was spoken slowly. Both men had been involved in currency smuggling— and it was because of this that they were made an offer they could not refuse: when, shortly after they left the army, they were each approached by a man who asked them to do some work for the Germans, it was made clear that their currency offences would be used against them if they refused. They accepted the offer.

The other couple, Waldberg and Meier, did not have to be black-mailed. Waldberg had already worked with the German espionage service for two years before the ill-fated trip to England. He was born in Mayence of a German father and a French mother. He spoke both those languages well—but not one word of English. On reaching Britain he was to find out what divisions and brigades were on the south coast, what the nature of the fortifications were, and what type of guns they had. Meier claimed that he was Dutch, although he had been born in Coblenz in 1916 and possessed a passport issued to him at Innsbruck in November 1938. He had worked at The Hague before the war, but, towards the end of July 1940, when the armistice between Holland and Germany had been signed, a captain in the German cavalry had asked him if he would be willing to work for the Germans. His answer was 'yes'.

A luncheon party, described as a merry affair by Waldberg, was given for the four spies in Le Touquet on 2nd September. Quite what happened on the Channel trip after that is a mystery. All had confused memories of the journey, possibly because they were drunk. Waldberg, for example, says that he and Meier were not joined by the other couple in the cutter which took them across. One of the men said that the fishing boat's crew consisted, improbably, of three Russians and a Latvian, while another said it was manned by two Norwegians and one Russian. Waldberg says two German mine-sweepers escorted the boat to about seven miles east of Dungeness and then ordered her to go due north for twenty minutes, when the men were to get into dinghies and follow the same course. Kieboom said they were put in their dinghy at midnight or 1am, although it is thought they did not land much before 5am. But however they came across the Channel, it is clear that each couple made its own way to the shore in a separate dinghy.

Kieboom and Pons landed near the Grand Redoubt at West Hythe. Their dinghy also carried a suitcase full of clothes, a radio-set and a sack of such provisions as tinned meat, chocolate and cigarettes. Their instructions were to look out for information of military importance and to send messages in code between 5am–8am and 8pm–2am. The code, which they carried with them, came in the form of a brown linen cloth perforated with holes; it was used in conjunction with a corresponding grid of letters.

They did not get far. At about 5am an incredulous private of the Somerset Light Infantry was startled to see the shadow of a man move across the road and disappear into the grass beside the sea wall. The soldier's "Halt, who goes there" was greeted with "I do not know your code word."

The man was the oriental-looking Kieboom, dressed in civilian clothes and white shoes, and with binoculars and another pair of shoes slung round his neck. He said: "I have come across the water. I am a Dutch refugee, and if I can see one of your officers, I can explain the position." The officer to whom he was taken searched him for arms and found that he had a loaded pistol on him. About fifteen minutes after Kieboom's capture, another private from the Infantry searched the area near which he had been seen and found the sack and the suitcase. The case containing the wireless-set, a plug, a valve and two aerials was found by a lance corporal later that afternoon. It was lying flat on the ground with grass bent over it. Kieboom managed to get rid of his code by flushing it down a toilet after his capture.

Pons did not remain free for much longer. At about 5.25 that morning another soldier noticed a figure moving in a field and asked him what he was doing. The man, Pons, replied that he was a Dutchman. The soldier then told him to stay where he was and sent out men to surround him.

Waldberg and Meier, meanwhile, were having their own problems. Their dinghy contained a wireless-set and batteries, two small bags filled with their personal belongings, a big sack of food and two small spades about 18 inches long. When they were about 200 metres off the shore, they saw, or thought they saw, a small boat approaching them. When it was about 100 metres away, Waldberg dropped his pistol, secret codes and maps overboard. But their landing near Dungeness was not interrupted. They came ashore and put most of their stuff in a disused boat, the wireless-set and batteries behind an overturned road-sign, and then went to sleep nearby.

They looked for a better place to put the wireless early next morning and chose a tree a short distance from the shore. Waldberg fixed his aerial up so that he could send and receive messages. By this time he was thirsty. There were provisions in the dinghy, but it was decided it was too risky to try to retrieve them from the boat in daylight. So Meier—the only one of the four with fluent English—walked into Lydd along New Street and went into the 'Rising Sun' pub at 9.30am. His request for some champagne cider was met by the publican's wife at first with surprise and then suspicion—for the pub did not open until 10am. She told him he would have to come back later and sent him across the road to buy the cigarettes he wanted. Once he had left, she sent a note to her husband, who also owned the butcher's shop a hundred yards away. But when Meier returned to the pub it was not her husband but an RAF officer who lived a few doors away who was waiting for him. The game was up. He did not have the required permit to travel so near the coast, a banned area, and he was taken to the local police station in the charge of a police sergeant.

He never mentioned a companion, but early the following day the police saw a man walking towards the beach across Boulder Well Farm, now mostly occupied by a gravel pit. When asked where he had slept, the man, Waldberg, pointed towards a pumping station, and they walked in that direction. There he took police to a large tree which stood surrounded by bushes about 400 yards from the Lydd to Dungeness road. The boughs of the tree reached to the ground, and inside them was an open space. In the fork of the trees were two cases, one containing the wireless-set and the other the five batteries and a morse-key. There were also two suitcases and a raincoat. An aerial ran from the tree to a large bush. A notebook was found on Waldberg which contained three messages he had apparently sent in French to his controllers. They were:

> Arrived safely document destroyed English patrol two hundred metres from coast beach with brown nets and railway sleepers at a distance of fifty metres no mines few soldiers unfinished block house new road Waldberg.
>
> Meier prisoner English police searching for me am cornered situation difficult I can resist thirst until Saturday if I am to resist send aeroplanes Wednesday evening eleven o'clock am three km north of [point of] arrival long live Germany Waldberg.
>
> This is exact position yesterday evening six o'clock three messerschmitt fired machine guns in my direction three hundred metres south water reservoir painted red Meier prisoner.

Kieboom and Pons in particular had been given to understand that an invasion of the Kentish coast was imminent, and there can be little doubt that all four spies had been sent over to find out information which would help Operation Sealion reach a successful conclusion. These three pathetic messages are all that came from their mission; and Sealion was, of course, called off when the Luftwaffe failed to achieve air supremacy during the Battle of Britain.

The four agents appeared at the Old Bailey together on 22nd November 1940 and were tried in secret under the Treason Act of that year. The defence for Kieboom and Pons was that they had been forced to become spies and had intended to give themselves up to the

British as soon as they landed—a fact not borne out by their actions when they did land. The jury, however, found Pons not guilty; a different verdict was returned on his three companions. Waldberg and Meier were hanged together in Pentonville on 10th December, and Kieboom went to the gallows there a week later, on 17th December.

These four ill-trained spies had found quickly that Britain's coastline was not entirely unguarded or defenceless. But what neither they nor the public in Britain knew was the extent of the anti-invasion preparations being made at that time.

The best kept secret of them all was the fact that down in Kent and Sussex small resistance patrols were being formed. Their members were civilians; their bases were underground and well hidden; and few, often not even their wives, knew that they led a dual existence. They were Britain's secret army—a web of resistance whose members would come out of the ground to harass the Germans once they had passed overhead. They were armed guerrillas, and they were ready to wreak havoc when the time came.

The task of forming the first guerrilla unit in Kent was given to Peter Fleming, brother of the creator of 'James Bond', an explorer, author and journalist, and then a captain in the Grenadier Guards. He needed a base and requisitioned as his HQ the Garth at Bilting, near Ashford. It was an ideal setting for his purpose, close to the main road from Ashford to Canterbury, and close to the likely centre of action in an invasion, yet tucked away on the Downs and right on the edge of Challock Forest. Captain Fleming moved in that summer with a captain and a sergeant who were demolition experts, another sergeant and a private to do the clerical work, several drivers and two batmen. Two RAF radio-operators used a room at the back of the house. He also had with him a platoon of Lovat Scouts.

Their recruits were civilians who knew their area well. Each patrol had between four and eight men and its own hide-out as a base; each patrol operated independently for the sake of security, and names were not recorded on paper. They were called 'Auxiliary Units' and were grouped into three Home Guard battalions known as '201', which was south of the Thames, '202' north of the Thames and '203' in Scotland. These recruits eventually received Home Guard uniforms, even though they were unpaid civilians; but because their units appeared on no official register, they were outside the rules of the Geneva Convention and would probably have been shot on capture.

Most of those men would have been sent at some time for training at the Units' national headquarters at Coleshill, near Swindon. There they would have gone to classes which taught how to kill silently. Pupils watched as new members, pretending to be German sentries, were sneaked up on by their tutor and 'stabbed' before they had time to cry out. Each man was given a pistol, a rubber truncheon and a commando knife and boots; each patrol was issued with a tommy gun, two rifles, hand-grenades and plastic explosives. They even took priority over ordinary troops, and the patrols in Kent were the first soldiers in the county to receive sub-machine guns.

Training was also carried out on the sloping fields round The Garth, where fifty to eighty men attended demonstrations in 1940, usually at weekends. They were taught how to use guns and how to handle explosives—the local people putting the loud bangs they heard down to Home Guard practice. The resistance men would have been doing most of their work at night so they often wore smoked-glass goggles when they carried out their daytime manoeuvres, attacking other goggled patrols who played the part of Germans. The other men sat higher on the hillside at these sessions to see how the exercises were going.

The big barn next to The Garth was packed with explosives (often stored in milk churns) ammunition and weapons, including six long-bows. Fleming was an expert archer who could kill a deer at a hundred yards, and he wanted his men trained so they could use the bows to send incendiary charges flying into German petrol-dumps and to pick off sentries silently. That plan never got far—but legends sprang up about bands of bowmen who wandered the fields and woods of Kent in search of Germans.

Another story which stems from this time concerns Fleming's brother Ian—that one afternoon Peter Fleming was at Bilting when the orderly-sergeant rushed into his office to report that a German airman was asking for him in the officers' mess: the airman was Ian. The story is not true, but it is based on a grain of truth.

At that time Ian was working for Naval Intelligence and—as be-fitted the creator of James Bond—often used to come up with imaginative ideas for combating the enemy. His latest idea was to stage a dummy crash in the Channel, near the French coast, using a captured German aircraft and a German-speaking British crew. He intended to lure a German rescue-launch to the scene and overpower its crew, capturing the code-ciphers on board which were of great value to British cryptographers. He himself planned to take charge of the operation. The scheme was approved. He was issued with a

A holiday-maker leaving Aylesford during the last week of August 1939 makes his feelings clear — but he had only a few days of peace in which to enjoy himself.

One of the 207 trains which stopped at Headcorn with troops returning from Dunkirk. About 145,000 men were fed by volunteers at this station, where they had their first decent meal in days.

One of many road-barriers erected quickly throughout Kent after Dunkirk in case of a German invasion.

These vapour-trails in the sky over the Medway area tell of dog-fights during the Battle of Britain, September 1940.

Anti-tank blocks on the bridge over the Medway at Maidstone leave just enough room for buses to pass through.

Fifty buses were destroyed when this Maidstone and District depot at Gillingham was wrecked by bombs on 27th August 1940. The attack on the town also killed twenty people, seriously injured twenty-two and slightly hurt eighteen.

A view of Mill Street, Maidstone, after bombs fell on the town on 31st October 1940 and killed three people, seriously injured fourteen and slightly hurt nineteen.

An RAF guard stands by a Messerschmitt 110 which crashed at Lenham—one of 374 enemy aircraft which came down in Kent during the war.

Caves like this in the cliffs at Dover could accommodate thousands of people during air-raids.

Wreckage of the 'Star' pub in Swanscombe, destroyed by a bomb while a darts match was in progress on the evening of 10th November 1940. Twenty-seven people were killed in this raid, six seriously injured and five slightly hurt.

A boy wanders in the wreckage caused by two parachute mines which fell on Chatham on 14th December 1940. It was the town's worst raid: fifteen people were killed, twenty seriously injured and 103 slightly hurt.

The aftermath of parachute bombs which fell on Rochester on 8th April 1941. Eleven people were killed, twenty-eight seriously injured and sixty-six slightly hurt.

The village centre of Sturry was devastated when two parachute mines fell on it on 18th November 1941, killing fifteen people and seriously injuring eleven others.

A greengrocer's and an ironmonger's shop lay ruined in Deal High Street as the result of the town's worst bombing raid on 22nd October 1942, which left sixteen people dead, seven seriously injured and fifteen slightly hurt.

Victims of the worst raid on Strood on 2nd March 1944 were buried under these piles of rubble which had once been their homes. Eighteen people were killed, eight seriously injured and thirty-eight slightly hurt.

weapon and selected authentic German flying-kit from a depot where captured enemy uniforms and equipment were stored in an RAF hangar. Ian Fleming had this kit with him in a suitcase when he stayed one night at Bilting, but no one but Peter knew what he was up to; and he was not wearing the uniform at the time. The plan fell through suddenly because Ian was unable to get a captured bomber for the operation.

In November 1940 Peter Fleming was replaced at Bilting by Lieutenant-Colonel Norman Field, then a twenty-three-year-old second lieutenant. Lieutenant-Colonel Field had been wounded at Dunkirk and was on sick leave in Somerset when he received a mysterious telegram telling him to report for duty at the post office at Highworth in Wiltshire. When he arrived, he was directed to a mansion in the neighbouring village of Coleshill, where he was interviewed and made an Intelligence Officer in the Auxiliary Units. He was sent to Kent the following day and on arrival was promoted to captain. (Lieutenant-Colonel Field has lived at Bilting since 1955 in a house close to The Garth, now known as Bilting Court.) In addition to his small staff, he was also in charge of two sections of soldiers, the Buffs and The Royal West Kents, which helped with the training of the civilians. Each section consisted of about twenty men, led by a lieutenant; one section was based at Bilting, the other just outside Cranbrook.

One of the most intriguing things about the resistance in Kent is that its members managed to dig a series of hide-outs throughout the county without anyone's knowing about them. This veil of secrecy was sometimes torn—as we shall see, but even now there can be few people who know the site of even one of those holes. There were about twenty-five hide-outs in Kent by the time Lieutenant-Colonel Field arrived at The Garth. His personal refuge was Big Kate, an underground hide-out in Challock Forest where fourteen men could stay for three weeks if necessary. Its entrance was a trapdoor concealed by a tree stump.

But by far the most spectacular of these hide-outs was Airship, a big underground chamber in Godmersham Park in the wooded hills above The Garth. Its unique feature was that it was a hole beneath a hole. Peter Fleming had found a massive depression at the site about 60 feet long, 30 feet wide and 30 feet deep. (It was dug out in the First World War to house an airship.) He decided that the Germans would never look for a secret hole beneath a well-known one, so he made the hole deeper, built a shelter at the bottom of it and put enough earth back to restore the depression to its original shape. It was not intended as a base for any one patrol but as a sanctuary for resistance men on the run, housing enough food, water and sleeping-accommodation for 120 people. An entrance to the shelter through the top hole would have been too conspicuous, so a shaft was dug at the edge of a path about 15 yards from the rim of the hole, and the two were connected by a low tunnel. Its trapdoor was a tree trunk which weighed half a ton and was nearly six feet high. It was counterbalanced so well that, when you knew what you were doing, it could be pushed aside with a finger. This hole, like almost all the hide-outs, was demolished after the war and all that remains of it now is a shallow depression which has been taken over again by the surrounding woods.

The hide-outs were dug by a Unit patrol, Royal Engineer tunnelling companies or sapper soldiers; and they had to be dug, for security reasons, without any other patrol knowing where they were. Hide-outs on Romney Marsh were below sea-level and had to be watertight constructions built by experts. Civilian workmen to do this were brought in from the other side of Kent, so they would probably not have been able to find their way back to the hide-outs again, should they ever have tried. It was that sort of secrecy that led the wife of a farm-worker near Dover to believe for more than twenty years that her husband was having an affaire during the war on his nights away from home—when he was really doing Unit work.

A major problem in maintaining this secrecy was the earth from the hide-outs. Ingenious methods were devised to get rid of the dirt so that no tell-tale signs littered the county. When the digging of a hide-out in Stocking Wood, near Baddlesmere, south of Faversham, left Lieutenant-Colonel Field with a load of chalky subsoil that was difficult to conceal, his solution was to have the soil put in a natural hole in the wood. He then mined the hole and set more mines in a line across the wood at 50-yard intervals. The next time German bombers flew overhead, he blew up the mines so that it appeared as though a stick of bombs had been dropped. The chalky craters would raise no eyebrows after that.

The Kent River Board indirectly helped with another hide-out being made at Wickhambreaux, near the mouth of the River Stour. The board had begun to build an anti-flood barrier on the other side of the river, so the local patrol simply constructed an aerial ropeway over the water and moved their earth to the barrier. When Lieutenant-Colonel Field decided to dig an underground observation post on the crest of Charing Hill, he realized that any men working there would be seen from miles away. He solved that problem by pretending that the site was an anti-aircraft gun emplacement. His men filled sandbags with earth from their hole and then used the bags to shield it. They finished the observation post behind this screen, and after several weeks an Army truck took the sandbags away. All that was left on the hill was the concealed hide-out.

Good use was made of old holes where possible. An enlarged badger-sett on the edge of a chalk pit at Challock provided one hide-out, while the cellars of Evington Manor at Hastingleigh, near Wye, which had been destroyed by fire long before, provided another. A patrol at Manston sited its base in a man-made cave, believed to have been tunnelled into the chalk by members of a religious order in the seventeenth century. The hide-out was situated in a new branch made for this purpose and concealed from the old passages by a massive block of chalk mounted on rollers. More tunnels, thought to have been made by smugglers, were used by the Thanet resistance group. When one old tunnel in this network was found to reach to the edge of Manston airfield, it was decided that this passage would be useful for patrol saboteurs to get in and out of the airfield should it be captured by the Germans. A team of sappers was to have been called in to clear a blockage along this tunnel, but a bomb which landed in the middle of the airfield blocked it for good.

Material such as wood and corrugated iron for many of the hide-outs in Kent came from the two main military engineering depots at Ashford and Charing. Most were eventually made big enough to house six or seven men, and all were eventually provided with bunks, stoves, lamps and food and water for at least two weeks. Most hide-outs had room for the patrols' arms, ammunition and sabotage material. The average base was high enough for its occupants to stand up in, 20 feet long and 10 feet wide. They were so well hidden that anyone walking over them would not notice the hollow ground beneath their feet. The most common trapdoors on them were oak or elm boxes filled with a foot-thick layer of earth, most of which had to be lifted out. But there were other types of entrances: one hide-out near Wootton, just south of the junction of the Dover and Folkestone roads, was entered through the false bottom of a manger against a hillside; another, under a brickyard at Lydden, near Margate, was entered by moving what seemed to be a solid wooden wall.

In addition to the places already mentioned, there were also hide-outs at Minster on Sheppey, Staplehurst, Sutton Valence, Frith Wood near Hawkhurst, Rolvenden, Tenterden, Bethersden, Brookland,

Ash and Pluckley.

The secrecy which surrounded the Auxiliary Units kept even Montgomery in the dark for a while. When Lieutenant-Colonel Field arrived at Bilting, the 12th Army Corps in Kent and Sussex—responsible for the defence of that area—was under Lieutenant-General Andrew Thorne, who had had a hand in the formation of the Units. But the then General Montgomery took command of the Corps in April 1941 and was there until that December, when he left to take over South-East Command. Lieutenant-Colonel Field had been at The Garth for ten months when he rang Montgomery's underground headquarters on the southern outskirts of Tunbridge Wells to ask for some leave. He was put in touch with an ADC because the General was out. Brigadier Simpson, the Chief of Staff, phoned back that evening to say that Montgomery saw no reason why he should not go on leave, but he did not know who he was and would like to meet him. Lieutenant-Colonel Field had not realized that General Thorne had been replaced, so he went to Tunbridge Wells to explain to Montgomery the work of the Auxiliary Units. Montgomery was at first concerned that a unit which he had not heard of was operating in this area of command, but he was reassured by what he heard and said he would like to meet some of the resistance men and see some of the hide-outs. The two men made an appointment to meet at the A20 crossroads below Lenham Chest Hospital.

Lieutenant-Colonel Field took the General to a spinney at the side of a lane on the rise near the present 'Three Musketeers' motel. When Montgomery asked what they were doing, there, he was told that within five feet of him there were ten men with weapons, explosives and provisions for three weeks. Montgomery seemed a little incredulous and was even more surprised when Lieutenant-Colonel Field dropped a marble into a mousehole on a bank. This hole was connected to a 12-foot length of pipe; the marble ran down it to clatter into an empty biscuit tin in the hide-out below—a signal which told those underground that it was safe to open the previously invisible trapdoor concealed in the ivy-covered roots of an old tree. This meeting, much to Lieutenant-Colonel Field's disappointment, brought his involvement with the Units to an end; within a short time he had joined Montgomery's staff at Tunbridge Wells.

There were about three hundred hide-outs already in use throughout the country by the end of 1940, and another sixty-one were ready by the spring of 1941, rising to about 534 by the end of that year. No later figures are available, but up to about a thousand hide-outs existed by the time the patrols were disbanded. Although the threat of a German invasion diminished as the war developed, the patrols continued to meet and exercise twice a week. By November 1944, when the Auxiliary Units were stood down, about three thousand men were members of this secret body.

Peter Fleming said of these men:

> It seems unlikely that in place the Auxiliary Units would have been able to achieve very much. Nevertheless, even assuming that the British resistance movement would have melted away in the white heat of German ruthlessness, it might have struck some useful blows before doing so; and within a bridgehead under heavy counter-attack, its diversionary activities would have had a value wholly disproportionate to the number of guerrillas involved. It is difficult to find fault with Churchill's estimate of Auxiliary Units as "a useful addition to the regular forces".

9. "Glass fell everywhere"

The Battle of Britain might have ended, but that did not mean that German raiders no longer crossed the coastline. Two people were killed when bombs fell on Newtown in Ashford on 16th September, and before the year was out, there were to be twenty-two bombing incidents in Kent in which five or more people died. The first town to suffer in this way was Gillingham: a raid on the borough at 12.55pm on Wednesday 18th September dropped about ten high-explosive bombs in the Milburn Road area; at least seven homes were wrecked and many more seriously damaged; five people were killed, twenty-two seriously injured and thirty-one slightly hurt.

It was Ashford's turn next. A short attack on the town in the afternoon of Thursday 26th September left seven people dead and two seriously injured. The worst damage was in the Regent's Place/East Street area. One man was killed when his car received a direct hit as he was driving into the Co-operative yard, and a warden in Godinton Road had to fling himself under an archway to save himself.

But by far the worst incident between then and the end of 1940 was the bombing of Maidstone on Friday 27th September. It was to be the worst raid the town experienced during the war.

A short dive-bombing attack was carried out at noon by about sixteen enemy aircraft. A total of ten men, eleven women and a child were killed, twenty-one men, twenty-two women and a child seriously injured, and twenty men, twenty-four women and four children slightly hurt. Damage stretched from Barton Road in the south to the Allington Castle area in the north. Two bombs fell in the Museum gardens, and one dropped close to St Faith's Church, making a crater 15 feet deep and 30 feet across. The church tower was split almost from top to bottom, the long crack passing through the dial of the church clock. This bomb uprooted shrubs and iron railings, which were twisted into fantastic shapes by the blast. Two gables of the Museum were damaged, one of them over the reading-room, although that was empty at the time. The gardener's cottage next to the gardens was wrecked, and almshouses on the other side of the road were damaged. Another bomb fell in a goods yard, overturning five vehicles and making a crater 10 feet deep and 20 yards across. The railway line itself was also damaged, and only one line was open until much later in the evening.

A bomb which fell in the Medway exploded and sent up a column of water like a depth-charge, while another fell on a nearby wharf. One incendiary bomb fell through the roof of the big Hills and Steele store in Week Street, setting clothes, hats and toys alight and creating a big fire within a few minutes. Two fire-engines were quickly on the scene, and the blaze was soon under control. One large bomb fell on the Walls ice-cream depot next to the temporary fire-station in Hope Street occupied by the Auxiliary Fire Service, injuring two firemen and damaging several fire-pumps and houses in the neighbourhood, including some homes in Cambridge Square.

A man who lived in a house opposite said: "I was having some biscuits and cheese with my wife when I heard a whistling sound, getting nearer every moment. I grasped my wife and put her beneath the sink in the scullery and stood over her. There was a loud explosion, and the house rocked. Everything seemed to fall over, and glass fell everywhere. Curiously enough, we found afterwards that only the windows had gone; mirrors in the house were not touched, and a china clock which fell into the fender was undamaged."

A one-legged man who kept a boot-repairing shop opposite was killed by the blast. He took cover in the public air-raid shelter normally, but he had a customer in his shop at the time. The public brick-built shelter itself was hardly damaged, although its roof was raised slightly. Windows were smashed in All Saints' School, and fragments from the bomb flew 200 yards and smashed the windows of a bus full of hop-pickers, but the pickers had heard the explosions and had thrown themselves on the floor of the bus, so no one was hurt even though a piece of concrete landed in the driver's cab. Another bomb fell near a bus loaded with soldiers, slightly injuring three of them, and one fell on the edge of the pavement outside the Lyons Restaurant in the High Street, making another large crater.

Glass embedded itself in walls and joints of meat when the plate-glass window of a butcher's shop in Sandling Road was blown in by a bomb. Kettles tied to the ceiling of the hardware shop next door showered down on the owner, who was behind the counter, but he escaped with cuts to his head. A 25-gallon tank of oil was thrown 30 yards from the yard and into the scullery without spilling a drop. Seventy employees were at work in a large machine-room of the Esgate and Chamberlain box-printing factory when a bomb hit the building: four of the staff were killed, but a plane-spotter who was blown off the roof and into a tree before the alarm could be sounded was unhurt.

About fifty high-explosive and incendiary bombs had been dropped across the town by the raiders, damaging between seventy and a hundred houses on one estate, some of them badly. Property had been hit in Barton Road, Loose Road, Rawdon Road, Brunswick Street, Priory Road, Square Hill Road, Mote Road, Foster Street, Springfield Avenue, Monckton Avenue, the High Street, East Station, the Barracks and Sandling Road.

Later that afternoon a raiding Junkers 88 was forced down at Graveney, near Faversham, when it ran out of petrol over Cleve Hill. The machine was hardly damaged, and the crew was able to scramble out unhurt, and when men of the London Irish Rifles closed in on the machine, the crew opened fire on them. A short gunfight took place before the Germans, two of whom were wounded in the action, surrendered. It was the first time that British land forces—apart from anti-aircraft and coastal artillery—had gone into action on British soil since 1797. An officer, who was later awarded the George Medal for his bravery, entered the bomber and dismantled the two time-bombs with which it was equipped, and so the plane, a new type and therefore a valuable prize, fell intact into the hands of the British.

Two days later, early in the evening of Sunday 29th September, Sittingbourne was attacked by a lone raider who came out of a bank of low-lying cloud and dropped three bombs on the outskirts of the town. These failed to do any damage, but the aircraft then disappeared back into the clouds before crossing the town a few minutes later and dropping a stick of bombs near the centre. Eight people were killed and fifteen slightly injured. The bombs fell near the bottom of Park Road, wrecking several shops and damaging many other businesses and homes. Thirty cars were destroyed when Pullen's garage was gutted, but fire-fighters managed to save the petrol-supply, which was the only stock of fuel in the town. A chemist's shop was reduced to a heap of rubble, and a policeman in the War Reserve was injured when the nearby police station was damaged. Windows in the Holy Trinity church were broken, and an elderly woman on her way to church was killed. The dead also included a woman and her two-month-old baby, who were getting ready to go for a walk when the bombs fell.

Less than a week after that, on Friday 4th October, Deal received one of its most serious raids of the war. Enemy aircraft appeared overhead shortly after 1pm and left a trail of devastation from Upper Walmer to Union Street. Eight people were killed, four seriously injured and one slightly hurt. A soldier who was probably a victim of that attack was not found until the following spring, when workmen repairing the roof of the Clarendon Hotel discovered his remains. A boy of six who was in a shop was told to hurry home when the siren sounded; he was killed in the street by flying debris.

All the dead people were in Middle Street or Union Street. The old 'Victory' pub in Middle Street and four other houses on the south side of Short Street were wrecked by bombs, and rescue-parties searched for hours in the debris for the bodies known to be there. One child of three was heard crying and was rescued from its dead mother's side. At least twenty houses were wrecked, fifty-one seriously damaged and 127 slightly damaged in the raid. A policeman who lay on a footpath when he heard the bombs coming down close by was moved about four yards by the blast. Another heavy bomb fell in the middle of Dover Road, south of the Walmer Baptist Church, and caused the road to be closed for weeks when it burst a water main. Hundreds of leaflets with the message "Try Wood's Soothing Powders" were scattered in the road of the Strand by the bombing. And conkers brought down in the raid cluttered up the roads in scores; it was a schoolboy's dream—but the evacuated youngsters were not on hand to enjoy it.

The three-man crew of a tug were blown up by a mine on the Swale at 9.35am that day.

A large number of enemy aircraft streaking towards the French coast on Saturday 5th October were followed by a smaller number flying in the same direction. Some of the planes from this second group swooped low over Chatham at 11.32am and dropped a number of high-explosive bombs. Some fell harmlessly, but others fell on the thickly-populated districts in the Ordnance Street and Rochester Street area, blocking those roads and wrecking at least three houses and damaging many more. One of the first bombs fell at the entrance to the old Napoleonic fort. A nearby soldier had a lucky escape when he flung himself to the ground and was blown 10 feet into the air by a bomb blast: he was able to walk away suffering only from shock. A girl of fourteen saved the lives of her nephew and a neighbour's baby by shielding them from falling debris with her body: the Mayor, on behalf of the staff of a first-aid post, presented her with a watch for her conspicuous bravery. This raid killed eight people, seriously injured three and slightly hurt twenty more.

The following day Folkestone was bombed twice, once in the morning by a single bomber and again in the afternoon. The morning raid came at 10.28am, and damage was spread over a wide area. ARP personnel worked for hours to release people buried under the ruins of their homes; but some were dead by the time their would-be rescuers reached them. One of those killed was the wife of a soldier. She left three children, the youngest of whom was found under the wreckage many hours later. Most of the casualties came from the two streets of small homes most seriously affected in the attack. A tree in one street was blown up in the second raid at 3.22pm and thrown 150 yards before it fell on a pub in another street, penetrating the roof. Another bomb fell on an Anderson shelter which was empty at the time because the family had stayed in their home. Nine people were killed in those raids, seven seriously injured and twenty-two others slightly hurt. A second officer of Folkestone fire-brigade and another man received the OBE for saving the life of a child trapped when a bomb wrecked several cottages that day. The man jacked up some boards so they could crawl underneath and dig in the rubble until they came across the head and shoulders of the child, who was not badly injured.

Raiders dropped at least three high-explosive bombs and several incendiary bombs on a hop-garden at Beltring at 8.42pm on Tuesday 8th October. Three women and three children were killed and eleven others seriously injured. The first of the bombs fell on three rows of hoppers' huts, wrecking all ten in each row. All that was left of one hut was a pile of matchwood and crumpled pieces of corrugated iron which were scattered over a wide area. One girl of seventeen was blown off her feet and her body found 100 yards away with all the clothes stripped from it. Clothing was thrown to the tops of trees. More bombs fell in the wood yard next to the huts and wrecked the yard.

A peaceful flight over Maidstone on Thursday 10th October ended with the deaths of five children, three women and a man when a plane plunged into the town. Another man was seriously injured and a woman slightly hurt. All the casualties occurred when a Hurricane dived out of control over the town at 3.55pm. The pilot had suddenly gone into a steep dive while on patrol with a formation of eight other Hurricanes over the eastern outskirts of Maidstone at 20,000 feet; he had suffered from oxygen-failure. People who saw the aircraft say that the pilot tried to steer it at the last minute towards open ground in an attempt to avoid the town. He failed, if indeed he ever regained consciousness. His plane skimmed the roofs of several streets, sliced through the roof of Albion Stores and smashed into the two adjoining houses in Albion Place, near the top of Union Street. The wrecked buildings, which were drenched in petrol, burst into flames which shot 50 feet in the air and filled the street with smoke. Firemen soon had the blaze under control, but the ruins continued to smoulder while the rescue-parties set about retrieving the bodies. The body of the sergeant pilot was found in a cellar an hour later, together with his parachute and parts of the plane engine. The rescue-squads had to abandon work at 7.33pm because of an air-raid warning but started searching in the debris again at 7am the following day.

Several groups of bomb-carrying Me109s crossed the coast during the morning of Friday 11th October, with fighter protection above 30,000 feet, and scattered their bombs over Ashford, Canterbury and Folkestone. The most serious of these raids was the one carried out on Canterbury at about 11am. Messerschmitts being chased by Spitfires dropped two loads of bombs within fifteen minutes of each other. The attack was unexpected, and people were taken by surprise as the first three bombs came whistling down.

The first of them scored a direct hit on a furrier's store in Burgate Street and severely damaged others close to it. The owner of the store, Mr Irvine Williams, who had been the victim of a £500 fur-robbery a few months before, was killed in the raid, together with his assistants and customers and one of the woman partners of the bookshop next door to them. The tailor and his assistant in the shop next to the bookshop had saved themselves by crouching in a cupboard. The tailor escaped with cuts caused by flying glass, but his daughter's fate remained a mystery for some time. Cries for help eventually led rescuers to the cellar into which she had dashed and been trapped; she was brought out unhurt through the pavement grating. Nine people were killed in the raid, two seriously injured and six slightly hurt. The cathedral was less than a hundred yards from the place where one bomb fell, and flying debris and the blast from the bombs smashed and blew out a number of nineteenth-century stained-glass windows. Cows in a field where one bomb fell were lifted into the air by the blast; they landed on their feet and went on with their grazing.

The parlour at the Royal Oak Inn at Wrotham Heath was crowded on the evening of Tuesday 15th October when the village was hit by bombs. A stick of sixteen high-explosive bombs was dropped across the area at about 9.30pm, one of them scoring a direct hit on the roof of the inn, killing at least three people inside. The woman proprietor of a sweetshop nearby was blown across the room; when she got up she found that sweets in the jars had been melted by the heat of the blast. Wrotham Place, a café, a garage and an AA box at the junction close by were all damaged in the raid, and telephone wires were brought down. Nine people were killed in this raid, six seriously injured and two slightly hurt.

The next bad raid came at 9.40pm on Tuesday 17th October when several bombs fell on Rochester and Strood. One fell near an ARP post in Elaine Avenue and killed an auxiliary fireman and an ambulance driver. Another fell at Fort Bridge Wood and killed three ATS women and a sergeant who was on guard. One of the victims had been slightly hurt when a bomb fell in Borstal Street at that time. The total casualties from this attack were seven dead, two seriously injured and eight slightly hurt.

Maidstone was attacked again at noon on Friday 25th October when seven high-explosive bombs were dropped across the town. The bottling department of the Style Winch brewery was damaged, and bomb blasts also smashed windows in St Peter's Church and damaged the roof there. Another bomb fell near a paper-mill, making a huge crater in the road and cutting gas and water mains, causing the crater to fill quickly with water. A bomb which fell in a wood near another paper-mill did not damage the property. Bombs had fallen in the areas of Portley Road, Campbell Road, Muir Road, St Peter's Street and Buckland Hill. Seven people were killed and eight seriously injured in the attack. The raiders were attacked by British fighters soon after they dropped their bombs, and one plane crashed in flames at Mote Park on the outskirts of the town, the pilot having baled out. A Messerschmitt which had taken part in the raid was later brought down at Marden, and the pilot taken to hospital injured.

Two days later bombs fell at Smarts Hill, Penshurst, and killed six people. The cottages wrecked in this attack were made mostly of wood and stood close together. One incendiary bomb set fire to one of the homes, and its two occupants were burned beyond recognition. Two other cottages were destroyed when a high-explosive bomb fell on them, killing all the people inside. One person was also seriously injured in this bombing, and four others were slightly hurt. A first-aid party which had been called out from Edenbridge was held up because someone had tried to steal their car. This was done by soldiers apparently, who had wrecked the wiring in the car before giving up the attempt.

In the early evening of Tuesday 29th October enemy aircraft dropped bombs in front of the officers' mess at the Royal Marines depot at Deal, killing eight men. Bombs were also dropped on the railway line; homes in Telegraph Road were made unfit to live in, and telephone wires were brought down. It is thought that the planes which carried out this attack were Italian. Their appearance in the skies over Kent was rare but quite likely in this case since it is known that fifteen Italian Fiat BR20 bombers, escorted by Fiat CR42 bi-planes, took part in a raid on Ramsgate that day.

Life was getting back to normal in Ramsgate on the morning of Saturday 2nd November after an alert which had sent people hurrying for shelter. When the All Clear sounded, people began returning to work and their shopping, but fifteen minutes later, without warning, twenty-five bombers swooped out of the clouds and attacked the town. They released about sixty to a hundred bombs over the area at 11.25am—and the warning siren did not sound until seven minutes after the attack had begun. Most of the damage occurred in the area round the gas-works, although a cemetery was also bombed, and tombstones, coffins and bones were flung in all directions when hundreds of graves were wrecked.

A grandmother, a mother and her two children had sheltered in a tunnel away from their house during the first warning. They came out when the All Clear sounded before the raid, and the grandmother and the two children were killed when a bomb fell on their house. The mother, who had gone out shopping, came back to find the place in ruins. Another woman was killed as she was heading towards shelter. One man was already in this garden shelter when the bombs began to fall: a bomb burst in the garden, and his body was later found in the garden next door; his wife was also out shopping at the time. The raid killed eight people, seriously injured five and slightly hurt eighteen others. Thirteen homes were wrecked, a hundred seriously damaged and eight hundred more slightly damaged.

This raid was followed on Tuesday 5th November by an attack on Sittingbourne at 4.10pm. One of the bombs fell outside a green-grocer's shop in Shortlands Road and was responsible for the entire death-toll in the town on that day. Five people were killed: a mother and her two-month-old baby and three other children. The mother and child had just stopped outside the shop when the bomb fell a few feet away. Two other babies escaped with nothing worse than slight shock when their prams were wrecked. At least two houses were destroyed, twenty seriously damaged and forty others slightly damaged in the bombing, and four people were seriously injured and five others slightly hurt.

The 'Star' pub in Swanscombe was crowded on the evening of Sunday 10th November with people who had turned up for a darts match. Shortly after 8pm a bomb scored a direct hit on the pub. All that was left of the small bars where the pub had stood was a heap of bricks and twisted rafters round the gaping hole of the cellar, although the staircase leading to the clubroom upstairs poked out of the wreckage. Distressing scenes occurred as the families of men and women known to be in the pub at the time gathered to await news of the casualties. One by one the bodies were recovered from the ruins. Little knots of women stood at street corners while they waited for the official casualty lists to be posted. Gradually it became known: the death-toll rose to twenty-seven, with six seriously injured and five slightly hurt. It was Swanscombe's worst bombing incident.

The landlord was among the dead, although his wife and daughter survived. The barmaid who was killed had given notice the week before the raid but had stayed on that evening because of the match. One of the other victims was a merchant-seaman on seven days' leave who had spent two days travelling from Scotland to see his wife and children and was having a drink with his father in the pub at the time of the bombing; both were killed. There was a big audience at the local cinema, but the bombing did not even interrupt the film—one woman, however, heard the crashing of bombs and went to her home nearby to see that her family was safe; she then returned to the cinema for the rest of the film.

At least five houses were wrecked at Wickens Place in the West Malling area the following day when a string of eight high-explosive bombs was dropped across the area at 7.15pm. Other bombs fell on Cascade Avenue, cutting gas mains. Another five houses were seriously damaged and thirty-four slightly damaged. The casualties consisted of seven dead, five seriously injured and one slightly hurt.

Raiders flying high above Dartford on Tuesday 12th November dropped a stick of thirteen bombs across the town at 8pm. Most of the damage was in Essex Road and Highfield Road, close to the hospital which had been bombed on 6th September. Another of the bombs fell on a bowling-green at the side of the working men's club, shattering the doors and windows. Men and women in the club were injured by flying glass, and some men holding glasses of beer were blown off their feet. Windows of shops in the nearby High Street were blown out, and the road was strewn with broken glass. Five people were killed and six seriously injured in the raid.

The following day several heavy bombs were dropped on Dover shortly after 2pm. One fell in front of the Salvation Army Citadel in the High Street, wrecking the building and killing people in the area. At least ten shops were seriously damaged, eighty shops and a hundred houses badly damaged, and slight damage was done to gas and water mains. The High Street near the Royal Victoria Hospital was closed, and traffic was diverted until it was cleared. Six people were killed altogether, twelve seriously injured and twelve others slightly hurt.

Damage was spread over a wide area near the station and harbour in Folkestone on Monday 18th November when two parachute-mines were dropped without warning on the town shortly after 4am. A number of people were buried in the ruins of shops and homes. Some were either rescued alive or managed to crawl out of the debris by themselves, but others were found dead after the rescue-squads had worked for hours to reach them. One old man was trapped under his house for nearly eleven hours before being rescued by soldiers; his wife was found dead in the ruins, and the man died later in hospital.

Flames lit up the sky when fire broke out in the wreckage of one shop after the attack, but firemen soon had the blaze under control. Several pubs, a small baker's shop, cafés and restaurants were among the buildings in this area wrecked by the mines. One small tea-shop was badly twisted and had its windows blown out by the blast; the proprietress, however, could be found later that morning serving hot drinks in the shop. Many homes were wrecked in this area, and an emergency feeding-centre was set up while help was called in from other areas. Fourteen people were killed in the raid, fourteen seriously injured and forty-six slightly hurt. Two fish-hawkers pulled up their barrows and began selling herrings in the scene of devastation the following day.

The Channel ports were by this time becoming used to being shelled. But the Germans set their sights a little higher in November. On Tuesday and Wednesday 19th and 20th November craters were made near Rainham by what at first were thought to be bombs. The splinters found in the area were studied, however, and it was decided instead that the fragments came from 11-inch shells. Similar splinters were also thrown up at Bearsted when shells burst there on Sunday 24th November. No warning whine of their approach was heard, and the explosions reported fitted those of a high-speed shell. Ten of them

exploded altogether, eight over Rainham and two at Bearsted. The
were fired probably from the Cap Griz Nez area of France—whicl
was 55 miles away. Although that distance was a considerable increas
on the range of the guns used against Dover, it was still some wa'
short of those used to shell Paris in 1918. Enemy reconnaissance plane
were spotted during these incidents. No one was killed during th
shelling, and the experiment—if it was one—seems to have been :
failure. No more shells are known to have fallen that far inland unti
the early hours of 13th June 1944, when several shells fell on Maid
stone and killed a woman.

Nine people from one family, including five children, were killee
on Sunday 8th December when a bomb fell on two houses in St Jame
Lane, Stone, near Dartford, shortly before 11pm. The bomb made :
large crater and reduced the houses, which were on the edge of fields
to a pile of rubble. All nine were buried under the debris, and rescue
work began by the light of the moon. Rescue-squads got two bodie
out but had to call off work until daylight. A horse which had been i
its stable nearby was also killed in the bombing.

Two men became the first people in the county to receive the
George Medal for following their ordinary occupation in December
Mr William Harris and Mr Reginald Blunt were given the medals i
recognition of the contribution they made to the war-effort by carry
ing on their farm work while the Battle of Britain was at its height
The men operated their threshing-machine for nine critical weeks or
farms in the Deal area—within range of the guns in France and while
enemy aircraft sprayed the area with cannon and machine-gun fire
They worked from dawn to dusk, with the help of farm labourer:
during the last part of threshing.

The last big raid of the year took place on Saturday 14th Decembe
when two parachute-mines were dropped on Chatham at 6.30pm
One scored a direct hit on homes in Ordnance Street, quite near the
railway station, and the other fell on open ground near Boundary
Road. It was the worst attack Chatham suffered. An area about 25(
yards square was blocked by debris, about sixty houses were wrecked
seven hundred others damaged and gas and water mains fractured
Fifteen people were killed in the bombing, twenty seriously injurec
and 103 more slightly hurt.

Rescue-parties worked for hours to reach people trapped in the
ruins of their homes. A special constable was rescued quickly afte
being trapped with his wife and two sons, but his wife and their baby
son were not brought out for another six hours; their other son hac

been killed. A boy of eighteen threw himself on his two small nephews during the attack: all three were buried and freed only after hours of digging; the children were safe, but their young uncle was badly injured and died soon afterwards. A man who lost his wife in a previous raid rescued his neighbour, a widow of sixty-five, from the debris which pinned her down. Her son hung up a notice on their door which said "Bombed out. We still live here, but in the Anderson shelter! Please, postman, bring the letters round the back."

One family had moved to Chatham from the East End of London after being bombed out of their home. The woman had just got her four children into the cellar when one of the mines fell nearby and made part of the house collapse. The woman heard her husband groaning. He had been getting changed upstairs, and she worked out where he was by the sound he made. She tore down part of the ceiling, cutting her hands in the process, and pulled floor boards aside to make a gap through which he could get to the ground floor. He was taken to hospital badly injured.

Hundreds of people were made homeless in the attack, and at least 250 of them had been evacuated by the following afternoon. First-aid repairs on those homes damaged began quickly, but by the afternoon of 19th December the repair-parties still had five hundred roofs to cover with tarpaulins.

10. "Take your trousers off"

Every bit of grassland that could be spared had to be ploughed up for crops during the war. The Kent War Agricultural Committee, which was guided by district committees made up of farmers, was given powers under the Defence Regulations to say what land had to be used in this way, and any farmer who ignored one of its orders was likely to find himself in court.

Farmers were given a subsidy of £2 for every acre of grassland ploughed, and before the end of the war farmers in Kent were even using the land between trees in their orchards for crops. The number of arable acres in the county rose during the first three years of the war from 167,000 to 290,000 The area of wheat in the county was more than doubled, and a million and a quarter bushels more were produced in 1942 than in 1939.

All that was in the future, however, when a man from Staplehurst became the first farmer in Kent to be fined for ignoring an order by the Kent War Agricultural Committee to plough up certain land. Mr Joseph Sorrell, of Highbury, had been fined £60 and ordered to pay £6 6s 0d costs when his case came before the Cranbrook court on 5th August 1940. But in January 1941 he appealed against the conviction at the sitting of the West Kent Appeals Committee in Maidstone. A member of the district committee had been told by Mr Sorrell in December 1939 that he would plough up whatever land he was asked to. On 11th January 1940 he was told to plough up a six-acre field at Staplehurst. This order was not carried out, so on 5th April he was told to plough up the land by 30th April and to produce a crop to be harvested in 1940. He made excuses about the bad weather on 12th April and later sent a letter saying that snow had prevented him from ploughing and that it was now too late for cropping. He would plough it next year, he said. He then complained about the way he had been treated by the War Office and said that farmers were sick of the war they were being treated. He said in another letter that he had ploughed up extra land at Headcorn instead. But this was only an extra acre, said the prosecution, and it was not ploughed until October, even though the land was fit to plough before 30th April. Sorrell said that the January notice did not specify when the work was to be done and denied the suggestion that he had refused to plough up the land because it would earn more money if it were kept for grazing. The appeal was dismissed with costs, and the conviction and fine were confirmed.

At the end of January tribute was paid to the "wonderful standard of resistance and discipline of the people of Kent" by Sir Auckland Geddes, the regional commissioner for the south-east, when he met the mayors of Kent at a luncheon in Maidstone. It was certain that they had some difficult experiences ahead, he said, and he anticipated many more fire-attacks. There might be other trials ahead, such as invasion, he added. He said:

> If the enemy arrive, we may have something to say about their destina-
> tion. If they do come, it is extremely probable we shall all be on the
> reception committee. I trust that everywhere the reception will be
> warm, not to say hot. The soldiers will play their part, and we on the civil
> side will have to play ours. We have to remember that we may get a fire
> blitz on many of our towns, immediately followed by invasion. Then
> the people will be tested to the utmost of their fibre, and you, gentle-
> men, are going to be tested in the power of leadership and control over
> the people.

The first deaths through bombing in Kent in 1941 had occurred as early as 4th January, when four people were killed at Ramsgate. This was followed by six other fatal bombings in Kent during the next week. Another three people were killed at Ramsgate on 3rd February. But the worst raid of the year so far came on Tuesday 4th February when two bombs fell on Marden at 9.44pm, wrecking two cottages and two shops on the main Maidstone-to-Marden road, blocking the road and damaging water and gas mains, sewers, the electricity cables and telephone wires. In addition to five people killed in the bombing, three people were seriously injured and four others slightly hurt. Ten soldiers were killed and four others injured when land-mines on the beach near the gasworks at Hythe exploded at about 11.30am on 24th February. And another five people were killed at Crockenhill, near Dartford, on 11th March when four houses there were wrecked by bombs at 10.15pm. Two people had also been seriously injured and another five slightly hurt in this raid.

Hundreds of houses and shops over a wide area were damaged, and hundreds of people made homeless temporarily when parachute-mines fell on Rochester between 3.20am and 4.30am on Tuesday 8th April. About a thousand incendiary bombs were dropped at the same time. The most serious damage was in the Wickham Street-St William's Way-Amherst Road area, where huge flames came shooting out of the ruins. Eleven people were killed altogether, twenty-eight seriously injured and sixty-six slightly hurt. Two members of the Auxiliary Fire Service were killed when the AFS sub-station received a direct hit.

Two of the mines fell at Shorts seaplane works on the Esplanade. The main offices and a workshop were burned out and several other workshops and offices damaged. Men tackled the fires there while mobile canteens were sent to the works from Chatham, Northfleet and Betteshanger. The factory was closed for repairs until 15th April, when it opened for full production. Elsewhere in the city, windows at Rochester Girls' Grammar School were broken and doors blown off their hinges by the blast. At least ten houses were wrecked, 120 seriously damaged and three hundred others slightly damaged. Two rescue-parties were sent to the scene from Chatham, together with two from Gillingham, one from Gravesend and another from Sitting-bourne. Cars were commandeered to take some of the homeless to friends in other parts of the district while the rest were taken to rest-centres.

Enemy aircraft dropped two high-explosive bombs on Dartford at 1.44am on the morning of Sunday 20th April. At least six houses were wrecked and fifty others damaged beyond repair. Kent Road, near the railway station, was blocked. Rescue-workers, wardens and police rushed to the scene and began to dig bodies from the ruins and help the injured from what was left of their homes. Two people were found lying in a yard some way from their wrecked home, still wrapped in the blankets they had been sleeping in; other bodies were buried completely and not recovered until after hours of digging. The rescue-work was accompanied by the drone of the bombers and the roar of the anti-aircraft guns. Thirteen people were killed, six seriously injured and fifteen slightly hurt.

Enemy aircraft continued to be shot down over Kent, and their pilots, when still alive, continued to be rounded up by the police, the Home Guard or whoever else was first on the scene. Their appearance when they stepped from their plane, or released their parachute harness, seems to have been greeted with bemusement rather than hostility. But the most unusual reception must be that given an airman who dropped out of the skies at this time. The *Kentish Express* newspaper reported on 2nd May 1941:

> German bombers crashing to destruction have become almost a commonplace in the lives of Romney Marsh folk since last summer. But one day recently a lone shepherd working with his lambs near Rye saw a parachute come down just after a bomber had been shot to earth. Striding towards the young airman, he made the German hold up his hands in surrender. Although he was armed, the Nazi decided to obey the determined shepherd. Now came the problem. Some ewes needed attention—but so did the airman. He must not be allowed to make a get-away. The sooner he was under lock and key, the better. The shepherd solved the quandary. "I'm too busy to worry about you," he said. "Take your trousers off." Meekly the Nazi did as he was told and sat watching the shepherd tend his sheep. When the last ewe was comfortable, his trousers were returned to him, and with his wary escort he set off to captivity.

A low-flying raider bombed the Aylesham Central School and surrounding homes on the night of Tuesday 6th May. Nine people were killed, including three children; two people were seriously injured, and another three slightly hurt. One man was rescued alive from the wreckage. At least four houses were destroyed and seven seriously damaged. Up to six hundred people were accommodated in rest-centres, and the temporary evacuees did not begin returning home until an unexploded bomb at the school was made harmless the following afternoon.

A train had just left Sandwich station for Deal on the cloudless evening of Saturday 10th May when six enemy aircraft roared over it at little more than roof-top height and raked it with machine-gun fire. The fireman sheltered as bullets rattled against the engine and then went to the driver, Percy Goldsack, and advised him to brake. The planes were streaking home towards France as the train came to a halt and the two men jumped down on to the line. Goldsack collapsed, dying from a wound in his chest; the fireman himself was wounded in the arm, thigh and leg, and—as he found later—also in the foot. But he shouted that he was not badly hurt and staggered down the train towards the guard before fainting. This guard had twice been in trains that were attacked, another driver dying in one of the incidents. He knew his first aid and saved the fireman's life by making a tourniquet for his arm, in which an artery had been cut.

A passenger had been slightly hurt in the foot in the attack, and the engine and two front coaches had been damaged. Marines stationed nearby came to help; one was sent by the guard to fetch their doctor, another to Deal station to ask that another train be sent to pick up casualties. Only a light engine came, instead. The Marines made a human chain to pass buckets of water to the crippled engine so that its fire could be put out. A message was sent asking for an ambulance to be waiting, and the injured men were made comfortable on stretchers made of corridor tables. The light engine was attached to the back of the train, which it drew to Walmer. The fireman insisted on being let out of hospital within five days and was back at work within six weeks.

The Mayor and Mayoress of Folkestone were among thirteen people killed in the air-raid on their town at about 2am on Thursday 29th May. Alderman George Gurr, aged fifty-nine, and his wife died instantly when a large bomb fell on the house next door. Their bodies were not brought out of the bricks and rubble of what had been their home until several hours later. A policeman who had been decorated by the King for bravery rescued the Mayor's son-in-law, who was in the same house as the couple. He had been in the room below them on the first floor and was found lying on a small strip of what had been the floor; nothing else remained standing except for part of one wall. The policeman also rescued an elderly woman, who was crippled, after she was heard calling for help from the wreckage of a room in her house which had fallen on her.

At least forty homes in the town were badly damaged in the raid and up to three hundred slightly damaged. People searching for the injured were hindered by the darkness, and they could not use lights because German aircraft were overhead from time to time. A soldier's wife and her baby were stranded on a small ledge at the top of a house, but rescuers heard their cries for help and climbed a ladder to bring them down safely. The blasts from the raid played some strange tricks: bottles in a chemist's shop only a hundred yards from the scene were not disturbed, although other bottles were thrown off shelves in homes half a mile away. In addition to those killed, four people were seriously injured in the attack and thirty-two slightly hurt.

An alert had sounded in Dover thirty minutes after midnight on Thursday 12th June. Most people had gone back to bed, but those still awake at 3.50am heard a low-flying plane, closely followed by a terrific explosion and a blinding flash which was seen over a wide area. This one parachute-mine which fell on the town caused one of the highest death-tolls in the war in Dover: fifteen people killed, twenty seriously injured and twenty-three slightly hurt. It fell behind houses near the bottom of Randolph Road, about a hundred yards from the gasworks in Union Road. The gas supply was cut for five hours. All the forty homes in Union Road had to be demolished, and a hundred people were made homeless in the attack. About 150 houses were seriously damaged in the blast, and another four hundred slightly damaged. Eight firms of builders were called to the town to carry out first-aid repair-work on the homes.

Many of the people in the wrecked homes had been asleep when the mine fell, and many were buried in the ruins. Rescue-work began immediately by torchlight, and soldiers worked in relays to help clear the rubble. Most of the casualties came from two families. Some of the dead were brought out in the first few hours and others taken to hospital.

One man, who volunteered to rescue a woman he could hear crying beneath the debris, made a tunnel under the rubble, propping it up with bits of wood as he went along. When he came across the handle of a pram, he pulled bricks out of the way and found a baby in it; he removed dust from its mouth and brought it out unhurt. When he went back into the tunnel, he found the baby's mother trapped by an overturned bed and a piece of pipe which was across her legs. He cut through the pipe with a hacksaw and slit a hole in the bed mattress to free the woman, who was only slightly hurt. Another child that the man found on his third trip into the tunnel was, however dead.

The restrictions on food caused by rationing, and the scarcity of food not rationed, meant that everyone had to adjust to a single item of food being much more valuable that it had been. A Gravesend schoolgirl, for example, was admonished for peeling apples too thick in a cookery lesson and was told to peel the peel. A girl at a technical school in Tonbridge remembers using pea-pods, as well as peas, in pea soup, while young dandelion-leaves were washed and used as lettuce. A woman from Tenterden gave up her egg ration for three bantams—which never laid an egg and which had the habit of perching in the apple-tree at night. A woman from Tunbridge Wells, sent a box of lemons from her nephew with the Army in Sicily, showed them proudly to her greengrocer, who had not seen one for years. The Women's Institute set up a network of Preservation Centres to prevent fruit being wasted. The five remaining Institute members at Hawkinge alone produced 14 hundredweight of jam in the summer of 1941. And some fruit was so rare it could be used in other ways: a girl who had been sent a lemon in one office in Tunbridge Wells raised 35 shillings when she raffled it with sixpenny tickets.

Meals in restaurants were not rationed, but it became illegal in July 1940 to serve more than one main course at any meal, and in June 1942 a five-shilling maximum was introduced for these meals. The diet which rationing forced on people was adequate for their health but sometimes not for their appetite, so the government expected all families to eat out, on average, one day a month. To meet these needs the government introduced the British Restaurants, which, using self-service, provided a filling meal cheaply—usually 10d or a shilling a person. A total of 2,160 of them had been opened by September 1943. They were provided on a non-profit-making basis by local authorities and guaranteed against loss by the government.

When one of these restaurants was opened at New Romney in June 1941, a military band played in the open air, a large group of local dignitaries was present, and the ceremony had an almost pre-war gala atmosphere. Mr L. Devereux, representing the Ministry of Food, conveyed the special congratulations of Lord Woolton, the Food Minister, on the opening of the restaurant. The Honourable Mrs Petherick, the county organizer of the WVS, said that in every British Restaurant in Kent the cooking and serving of meals was done by her organization—every village in the county now had its WVS group, she added. Mrs W. Spens, wife of the Ashford MP, said that men in New Romney whose wives were evacuated would now be sure of getting a hot midday meal. The menu at the restaurant was varied each day. On the day it opened, it consisted of soup and bread for 2d, meat and two vegetables for 8d, sweet or pudding for 2d and a cup of tea for a penny.

The British Restaurant at Maidstone was also opened in June at a room in the Corn Exchange used for many other purposes so that opening hours in the restaurant were limited from noon to 2pm. The cost of a meal there was 9d, with soup for a penny and tea at the same price. Between June 1941 and December 1942 it sold 164,540 midday meals, at an average of 2,256 a week, with takings of £6,411 5s 6d.

The new British Restaurant in Canterbury was opened in the Parry Hall at the King's School at the end of September by the Archbishop of Canterbury, Cosmo Lang. The Mayor of Canterbury, Alderman Charles Lefevre, welcomed the Archbishop. Family meals, he said, had been a means of fostering family feeling, but communal feeding encouraged the sense of neighbourliness. Those present then sat down to a meal of vegetable soup, roast lamb, beans and potatoes, rhubarb tart and custard—all for 9d.

It was on 22nd June 1941 that Germany invaded Russia.

Another of the many exercises carried out by the troops and the Home Guard in Kent during the war took place at Hawkhurst in July 1941. Members of the Home Guard from Hawkhurst, Cranbrook, Ticehurst and Sandhurst, in conjunction with the ARP services, took part in a large-scale mock battle at end of the month, when the members from Ticehurst, Cranbrook and Sandhurst carried out an 'enemy' attack on the village. The Ticehurst section was spotted while trying to break through the defences at Oakfield, and all its members were taken prisoner after one of the four defending platoons trapped them with a flanking movement. The men from Sandhurst later attacked from two directions in the east. They encountered another platoon which took about fifty prisoners and two cars which were meant to be armoured vehicles. The Cranbrook section continued to harass a third platoon until they were taken in the rear and mopped up. The ARP services dealt with a number of imaginary fires, rescued people 'trapped in burning buildings' and took 'serious casualties' to hospital. The exercise was considered to be of great value should a real attack ever take place.

Hundreds of members of the Kent Woman's Land Army took part in a rally at Maidstone Zoo Park on the same day. Many of the girls had worked on as dog-fights went on overhead in the Battle of Britain, and nine of the girls were presented with badges at the rally for "sustained courage under dangerous conditions". One had stayed at her post when a nearby airfield was being heavily bombed; another carried on work when cowsheds close to her were wrecked, while others had remained at work in greenhouses when bombs fell. Lord Cornwallis, chairman of the Kent War Agricultural Committee, thanked the girls for the splendid work they were doing and said: "I do not think we could have carried on without you." There were more than a thousand Land Girls in Kent, he said, and another five hundred girls from other counties would be joining them shortly for the threshing. He then read a message from Mr R. Hudson, the Minister of Agriculture, which said: "I am very happy to be able to congratulate Kent—and Kent Land Girls—on being the first county to have more than a thousand members of the Women's Land Army in employ-ment. I congratulate you all, and many others like you in all parts of the country, on the good work you have been doing and the way in which you have been sticking to your jobs, very often in dangerous areas."

Broadstairs received its worst air-raid of the war a few weeks later.

Broadstairs suffered much less from bombing than its neighbouring towns of Margate and Ramsgate. Only seven people were killed in the town in the whole war, and five of those deaths were caused when a single plane dropped bombs on the town at 9.31pm on Saturday 16th August. The five people who died in that raid were all members of the fire brigade. Three of them had been standing outside their sleeping-quarters when two bombs fell in the grounds and killed them; another was taken to hospital with serious injuries, where he died two days later. The chief fire-officer, Mr Arthur Bates, walking along the road with the second officer shortly before the attack, told his colleague to go on ahead when the raid began because he could not keep up with him. The second officer ran up the hill and had just turned into a side road when bombs exploded. Mr Bates was found dead in the street; his colleague escaped with cuts and bruises. The bombs had fallen in the centre of the town, blocking the High Street with craters and damaging many homes and other buildings.

On Sunday 7th September people on the cliffs at Ramsgate were watching British planes bomb the French coast when enemy aircraft carried out their own attack on the town. Ten high-explosive bombs fell on an area near Ramsgate harbour in this raid at 10.23pm. Eight people were killed, four seriously injured and nine slightly hurt. One pub received a direct hit, and bombs fell outside two others. The worst damage was in the area of Townley Street, Liverpool Lawn, Adelaide Gardens, Prospect Terrace and part of Sion Hill, which were all blocked after the attack. One man was blown through a hole in the floor of his house and into the cellar but clawed his way out of the wreckage and rescued his wife and thirteen-year-old daughter, who were trapped in a dug-out in the cellar. He then went to the front of the house to help two injured men who were later taken to hospital. His home, which was wrecked in the bombing, had thirty canaries on the verandah at the time; twenty-one of them were still alive after the raid. Two dead bodies found were those of a father and the teenage son he had been trying to shield; one man was killed while running towards his home. A total of 120 people were made homeless in the attack. All rescue-work was completed shortly after midnight, except for the recovery of one body in a building in danger of collapse.

One of the worst dive-bombing attacks made on Dover occurred on Thursday 2nd October when the town was hit by three different waves of planes between 7.30pm and midnight. Most of the bombs in the first raid fell in the St Margaret's area and were thought to have been aimed at the anti-aircraft guns; but at least one bomb also fell in the town, at the bottom of Archcliffe Road. The second wave came shortly before 9.30pm. The worst incident was in the road near the 'Red Cow' pub in Folkestone Road, although other bombs fell on either side of the nearby Priory Station at about that time. A concert at the Wesley Hall in Folkestone Road had just ended, and the audience was making its way home. One soldier probably saved a woman's life when he threw her to the floor and shielded her with his body; he was seriously injured and had to have his leg amputated. The final attack came shortly before 11.30pm. Four bombs wrecked many houses in Dour Street, north of the station, and about a hundred incendiary bombs were dropped on the slopes at Western Heights, starting seven small fires which were all quickly put out. About forty bombs had fallen in the raids, mostly in the area between Folkestone Road and the sea-front near the docks. Sixty people were made homeless when six houses were wrecked, and eighteen hundred homes needed first-aid repairs of some kind. The bombing left eight people dead, thirteen seriously injured and thirty-two slightly hurt.

Bad luck on the part of a German bomber pilot and successful work by the RAF helped bring an enemy aircraft down in Kent on Tuesday 21st October. A Dornier 217 was heading back to France after a re-connaissance trip over the Atlantic when it came across unexpectedly strong winds. The plane drifted far north of the route it should have been on, although its crew did not realize it. The pilot did not cross the west coast of France when he expected to, so he flew north to get a fix off the south coast of England. He reached Pembrokeshire in Wales, which he thought was Cornwall, and turned south to cross the north coast of Devon, which the navigator thought was Brittany. The Germans had a system of navigational beams which were transmitted from France to guide their planes over Brittany, but the RAF was now able to blot out those beams with its own equipment—which is what they did in the case of this bomber. The pilot was amazed when, quite lost, he turned south and came across yet another coastline. He had nearly run out of fuel by that time and had to land at the first airfield he came across, which was Lydd. The Dornier was the first example of the new bomber to fall into the hands of British Intelligence.

11. The dash up the Channel

Parachute-troops landed on the outskirts of Canterbury at dawn one Sunday at the end of October and began heading towards the city. The noise of gunfire as they made their attack woke some people from their sleep—but they had nothing to fear: the 'attack' was an exercise to test the liaison between the military and civil authorities; and the 'enemy' troops were really British. A number of high-ranking officers from Allied countries watched with interest as members of the Civil Defence, the Home Guard and the Army carried out the manoeuvres.

Parachute-troops captured the East and West railway stations in the early stages of the fighting before going on to take the Westgate Towers—which was the scene of bitter street fighting. Various counter-attacks took place in that area but even dive-bombing could not shift the 'enemy'; they withdrew only when they discovered that reinforcements were nearby. 'Fifth Columnists' had elsewhere supplied parachute-troops with boats to cross the river. These troops were met by withering fire from the opposite bank, but they managed to storm across under the cover of a thick smoke-screen. Rescue, demolition and first-aid squads were meanwhile coping with incidents all over the city as the result of bombing. Gas was dropped at several points, and smoke hung over the whole town as war-vehicles of all types raced along diverted routes to one point or another.

Shortly before the end of the exercise, the Mayor, Alderman Charles Lefevre, and the town clerk, Mr George Marks, were 'blown up' at the control-room of the Civil Defence. They staggered outside 'seriously injured' and were put on stretchers as another bomb fell nearby. The Mayor, given one minute to make a brief message before he 'died', said: "Keep working at it, and save the people." In fact, the Mayor lived through the real bombing of the city the following year, while Mr Marks was killed by one of the first bombs that fell. The exercise was described as a complete success, and the co-operation was said to be about as good as it could be. The 'enemy', which had made such a good start, was withdrawing with heavy casualties by the end of the day.

Only a few weeks after that day of make-believe, the nearby village of Sturry—only a few miles from Canterbury—suffered a raid which turned it into the most damaged village of its size in Kent. Shortly after the alarm sounded on Tuesday 18th November, at about 7pm, an aircraft could be heard circling the village in the pitch-black. A few minutes later, at 7.07pm, there was a terrific flash and an explosion. Two parachute-mines had been dropped in the village. One fell on open ground near allotments, but the other fell in the main street outside the 'Red Lion' pub. Several buildings were wrecked, and every building in the street was damaged in some way. The raid left fifteen people dead and eleven seriously injured. One of the first bodies to be found was that of a small girl who had apparently been to the baker's shop: her body was found in the street—and she was still clutching a bag of buns.

The landlord at the 'Red Lion' was injured in the blast and his wife killed when their pub was demolished. The parish hall, which was used as a first-aid post and canteen, was also wrecked. People inside serving refreshments at the time looked up to see the walls caving in on them, followed by the roof. Everyone inside was rescued within minutes and found to be suffering from nothing more than minor injuries. Milner Court, a large house in the area, was turned into a first-aid post, and it was there that the injured were sent for treatment after they had been rescued. At least twenty-five people made home-less in the raid were also taken to the house for the night, moving to a rest-centre the following day for their billeting arrangements to be sorted out.

A woman escaped unhurt when a door fell across her and held up the debris from her ruined home. Her son was only slightly injured when he had his nightwear blown off him in bed; he was rescued naked and carried off wrapped in a curtain. The bodies of a married couple, their two children and a boy visitor were recovered from the wreckage of another house—the couple had returned to Britain a few years before after losing all their possessions in an earthquake in New Zealand. The body of one woman was found spreadeagled across the two bodies of her children—as though she had been trying to protect them. A local doctor went into the tunnels in the debris to give first aid to some trapped children, but they were dead before he could help them. One man, trapped in the debris of his house for eight hours, gave directions to those trying to reach him which enabled them to get to other trapped victims.

Rescue-work had to begin with the help of covered lights, for fear of pinpointing Sturry as a target for further bombers, but rescue-parties from Chislet Colliery brought lamps and flood-lights with them to help rescue many people alive from the rubble. Tiles, glass and debris were scattered everywhere by the mines. At least twelve houses and shops were wrecked in the bombing, twenty made unfit to live in and eighty other homes in need of first-aid repair-work. Gas and water were cut off for a day, and the A28 main road through the village was not open to single-line traffic until the afternoon of 21st November. Few windows were left in any building over a wide area, and houses a considerable distance away were hit by flying glass. The Civil Defence and Home Guard rescue-squads were also helped by troops.

Kent became the first county in the country in 1941 to buy a Spitfire squadron for the RAF. Spitfire funds had sprung up all over the country during the summer of the previous year. These fighters were priced at £5,000, and any town, group or individual giving that amount could 'buy' a new aircraft to bear the name of its choice. More than £13 million had been raised in this way nationally by April 1941, and by the end of the war nearly every big town in Britain had its name on a Spitfire. But Kent went several times better than every other county—by buying a whole squadron.

The fund started in the ordinary way with towns in Kent simply aiming at £5,000 to buy their own fighters, but by July 1941 the various Spitfire funds in the county had raised so much money that Colonel Moore-Brabazon, the new Minister of Aircraft Production, wrote to Lord Cornwallis, chairman of the Kent County Spitfire Fund: it had been the county's intention to supply only part of a squadron—but now a whole squadron was within reach of Kent, he pointed out. The county fund then stood at about £80,000; a squadron would be named when the fund reached £100,000, wrote Colonel Moore-Brabazon.

By November 1941 a total of £108,000 had been given to the fund, and Kent became the first county to have its own fighter squadron. The twenty-two planes its funds provided were given the following names: *Beckenham, Bexley, Bromley, Chatham, Fair Maid of Kent, Garden of England, Kentish Man, Man of Kent, Medway, Meteor, Chislehurst and Sidcup, Canterbury, Faversham, Folkestone and Hythe, Robinson, Gravesend Shrimp, Rochester, Royal Tunbridge Wells, Pride of Sheppey, Weald of Kent, Spirit of Kent* and *Yeoman of Kent.*

The squadron went on to make a name for itself in low-level strafing attacks in preparation for the invasion of Normandy. Five of its commanding officers were awarded the DFC. By 1945 the squadron was in India, where it was re-equipped with Thunderbolts, although it kept the motto '*Invicta*'. It was known by this time as 'the 131 (County of Kent) Fighter Squadron'. It was disbanded on 31st December 1945 "owing to the contraction of RAF numbers to peace-time staff".

Miners in Kent hit the headlines at the beginning of 1942 when three of their leaders were sent to jail during a strike at Betteshanger Colliery. An order passed by the government in the summer of 1940 had set up a National Arbitration Tribunal to handle pay-claims—and it also made strikes illegal. So the Ministry of Labour stepped in when 1,050 underground workers at the colliery went on strike over pay on 9th January. All the miners were prosecuted at the Wingham Petty Sessions held in Canterbury on 23rd January; about fifty miners, including their secretary and chairman, actually appeared in court.

The prosecution said that the court was not worried about the facts of the pay-claim, nor about any technical detail between the company and the miners. The summonses were taken out because the men had broken the law by coming out on strike; it was a serious offence. The legal representatives for the miners pleaded guilty. The three miners' leaders in court were the chairman of the Betteshanger branch of the Kent Mine Workers' Association, Tudor Davies, who was also a JP and a Deal councillor, secretary William Powell, another Deal councillor, and committee member Isaac Metheuen. Powell was sentenced to two months' hard labour, Davies and Metheuen to one month's hard labour, while the thirty-five or so workers at No. 2 face were fined £3 each and the rest of the miners £1 each. Lord Hawarden, passing sentence, said that coal was a munition of war—and it had not been treated as such at that colliery.

The strike itself, which lasted nineteen days, was settled in the miners' favour on Wednesday 28th January, and work began again on the night shift that night. A few days later, on 2nd February, the three leaders were released from Maidstone Prison, where they had served eleven days of their sentence. They went to the Welfare Club in Deal later that evening and were given a great welcome by the miners there. Crowds of men and women shook their hands, and many sang 'For they are jolly good fellows'. All three men were reinstated at the colliery. Only nine of the strikers eventually paid their fines. There was not enough room in jail for all those who had not paid, and no individual prosecutions were brought for fear of provoking a strike in sympathy.

One of the most audacious episodes of the year took place a few days later when the Germans made a break-through in the English Channel in broad daylight. The battleships *Scharnhorst* and *Gneisenau* and the cruiser *Prinz Eugen* had been based at Brest since May the previous year, but now Hitler wanted them in Norwegian waters because he feared an invasion of Norway by the British, so on the night of 11th February the three ships slipped their moorings shortly before 11pm and sailed out to sea to join their escort of destroyers, torpedo-boats and mine-sweepers. Hitler's aim was to take the British by surprise: the ships would sail up the Channel at high speed and pass the Straits of Dover at about noon, when the tide would be in their favour.

The plan had its share of luck—two RAF radar aircraft which might have spotted their movements both had defective sets, so the ships were only spotted by accident on 12th February when two Spitfires from Kenley chased two Messerschmitt 109s over the French coast. The British fighters suddenly found themselves right over the German battle-cruiser fleet. They dived through the curtain of flak coming up from the ships and streaked back to Kenley, landing at 11.10am. The hunt swung into action. The Vice-Admiral at Dover, Sir Bertram Ramsay, had five motor-torpedo boats and a squadron of torpedo-carrying Swordfish aircraft with which to launch his attack, and they left Dover at 11.55am, on their way to attack a group of vessels which consisted by this time of the three big ships, fifteen fast torpedo-boats, ten large destroyers, three flotillas of other torpedo-boats and a fighter aircraft escort of about fifty Messerschmitt 109s and Focke-Wulf 190s. All five British torpedo-boats fired their total of ten torpedoes, mostly at the *Prinz Eugen* through a gap in the smoke-screen that had been laid round her. The *Prinz Eugen* altered course when she saw the torpedoes coming—and all the missiles missed.

The Dover torpedo-boats were saved from destruction probably because the enemy fighters were keeping their ammunition for the Swordfish, six biplanes of Fleet Air Arm which were kept at Manston airfield in anticipation of a Channel break by these ships—although the British had always expected such a break to take place at night. Their fighter escort from Biggin Hill was late in coming, but the Swordfish were unable to wait, so they took off at 12.20pm, meeting up with ten Spitfires from Gravesend as they circled over Manston. The Spitfires and Swordfish sighted the German ships at 12.40pm, and the Swordfish went straight into the attack, ignoring the enemy fighters which were swarming all over the ships. Their leader, Lieutenant-Commander Esmonde, was shot down almost at once and killed. Every ship in the fleet was firing now, and before long all the Swordfish were shot down—and only some of their crews rescued. Esmonde was awarded the VC for his action. Two squadrons from Biggin Hill were on the scene by then. One Messerschmitt 109 was sent crashing down on the deck of a destroyer, and four other enemy aircraft were claimed destroyed. But it was the ships that mattered.

Various other attacks were made on the fleet by boats and aircraft later in the day, in spite of cloudy weather, but the German fleet survived them all. The only serious damage caused was to the *Gneisenau*, which hit a mine off the Dutch island of Terschelling during the evening. She was badly damaged by bombs while being repaired in dry dock and was not able to sail again.

The war continued to knock down the divisions between class and sex. Women were filling the thousands of factory jobs left by men who had joined the Forces—just as they had done in the Great War. A party which visited the Southern Railway works at Ashford in February to see some of them in action included union officials and Mr William Spens, the MP for Ashford; the visit was arranged in connection with the Maidstone War Workers Campaign. Nearly two hundred women had learned how to handle a variety of machines at the works over the previous year. The visiting party, impressed by the part women were playing, saw women in blue boiler-suits working at almost every type of machine. Mr Spens spotted his former parlour-maid working as a bench-hand; a former fruit-shop assistant was wielding a blacksmith's hammer. Mr Spens, at a lunch in the town after the trip, said that every bit of labour, male or female, should be put on to essential war work and agriculture. Mr H. Maxwell, from the Ministry of Information, said that every idle hand was a hand for Hitler and oppression, but every full, occupied hand was a hand for the Allies and Liberation.

The county was being ransacked meanwhile for every piece of waste metal that could be found. A meeting of local authorities, voluntary organizations and other interested bodies was held in Maidstone in March to impress on everyone the urgency of the problem. Mr George Hicks, the Parliamentary Secretary to the Ministry of Works and

Buildings, told the meeting that metal was needed urgently to mak
guns, tanks, ships and bombs. It was intended to clear away ever
village dump of scrap metal within the next few weeks.

Every type of metal object was handed in eventually. A farmer nea
Cranbrook gave the remains of a German oil-bomb, while a mason
yard in Tunbridge Wells yielded four tons of scrap. A man fro
Pembury presented two old floating mines from the last war; he ha
bought them in a sale ten years before and had intended turning the
into water-butts. The owner of the old windmill at Benenden offere
two large wheels, one about six feet across, which ought to hav
yielded about a ton of metal. Youngsters at Penshurst borrowe
horses and carts to search the neighbourhood for any odd bit of jun
they could find; local residents said they had never seen so man
broken iron bedsteads before. A farmer at Five Oak Green, nea
Tonbridge, gave one half of a threshing-machine—having kept th
other half for spares.

Every town and village throughout the country raised mone
during the war for one part or another of the war effort. The Spitfir
Funds, as we have seen, raised enough money in Kent to buy twenty
two aircraft, and staggering amounts were also collected for some o
the other official national funds: War Weapons Week in 1941, Wa
ship Weeks in 1942, Wings for Victory Weeks in 1943, and Salute th
Soldier Weeks in 1944. Each town would set itself a target-figure a
the start of the week—and usually pass it easily seven days later.

In Faversham, for example, the town set out in the spring of 1942 t
raise £120,000 in Warships Week to pay for the corvette HM
Armeria; its fund filled to overflowing at £190,583. Maidstone set ou
to collect £1 million, which represented £10 for every person wh
lived in the town, but it eventually ended up with £1,036,00
Tenterden, which aimed to buy two motor-launches for a flotill
commanded by a former local businessman, had reached £40,000 o
its £50,000 target by the middle of the week. Herne Bay raise
£70,000 to pay for a torpedo-boat, while Romney Marsh and distri
brought in £688 more than its target of £28,500. Hythe set out t
collect £40,000 and ended up with £63,146. Margate raised £162,01
Ramsgate raised £163,661, and Chatham, Rochester, Strood an
Gillingham brought in £806,359 between them. Deal, which intende
to raise £62,000 for a trawler-minesweeper, ended the week wit
£89,928.

The first recorded fatal raid of the year on Kent took place on 23r

March. The first of a series of moonlight attacks on Dover was carried out about 9pm after almost a week in the town without the air-raid sirens sounding. Four or five enemy aircraft circled the town before diving down from 20,000 feet to 10,000 feet and dropping twenty heavy bombs. The All Clear did not sound until an hour later, by which time sixteen people had been killed, six seriously injured and five slightly hurt. The worst incident was at the East Kent Road Car Company garage in St James Street, where a bomb fell on the air-raid shelter and killed most of the staff inside. Most of the other deaths were caused when a bomb hit one end of the Carlton Club, killing some of those inside and trapping the wife of the steward in the rubble for thirteen hours before she could be rescued.

Another moonlight raid was made on Dover on 3rd April, Good Friday, when eighteen bombs were dropped in an attack which began about half an hour after midnight. By the time the All Clear sounded at 2.10am, sixteen people had been killed, eighteen seriously injured and four slightly hurt. Nine people were killed instantly when a bomb wrecked one end of a concrete shelter under gardens in Union Road. About thirty people were sleeping in the shelter at the time. The Priory railway station was thought to have been the raiders' target. One of the worst incidents in the bombing occurred when two houses near the station, in Priory Gate Road, were hit by bombs and collapsed on those inside. Only some of the eight trapped in the wreckage were rescued alive at dawn. The body of a postman, whose wife died in hospital, was not recovered from the ruins until twenty-four hours later. Their two daughters were also injured in the raid.

Two men from Deal were badly injured when a bomb fell on the power-house at Betteshanger Colliery at about 8am on 26th April. A large number of men had to stay down the pits for some hours because of bomb-damage to the machinery. A total of eleven men were injured in this attack. One of the worst attacks on Deal itself was made at 6.25am on Wednesday 6th May. Several bombs were dropped from a low height on the north and south ends of the town. The raid left seven people dead, three seriously injured and seven others slightly hurt. A bus-driver, his sister and another woman, all from Park Lane, died in the bombing in the south of the town, while all the other deaths occurred in Alfred Square. Ten homes were wrecked, seventy-seven seriously damaged and 113 slightly damaged.

Three people died when bombs fell on Folkestone on 17th May— but the casualty-list might have been much higher: one of the bombs that Sunday fell on Christ Church and severely damaged the building only thirty minutes before Matins were due to be held there. The hundred or so people who would have formed the congregation late held a thanksgiving service for their escape in the church hall. One person was seriously injured in this attack on the town and another slightly hurt.

But the casualties were much worse in Canterbury two weeks later when German raiders attacked the city in the early hours of 1st June— the most devastating Kent raid of the war.

12. Alight from end to end

Families in Canterbury heard of a devastating RAF raid on Cologne for the first time one warm evening when they tuned in to the BBC news at 9pm. The RAF destroyed 600 acres of the city of Cologne for the loss of forty bombers from its force of 1,046 aircraft on the night of 30th May 1942. It was news of that raid—the first of its size—that the people of Canterbury might have listened to on Sunday 31st May with justifiable apprehension. Within a few hours of that broadcast, a third of the city-centre of Canterbury itself was destroyed by a reprisal raid.

The country had been hit since April 1942 by a series of what came to be known as 'Baedeker Raids', the first of which took place on 23rd April when Exeter was attacked in retaliation for a heavy RAF attack which razed large sections of the city of Lübeck. This was followed by raids on Bath, Norwich, York, Hull, Poole and Grimsby. The Baedeker Raids, launched against smaller and less well-defended cities, were so called because the targets were said to have been picked from the famous guide-books of that name. Canterbury was the next target to come from their pages.

Mrs Catherine Williamson, Mayor of Canterbury from 1938 to 1940, describes what happened after the city had settled down for the night that Sunday.

> The household where I was staying went to bed at about eleven o'clock, and I retired to my room although I did not go to bed. Sitting on the edge of the bed reading a book, I tried to while away the hours. All other Baedeker raids had occurred at about 12.45am, and so I did not worry myself very much until about 12.15am when the tension seemed to grow. Sure enough, about 12.45am a plane was heard in the distance, and almost simultaneously the siren sounded, together with the inner warning. I looked out of my window. By this time a few German raiders were circling over the city dropping flares. The city, with every fine detail of architecture, was picked out in the uncanny blue and yellow

light. Chandelier flares hung in the sky over the whole area of the city, and I knew that we must be prepared for the worst. After about three minutes there was an ominous sound of bombs dropping on the north side of the city.

Sixteen parachute-flares could be seen in the sky over the city at one time. They were dropped to illuminate the city for the fifty bombers which now swept in from the direction of Whitstable and Herne Bay in three waves. Mrs Williamson said:

> The hum of heavy bombers became almost deafening as more and more arrived to take up their places, and after about ten minutes dive-bombing was heard continuously and without relief. It seemed as if the whole city was being laid flat. After about an hour and a quarter of unmitigated terror, it appeared that the raid was gradually easing off. The gun-fire was less, and the interval between bombs dropped, longer. In another quarter of an hour planes were almost inaudible, and we emerged from our shelter to take stock of the damage done. The All Clear was sounded at 2.10am.
>
> In walking a considerable number of yards down the garden to a position where practically the whole length of Canterbury could be seen, it seemed at first sight that immense fires enveloped the whole city, the flames reaching so high that the Bell Harry Tower of the cathedral could not be observed. The sound of crashing masonry was almost deafening . . . all the houses on the city wall, as far as Rose Lane, and a very good deal of Watling Street, were on fire. Many of the buildings looked just about to crash. Many frontages of houses were leaning out at very dangerous angles, and in Watling Street the heat was intense.

Mr George Marks, the town clerk and ARP controller, aged forty-eight, was waiting for a break in the bombing to go to his control-centre when one of the first bombs fell on his house in St Augustine's Road, burying him and his wife beneath the debris for some time. While lying there with his wife, he heard the All Clear and said: "Now that the raid is over, I wonder how soon they will come and dig us out?" But he died before the rescue-workers could reach him.

The cathedral—thought to have been the main target—did not escape the night unscathed. The heaviest bomb ever dropped in that part of the country at the time—a four-tonner—fell about twenty yards from the entrance to the Warrior's Chapel, and the few stained-glass windows which remained in the nave were blown out. (Fortunately, all the valuable glass had been moved to a safe place before the war.) Some incendiary bombs did fall inside the cathedral, but they burned themselves out harmlessly on the stone floor. The cathedral precinct was not as lucky: the Victorian cathedral library was destroyed, as were the homes of Canons Shirley and Macnutt and Lady Davidson; the Norman staircase and a block of King's School buildings in the Green Court were damaged, and so was the four-teenth-century Chapter House and the block of buildings facing the Dark Entry.

The Archbishop of Canterbury, Dr William Temple, and his wife were in residence and spent the night sitting under the stone stairs in the Old Palace. He walked through the streets after the raid to help people where he could and later said that he "felt proud to think he had been a participant with Canterbury in that night of horror". (Dr Temple had been enthroned as Archbishop on 23rd April, replacing Cosmo Lang, who had resigned on 31st March.)

There were many people in Canterbury who needed help that night.

About a hundred high-explosive and six thousand incendiary bombs had been dropped by the raiders, gutting between four and six acres of the city centre. The fires spread quickly because the streets were narrow and a large amount of wood was used in the fabric of the buildings that lined them. A total of forty-three people were killed, forty-eight seriously injured and fifty slightly hurt. The body of one of the victims—a nineteen-year-old tailor who had been missing since the raid—was not discovered until 20th July, when it was found in the ruins of the late town clerk's house. A Ramsgate family of seven was wiped out when a block of houses was wrecked; the family had moved to the city after the bombing of their home town. The area of devasta-tion extended from Watling Street in the south-west to Burgate, already badly damaged in a raid in October 1940, in the north-east; St George's Place was also badly damaged, and there was a smaller pocket of destruction in St Dunstan's. The bombs had wrecked four hundred buildings, mostly by fire, seriously damaged fifteen hundred more and slightly damaged two thousand others.

Such devastation obviously presented appalling difficulties to those trying to carry out rescue-work; ambulance-drivers, for example, frequently found their routes blocked by fallen masonry and some-times drove over burning rubble and through sheets of flame to get the injured to hospital. A woman who experienced such nightmare rides was Miss G. Hann, a driver for the nursing division of the St John Ambulance Brigade and a qualified sister. She said:

> The cathedral stood silhouetted against a pall of fiery smoke. A horse neighed in terror, and now a dog rushed by, its tongue lolling out. A man

came past me, urging his wife along, who was sobbing as she ran
Around came the planes, and down came the bombs, until the whole city
seemed alight from end to end.

My ambulance attendant came, and we were given a message to
proceed to the top of St Martin's Hill. We had to find our own route, so
off we started: up Watling Street, along the top of the town. Fires were
burning on either side of us. The Dane John Terrace seemed alight from
end to end. We put the ambulance at a huge pile of bricks and rubble
near the junction of Ivy Lane, and after a good deal of shaking we got
through. Turning into St Paul's, we saw a very fierce fire, with showers
of sparks coming down into the road, and smoke blinding us, we felt our
way through into Longport Street. At the narrowest part of the St
Martin's Hill there was another large fire with more rubble in the road. I
wondered if we could get up a steep hill over so much debris to climb,
but there was no time to be lost with a patient waiting, so, changing
down into low, I nursed the engine until we were by, just a little scorched
by the fire. We arrived to find it too late—our patient had died.

A warden called to us that he had another waiting, and in no time we
had loaded up and started on our way to hospital. At St Paul's the road
had been roped off—the fire was too dangerous. But the warden decided
to let us take the risk, as all the smaller roads were blocked, so through
we went. As we approached the fire, the roof collapsed into the inferno,
window-frames, burning hard, came crashing into the roadway. Some
pieces fell on top of the ambulance, but I did not dare stop then. I
expected the engine to catch fire with the flames that licked at us. The
tyres smelled as though they, too, were burning. But again bumping
over the bricks, we cleared ourselves and turned the corner to start our
climb over the Co- perative Stores pile of debris. Our engine started
spluttering, and a few soldiers rushed to give me a push; just then a bomb
went off round the corner. It seemed to put life into our engine for we
went off in fine style and reached the hospital safely with our first
patient.

Two hundred firemen from all over Kent and London were rushed
in to tackle the blazes. One fireman from a coast town, who was
spending the weekend in the city, reported for duty clad only in
pyjamas, an old coat and trousers borrowed from a relative. He was
provided with a steel helmet two sizes too small and rubber boots two
sizes too big, the only ones available, before helping the Canterbury
pump-crew for several hours. Many of the firemen and other rescue
workers worked for more than twenty-four hours without sleep
although the main fires were mostly under control by daybreak. And
with the daybreak the full extent of the damage was revealed; the
scene was one of chaos and destruction. Mr Hubert Banner, the

Ministry of Information's chief regional officer for the south-east at the time, describes the view which confronted him when he arrived in Canterbury later that morning:

> By God's mercy the cathedral still stood four-square, though vast craters gaped in its green precincts, and the walls and windows bore grievous scars—a desecration as vile as when Becket fell beneath his murderers' swordblades. But the eastern half of the High Street was in a condition only comparable to that of Ypres during the last war. It presented an almost unbroken vista of desolation, and among the buildings battered into shapeless, rubble-heaps or irreparably damaged were many hallowed by antiquity.
>
> Through that first day and the days which followed, Canterbury presented a picture which seemed fantastically unreal to anyone familiar with its normal aspect. Along its streets lay miles and miles of snaky hosepipe. The gutters were full of sweepings of broken glass and other debris. Over great mountains of wreckage climbed swarms of human figures, dimly to be seen through a curtain of fine dust and ash . . . From morning to night the air was filled with the stroke of pick and shovel, the nerve-wracking clatter of pneumatic drills, the thudding of fire-pumps, men's shoutings, and every now and again the roar of collapsing masonry. Everywhere was the smell of burning.

It was not only God's mercy which allowed the cathedral to stand throughout this raid—the fire-guards played a large part in its protection. These men spent the duration of the attack crawling round the cathedral parapets and throwing burning and burned-out incendiary bombs onto the grass below.

The cathedral still stood, but much of historic Canterbury had been reduced to rubble in the raid. St George's Church—which, with St George's Street, was at the centre of the damage—was left a mere shell; its tower, all that remains of it, still stands in the shopping-centre which replaced the old buildings. The church of St Mary Bredin was also destroyed, as were 57 St George's Street, the birth-place of the playwright Marlowe, and 61 Burgate Street, the birth-place of the Rev. R.H. Barham, author of *The Ingoldsby Legends*. The Royal Fountain Hotel in St Margaret's Street, reputedly the oldest hotel in the country, and The Rose Hotel in the main street were both destroyed, and so was the reputed home of Uriah Heep in Lower Chantry Lane. St Martin's Church, St Thomas's RC Church in Burgate Street and the Kent War Memorial were all damaged by bomb-blast. Only one house was left standing at Lady Wootton's Green, where a heavy bomb had also badly scarred the nearby gateway to St Augustine's College. Parts of Wincheap School, the Payne-Smith Schools and the Simon Langton Schools were also destroyed in the attack.

The daylight revealed many pathetic sights. Crowds of people wandered from one street to another, gazing in a dazed way at what had happened; the homeless began to salvage some of their precious belongings; old people sat dazed and bewildered outside the wreckage of their homes; and at least one old couple walked aimlessly through this unreal scene, both injured and supporting each other. One house-proud and elderly woman, whose house was probably saved from destruction by soldiers who entered and removed a fire-bomb from a bedroom, complained that the men did not wipe their boots.

The British Restaurant in the Parry Hall at King's School, open from 8am to 6pm, served more than a thousand meals in one day after the raid. There were eight emergency feeding-centres in the city, staffed by 450 helpers who worked without break to serve meals and give out clothes, helped by a convoy of Queen's Messengers from Tonbridge and London, and YMCA officers. A Red Cross 'flying column' in the charge of the Viscountess Falmouth left London on the Tuesday for Canterbury, and the Salvation Army also helped with this work. So many people wanted to send telegrams to let relatives know that they were all right that special tables were set up in Stour Street for people to write their messages. Telegrams coming into the city from worried relatives were so numerous that they were delivered like letters by postmen and sometimes taken out in Post Office vans.

Now that the raid was over, and daybreak had come, the people of Canterbury began to get back to normal—or to something approaching that state. Loudspeaker cars toured all areas of the city from morning to night, repeating announcements and instructions with the new addresses of bombed-out organizations to which people might turn for first-aid repairs to buildings, for replacement of lost food or clothing coupons, for cash, emergency transport, sanitation and other health precautions.

Notices warning that water must be boiled for five minutes were put up round the city; boarded-up shops announced business as usual; Union Jacks appeared defiantly at the windows of damaged buildings; workmen continued to clear up rubble and repair buildings where they could, and where they could not, red flags on the pavement in front of a blitzed building showed that the walls were dangerous and likely to collapse; undamaged businesses shared their buildings with bombed-out firms; and the shell of St George's Church flew its saint's flag from a post on the pavement.

Then, two nights later, on the night of 2nd–3rd June, the raiders came back once more; and four nights after that, on the night of 6th–7th June, they came back yet again, but these further attacks were nothing like as serious as the first raid.

The first of these later raids lasted only an hour, causing further damage to businesses and homes, and destroying the Congregational Church in Watling Street by fire; thirty-four fires were started altogether, but these were all under control forty-five minutes later. The electricity grid-system near Canterbury was damaged, and power to Thanet was cut off for a time. Five people were killed, five seriously injured and eighteen slightly hurt. Most of the high-explosive and incendiary bombs dropped in the final attack fell on open ground, but three main and two local cables were damaged, and nine minor fires were started.

The only casualties in Canterbury occurred when a fire-engine overturned in a crater, killing one fireman and injuring two others. The death of this volunteer fireman came after the Sturry fire-service received a call at 1.35am to proceed to a fire in another district. The engine passed the glow of burning incendiary bombs before turning into a road which was in darkness. They were travelling without lights, the normal procedure when enemy aircraft were overhead, and were doing about 12–15mph in the centre of the road. The fire-engine toppled into a crater in the road after a short while and trapped the dead man for six hours until it could be removed by a large grab.

With the final June raid over, it was possible to assess the damage. The three attacks had left forty-nine people dead, forty-six seriously injured and sixty-one slightly hurt; 310 homes were destroyed and 2,500 others damaged; while two hundred other buildings had been wrecked and three hundred more damaged. A total of 697 people had been made homeless by the raids. In addition to the thousands of incendiary bombs which fell in this one black week, it was estimated that the number of high-explosive bombs dropped was: a hundred on 1st June, including fifteen unexploded; six on 3rd June, including two unexploded; and seventeen on 7th June, including two unexploded.

The only good thing about the timing of these raids was that they occurred in the middle of a short heat-wave, allowing repair-work to be carried out unhampered by rain or wind. First-aid work on the buildings began on 2nd June with 460 men, rising to 670 on the Wednesday and 920 on Thursday. The final building labour-force numbered 1,150. This house-repair army was drawn from thirteen different towns in Kent, and they used about 2,940 tarpaulins to cover roofs.

Many habitable houses now lacked occupants, however. Many people were frightened of further raids and took advantage of the fine weather to sleep in open fields, haystacks, woods and hedges—any-where, in fact, provided it was outside the city. Some people trekked out to get a good night's sleep in the hoppers' huts round Canterbury, coming into work daily from them; and some lay their bedding between the lines of the Tyler Hill railway tunnel, assured of a peaceful night. In mid-August that year it was reported that four hundred people had recently stayed overnight in the Dane John shelters; shelter-sleeping had become a habit.

Canterbury lacked the protection of London, but it was not without its defences. Anti-aircraft guns round the city had, together with night-fighters, brought down three of the bombers during the 1st June raid. And, after the 3rd June attack, barrage-balloons made their appearance in the skies over the city. But on Saturday 31st October the balloons were grounded for repairs—and that was when the raiders came back again.

The city was not without its distinguished visitors during the summer of 1942. The Duke of Kent toured the devastated areas of Canterbury on 4th June; and on 30th October it was the turn of Mrs Roosevelt and Mrs Churchill to come to the town. Mrs Roosevelt, wife of the American President, was in Britain to study the work which had been carried out by British women during the war. Had she come to the city a day later, she would have been able to observe at first hand how they coped with an air-raid.

Saturday has always been a busy day in Canterbury, and on the afternoon of 31st October the city was filled with people doing their weekend shopping. A big crowd of people waited outside a cinema to see *Gone With The Wind*. A bus carrying eight passengers, including a child, was heading along the Sturry road towards Sturry; shortly after 5pm they and the conductress were all dead, when their bus was tilted on its end by a bomb blast. But the driver escaped by pulling his collar over his head and ducking below the windscreen. The driver of another bus approaching the city from a nearby village, however, was shot through the heart by a machine-gun bullet from a plane. And two men repairing a roof were killed when they were hurled to the ground.

All those casualties were victims of a raid carried out by aircraft which came hedge-hopping over the countryside, almost skimming the roof-tops, before dropping their bombs and spraying the streets with machine-gun and cannon fire. The streets were crowded with shoppers who dived for shelter or threw themselves flat, many of them rushing to the cathedral to shelter in the crypt; many injuries were caused by flying debris of glass. Five minutes later it was all over.

This low-level attack was made by a force of thirty Focke-Wulf 190 fighter-bombers which flew with a similar number of fighters as close support and thirty more as rear support. Each of the planes carried a single delayed-action 1,100-kilo bomb fused to explode when the last of the attackers had got clear. They made for a point north-west of the city and turned through a semi-circle to run in for the attack. They were over England less than six minutes. Fighter Command put up sixty-three fighters to meet the raiders, and there were several combats with the German escorts. Three aircraft from the raiding force were destroyed by fighters or anti-aircraft fire.

Standing orders had been issued to the Kent ARP Mobile Reserves at Bridge Hill House after the June attacks stating that a striking force should be sent into Canterbury as soon as it was known that bombs had dropped, without waiting for instructions. The commandant there sent rescue-parties into the city as soon as he saw this happen, and within forty-five minutes of the attack the first people trapped alive had been rescued by the detachment. But rescue-work during the night was made difficult by two further raids.

The first of these took place in the area at about 8pm, although there were no incidents in the city itself. But the second attack, at 12.30am on 1st November, killed two people, severely injured seven, including three children, and did further damage to homes and businesses.

The people in the cinema queue were severely shocked when a bomb wrecked the back of the building in the afternoon. By the end of all the raids the other cinema was also damaged, as were two churches, the council buildings and industrial premises, including the electricity works; and the cathedral also suffered slightly from bomb-blast. A garage, two shops and three pubs were destroyed; and 110 homes were wrecked, 154 seriously damaged and two hundred slightly damaged. The estimated total number of bombs dropped on the city was fifty high-explosive, seven unexploded, forty-five 50-kilo incendiary bombs and four hundred smaller incendiary bombs.

Thirty-two people were killed in the attack, including six children and six service personnel, fifty-five seriously injured, including eighteen children and nine service personnel, and fifty-four slightly hurt, including four children. About 250 people were made homeless by the raid. A total of three hundred first-aid repair-men were drafted into the city on 1st November and during the day nearly a thousand tarpaulins were placed over damaged roofs. All transfers of building labour in East Kent were cancelled and by 4th November about nine hundred men were carrying out these repairs, having covered up seventy-five per cent of the roofs in spite of the wet weather. The city's two British Restaurants—in the Parry Hall and St Mary Bredin's School—and the mobile canteens run by WVS members served food to those in need, dishing up hundreds of meals the day after the raid.

Mrs Roosevelt sent a telegram to the Mayor, Alderman Charles Lefevre, in which she said: "The great kindness shown me when I visited Canterbury with Mrs Churchill made the attack on your beautiful city very real to me, and I wish you to convey my deepest sympathy to those who were injured or suffered."

The ruined area of Canterbury, devoid of new buildings, lay desolate for some years. William Townsend, writing shortly after the war, said:

> Spread out towards the cathedral is a tufted wilderness . . . Narrow lanes wander half-hidden through all this growth, and the main street, with only a scattered and diminished survivor here and there of its shops and houses in 200 yards of its length, reaches towards the centre of the city between chestnut fences and low edges of walls. It leads past rows of open cellars, where former proprietors have set up notice-boards to give their new addresses, and past the gutted ruin of St George's Church . . . It is difficult, without walking over the spot, to remember just what stood here or there, but in time all this will be built over again. . . .

Canterbury began to pick up the pieces, and eventually the wilderness was built over again.

13. "Killed on Active Service"

The bombing of Canterbury in June might have been the most tragic and devastating event of the year—but it was not the only incident in Kent that summer. Some of them, however, had happier endings. A Wellington bomber crash-landed near Lydd early in the morning of 26th June on its way back from a 1500-plane attack on Bremen. The pilot, who was only nineteen years old, had wanted to get down safely because his rear gunner's wife was expecting a baby. the most welcome sound they heard, he said, was an English voice telling barking dogs to shut up. The crew had not known if they were behind enemy lines or not until then.

The most patriotic housewife during the war was said to have kept four separate containers for the different types of salvage for which the government was always asking: one for scrap metal, another for paper and cardboard, a third for bones (which were said to be made into glue for aircraft or glycerine for explosives), and a fourth for waste food for pigs. All manner of ingenious schemes were devised to encourage people to part with their unwanted odds and ends during a salvage drive in Kent in July. People could get in free to many cinemas in the county if they handed over books and paper on their way in; and the cinema at Broadstairs was giving free seats every morning to youngsters who had distinguished themselves by their own salvage efforts. Elsewhere in Broadstairs, people could get a boat-ride on the lake by donating two books, and they could attend a concert at the Grand Pavilion by handing over books or paper—4lbs worth would get them a seat in the stalls, 2lbs worth any other seat.

Beach donkeys equipped like pack-mules paraded with refuse-vans through Margate, together with a military band and loud-speaker vans. The public at Ramsgate were invited to throw their books at a knock-down effigy of Hitler. A total of 150 bone-bins, converted from ex-Army four-gallon petrol-cans, hung on posts throughout the

Hollingbourne area—and every bin was filled to overflowing. Three hundred shop-windows in Ashford carried salvage slogans in bright chrome lettering, while a decorated concrete dump was set up in the High Street. Loudspeaker appeals in Maidstone were followed by daily collections of salvage—and refuse-collections were suspended People at Broadstairs could also go to special book-exchange libraries where three old books for salvage could be exchanged for one new book. And Canterbury, which was still recovering from its June raids managed to collect 20 tons a week during the salvage-drive.

Eight enemy aircraft flew in low from the sea about 6pm on the evening of Tuesday 11th August and carried out a bombing and machine-gun attack on Deal. Many people were caught in the streets and had to throw themselves to the ground or dive into public shelters A boy of sixteen was killed while he was cycling over the bridge, and two women died when they were buried under the debris of a house which received a direct hit. The women were thought to have been on their way to the cinema at the time; the Odeon cinema itself was severely shaken in the bombing, had its roof stripped and had to be closed for repairs for several weeks. The raid left eight people dead six seriously injured and fifty-five slightly hurt.

The chief constable of Folkestone found it necessary to outline the regulations concerning banned coastal areas of Kent a few days later on 14th August. People were allowed to enter a Defence Area to visit parents, children or a husband or wife, he said. Uncles or sisters did not count. He was speaking at the town's petty sessions, where two women had been fined £1 each for entering a defence area for a holiday. There were notices at London stations warning people not to enter such an area without permission.

The flags in Kent were flying at half-mast on 26th August when the county learned of the death the previous day of the Duke of Kent. The official statement about his death, issued shortly before midnight on 25th August, said: "The Air Ministry deeply regrets to announce that Air Commodore HRH the Duke of Kent was killed on active service this afternoon when a Sunderland flying-boat crashed in the north of Scotland. His Royal Highness, who was attached to the staff of the Inspector General of the RAF, was proceeding to Iceland on duty." The Duke was Colonel-in-Chief of the Queen's Own Royal West Kent Regiment and patron of the County Association, the Men of Kent and Kentish Men. He had inspected civil defence services at Tunbridge Wells and made a tour of bomb-damaged Canterbury in June, and in July had visited the King's School, Canterbury, at its war-time home in Cornwall. The Mayor of Canterbury, Alderman Charles Lefevre, sent a letter of sympathy to the Duchess of Kent.

Two workmen died on 29th September when a bomb fell on the fan-house at Betteshanger Colliery between 9am and 10am. Several other men were injured, and the men working below were brought to the surface. That was the fourth direct hit made on the colliery. It was out of action for several weeks, and half the men were transferred temporarily to other collieries nearby.

The most serious attack ever made on Deal took place on 22nd October when enemy aircraft bombed and machine-gunned the town at 9.18am. One bomb wrecked a greengrocer's shop in the High Street, killing the manager, his wife and two assistants. One of the assistants had not intended going to work that day, but he changed his mind—and lost his life. A soldier in the ironmonger's shop next door was killed when that was also ruined. A mother and her two babies and another woman all died when a bomb fell in College Road. The raid left sixteen people dead, including the soldier, seven seriously injured and fifteen slightly hurt. Work went on all day to rescue people trapped in the debris. A crushed parrot-cage was found in the rubble, with an unhurt parrot inside it. One of the places wrecked was the north wing of St George's parish hall, which was used as a storeroom for the Borough Restaurant—the windows and roof of the restaurant itself, which occupied the main part of the hall, had its windows and roof blasted. All those made homeless were found accommodation with friends. The bombing destroyed fifteen buildings, seriously damaged sixty-eight and slightly damaged ninety-six others.

Winston Churchill visited Dover the following day, 23rd October. When many women from that battered town—where about 120 people had so far been killed—rushed forward to shake his hand, Churchill told the policemen who were trying to hold them back: "Don't stop them. These hands are worth shaking."

Bombs had fallen at the railway works at Ashford as early as July 1940, but it was not until 26th October 1942 that the first serious damage occurred there. A lone raider, thought to be a Dornier, came in under cover of low cloud at lunchtime and dropped two bombs. One of them fell on the works, damaging the heavy-machine shops, the brass shop and the machine shop. Ten men and a woman at the works were killed—the total death-toll for the town in this attack. Several of the dead had been sheltering under a wall; they died when the bomb burst outside the building and blew the wall in. A few hours after this attack a second raider, also thought to be a Dornier, machine-gunned the town as it flew overhead—but there were no reports of damage or casualties.

The railway works at Ashford were the first in the country to be equipped with a light anti-aircraft gun, which was manned entirely by members of Southern Railway's own Home Guard unit. The works also made armour-plating for twelve armoured patrol trains used on various railways in the country. Southern had four such trains, one based at Canterbury, another at Tonbridge, one at Barnstaple in Devon and a fourth at Wadebridge in Cornwall. All of them were ready to move at any time and patrolled regularly at about 25mph. Their use was discontinued in the late summer of 1943.

Production at the works went on much as normal during the war, in spite of 4,925 signals and alerts, and sometimes the staff there excelled themselves. In the autumn of 1941, for example, the works received an order for a thousand open 12-ton freight-wagons for Russia—they were completed in less than ten weeks. Russian flags fluttered in the workshop, and Russian slogans were chalked up, while the people there worked double shifts day and night to produce double the normal output in each shift. Colonel Llewellin, then Parliamentary Secretary to the Minister of War Transport, came down to Ashford on 10th November and drove the last nail into the last packing-crate with an American hammer—to symbolize the unity of three Allied nations. Men and women at the works also made seventy-five ramp-wagons to carry tanks, repaired and converted forty-three 3·7 Howitzers and produced armour-plating for armoured trains; and other essential work carried out there included the production of bomb-trolleys and tank-fittings, such as turret-sets and breakdown-trains for the US Army.

A great welcome was given in Canterbury on 9th November—not for Churchill or royalty but for three members of the Russian Red Army, one of them a woman, who were on a short tour of the city. The trio, who had recently arrived in Britain, had killed hundreds of Germans between them by sniping, it was said. The woman, Lieutenant Lyudmila Pavilchenka, was said to have shot 309 invaders. She had been wounded four times in defence of Odessa and Sevastopol and been decorated with the Order of Lenin. The other two members of the party were Nicolai Krasavchenko, the leader of the Moscow Youth, and Lieutenant Vladimir Pchelintsev, who was said to have killed 152 Germans with 154 bullets. He was decorated as Hero of the

Soviet Union and with the Order of Lenin. The party was received by the Mayor of Canterbury, Alderman Charles Lefevre, before looking round the cathedral. Krasavchenko expressed their feelings for the heroic attitude of the British people and proposed a toast to the new offensive in Egypt and North Africa.

One of two Focke-Wulf 190s got more than it bargained for on 27th November when it attacked a train near Lydd—it was blown up by the railway engine it gunned. The two aircraft had carried out a machine-gunning raid on Ashford—where they killed a man—and were streaking back home towards the coast when they saw the train moving away from the station. One of the planes opened fire. The boiler of the engine was hit and exploded, and one of the enemy raiders crashed, probably struck by flying debris from the engine. The pilot was found dead in a field a hundred yards away, and bits of his plane were strewn over a radius of half a mile. The fireman on the engine suffered from shock and scalds, but the driver was unhurt.

So many Kent men were among the prisoners in one German camp in Austria by the end of 1942 that they formed their own branch of the Association of Men of Kent and Kentish Men, which already had more than forty members. More and more men from Kent were, in fact, being taken prisoner, and by the first week in December the county was fourth in a 'league' based on figures supplied by the Red Cross. These showed that four thousand Kent men were prisoners of war in German or Italian camps. This put the county fourth out of the fifty-two counties in England and Wales, beaten only by Yorkshire with 8,935 men, Lancashire with 7,840 and Durham with 4,270 men.

The year 1943 got off to a bad start when torrential rain fell on already saturated ground on the night of 13th January, disrupting rail services and flooding large areas in south-east England. About 1·5 inches of rain fell in five hours. The Rivers Medway, Rother and Stour overflowed, and thousands of acres disappeared under water which was several feet deep in places. All the low-lying parts of Ashford were flooded, and from Ashford to Canterbury and beyond there was often little more than vast stretches of water. Members of the Home Guard had to leave their parades early to catch buses to take them home through the water—which was too deep for pedestrians. And anti-aircraft gun and searchlight sites were marooned, although voluntary YMCA workers battled through in their cars to take refreshments to the men. It was the worst flooding in places for many years.

The first big attack of the year came on Wednesday 3rd February when four enemy raiders swept in over Ashford at roof-top height shortly after 8am. They flew in from the coast and were over the town for less than thirty seconds, but by the time they were flying home again, six people had been killed, eleven seriously injured and fifteen slightly hurt. The worst damage was in St John's Lane, Birling Road and the Penlee Point area. The bodies of an ex-soldier, his wife and their two-year-old daughter were recovered from one lot of ruins; policeman's wife and her adopted teenage son died in the house next door. Another bomb fell in the Co-operative Society's warehouse behind the cinema in the High Street, badly damaging several houses. The body of the sixth victim, reported missing during the day, was found there in the evening. Sixty sheep were waiting to be slaughtered in a nearby slaughterhouse; all but four were killed in the raid. Nearly all the windows in one part of the High Street were shattered, and Baptist chapel, hotel, bank and schoolroom were damaged in the blast. It was said that this raid, and a lighter attack carried out on Swanage in Dorset on the same day, were reprisals for the mounting scale of RAF attacks on Germany.

One of several bombers attempting to attack London early in the morning of Thursday 4th March was damaged before it could reach the capital. It jettisoned its bombs over Chatham before crashing in the country several miles away. Many people heard the bomber as it tried to gain height and avoid the anti-aircraft fire, which was fairly heavy. Others saw it burst into flames before it fell below the horizon. One member of the crew was found burned to death in the plane. Several houses were wrecked by the bombs it dropped; five people were killed, two seriously injured and five slightly hurt. One elderly couple and their grand-daughter died in one house, while another couple were killed a few streets away. A total of ninety-eight people were accommodated in the rest-centre.

But the worst death-toll from a single attack on any town in Kent during the war occurred shortly after 10am on Wednesday 24th March 1943, when a dozen Focke-Wulf 190s swept in at roof-top height over Ashford in three waves, bombing and machine-gunning as they went. The raid was over in less than three minutes, but in that time fifty people were killed, seventy-seven seriously injured and seventy-nine slightly hurt. It was an even more savage attack, in terms of lives lost, than the attack on Canterbury the previous June.

The fighter-bombers were seen approaching the town almost immediately after the warning siren went. Cannon shells and machine-gun bullets ripped into the streets and buildings only a few seconds before bombs exploded in different parts of the town. Some of the raiders turned and opened fire again. One plane caused widespread damage when it blew up over Godinton Road after being hit by anti-aircraft fire; another of the planes was also brought down.

Two spotters on duty on top of the Newtown Bath House helped keep the casualty figures down at the railway works. When they saw the aircraft flying in from the Mersham direction at less than 100 feet directly out of the sun, they immediately sounded the danger-signal and gave everyone in the works about twenty-five seconds warning, allowing most people to reach some kind of cover. But in spite of this warning eight men there were killed and forty-one people injured. Five bombs fell on the works. One dropped on the erecting shed and tossed 50-ton locomotives round like toys—a quarter of the shed was wrecked, and production came to a halt for three weeks, not rising to a hundred per cent again for some time afterwards. Two bombs fell on the running-shed; one hit a steam engine and killed the driver and the fireman.

Hundreds of youngsters had a narrow escape during the raid. Three hundred children aged between eight and eleven were at their lessons in the Victoria Road primary school when the warning siren went. They were hurried to nearby shelters only moments before a bomb scored a direct hit on the school. Two classrooms where eighty girls should have been studying were wrecked. The youngsters came out of the shelters to find their playground covered in debris, text-books and other school equipment. Worried parents and friends who rushed to the school found every child unhurt.

Two people were killed at the large Haywards Garage in New Street, one of the main roads leading into the town, when it received a direct hit. The garage was wrecked and inflammable supplies were set on fire, causing an extensive blaze. Cars stored there were ruined. The fire was controlled successfully by firemen, although they were still at work late into the afternoon making sure it did not flare up again. It was one of seven fires started by the bombing, and twenty fire-engines were ordered in from outside the town to help cope with them.

The five people killed when a baker's shop in Kent Avenue was hit were the baker, his wife and son and two people working in the building. Seven houses were wrecked and every house damaged in one road during the bombing. Two little girls and a dog escaped unhurt from the ruins; but a mother and her three-year-old daughter were not so lucky—their bodies were among those recovered from the wreckage. A woman of ninety and her housekeeper were killed in another of the houses, but another woman nearby had just got into her Anderson shelter when part of her house collapsed—covering her in dust from head to foot; her dog was found unhurt under the settee in the ruined front room. One of the bombs fell behind two clothing shops, and assistants could be found in the afternoon salvaging clothes and stocks from the wrecked departments and hanging them out on the tennis court next door.

The worst damage occurred in Milton Road, Dover Place, New Street, New Rents, Kent Avenue, Star Road and Hardinge Road. Windows were smashed over a wide area, and homes in many streets in the town were damaged in some way: slates were ripped from roofs, ceilings brought down and door-locks wrenched from their sockets. About fourteen homes were wrecked altogether in this raid, sixty-five badly damaged and another ninety-nine slightly damaged; superficial damage, such as lost slates, was caused to six hundred roofs. Rescuers continued to dig for people trapped in the rubble all day and through-out the night with the help of floodlights. They were assisted by soldiers and members of the Home Guard who went to the scene after finishing their normal day's work. Members of the Salvation Army and the WVS kept them supplied with food and hot drinks. House-wives and workers were hard at work sweeping up glass and clearing up the debris even before the All Clear sounded.

The plane shot down by anti-aircraft fire exploded over Godinton Road, and its tail fell in the back gardens of some council houses. The engine crashed through the back wall of a block separated from the first homes by a big allotment, severely damaging two buildings. No one was injured. One of its crew-members was thrown in flames from the aircraft and landed in a playing-field. The other raider destroyed was said to have been shot down over the sea by a fighter squadron.

Some of the victims of the air-raid were given a communal burial less than a week later, on the afternoon of 29th March. Their coffins, covered by Union Jacks, were carried to the cemetery from the mortuary in open Army and Civil Defence trucks. They passed through a guard of honour near the cemetery formed by members of the Army, ATS, Home Guard, Police and Civil Defence. The coffins of two Home Guard members were on the first truck, and at its side six of their colleagues walked as bearers. The Bishop of Dover was joined by local clergymen of all denominations for the service. Two local Home Guard companies provided the escort; and buglers from one company sounded the Last Post and Reveille as the service came to an end.

The Home Guard was in the news again on Sunday 11th April when members of the Kent (Bus) Battalion (later to become the West Kent HG Transport Column) took part in a convoy exercise. The idea was that the south-east had been invaded and the enemy had succeeded in establishing two bridgeheads. Heavy casualties were caused on both sides in subsequent operations. The sea-landings were supposed to have been made at a 'harbour' at Goudhurst. Parachute and glider landings had been taking place further inland meanwhile, with the aim of seizing airfields and other vital points, and disrupting and attacking lines of communications and areas at the rear. Most of the airborne troops had been dealt with, but some groups were still at large, and there was the possibility of further paratroop landings. The object of the Home Guard convoys was to take the slightly wounded to the harbour, brushing aside enemy interference on the way and making sure that their transport did not fall into the hands of the enemy. The three convoys had to supply their own protection against air attack and ambush.

They set off with this aim in mind from Maidstone, Tunbridge Wells and Hastings. Everything went well for one of the convoys for the first 10 miles, but then the head of the column came across a road-block at a narrow road just before a fork. Concealed 'enemy' guns picked off the despatch-riders, while a 'bomb' was thrown in the middle of a lorry containing a fighting force. Paratroops, represented in the exercise by men from the Regular Army, meanwhile fired at the convoy and bombed it from behind trees and hedges. The Home Guard, however, escaped this first surprise-attack, quickly adopted defensive measures and claimed that the ambushers were eventually wiped out.

The three convoys all reached the harbour after a time and dispersed and camouflaged their vehicles, throwing out protective screens, installing field-telephones and setting up their headquarters. Villagers passed by on their way to church; sheep grazed in the next field. Suddenly the peace was shattered. A shot rang out—the harbour was being attacked by a stronger force of the enemy. The alarm was sounded on the vehicle horns, and the drivers started up their engines so they could move off as quickly as possible if the attackers broke through. The defenders, however, prevented this from happening. Altogether, said a staff officer at the end of the day, the Home Guard had put up 'a good show'.

One of the strangest things to happen to an airfield occurred at West Malling on the night of 16th April 1943. A single-engined plane, thought to be a Defiant in distress, was heard circling the airfield, so a special van, operated by two WAAF girls, went to guide it in. The lighted FOLLOW ME panel on the van was switched on and the plane led to the tarmac. It was then realized that the plane, far from being a British Defiant, was a German Focke-Wulf 190. An officer who had left his revolver in his room stuck a pencil in the German's back and got him to surrender. No sooner had he been marched off for interrogation than another Focke-Wulf landed. An armoured car immediately set out for it. Wing Commander Peter Townsend, who had been given command of the airfield in January 1943, yelled at the car-crew not to shoot. But they did—setting the plane on fire. The pilot, also on fire, jumped to the ground to have his flames smothered by those nearby. His blazing aircraft, only 50 yards away, suddenly exploded. One fire-tender airman received a chest full of splinters, while the other had a hole in his neck from which blood was spurting. Both men were seriously injured. Pieces of this aircraft were found up to 300 yards away. The planes had become lost in the haze and had landed at West Malling, after spotting the flarepath, believing they were in France. The pilot of a third Focke-Wulf ended up with a fractured skull after undershooting and landing in a cherry orchard, and a fourth pilot was killed when his plane crashed at Staplehurst.

14. The Dam Busters

The police had meanwhile been busy near Herne Bay. At the end of March they began to cordon off an area one mile square, east of Reculver Towers. They were getting ready for the testing of a special sort of bomb—the bouncing bomb used by the Dam Busters, which had been designed by Barnes Wallis and was now at the prototype stage. A Lancaster bomber was to carry out a trial drop off the shore at Reculver Bay. So on Thursday 15th April Guy Gibson (who was to lead the raid) and Bob Hay, the group bombing-leader of their 617 Squadron, were sent down to the coast to watch this first trial.

Guy Gibson, who was to be awarded the VC for his attack on the dams, said:

> We had been told that things weren't quite ready, so we drove round the town of Margate to see what it looked like in time of war. It was pretty hard to realize, as we lounged on the beach, that this was the same old sunshine resort of peacetime; the hotels were all closed; Dreamland was an army barracks; barbed wire was everywhere, and the place was full of soldiers. The only thing that had remained was the fish. We had just stuffed ourselves full of Dover soles and now felt pleasantly lazy in the early afternoon, listening to the screaming of the gulls as they glided over the harbour. Suddenly there was a noise like the release of compressed air, then the chattering of cannon guns, followed by the full crump of bombs. Like a flash, glinting in the sun at 'nought' feet, four FW 109s rocketed over our heads going flat out towards France, followed closely by four Typhoons. The many Bofors parked along the front chattered after them, sending up red balls one after another in a gentle curve towards the whole ensemble, enemy and friend.

They joined Barnes Wallis early the next morning at a bare beach near Reculver. Barbed wire surrounded the area, and special policemen patrolled the boundary to make sure that no strangers stumbled on the scene. Two white buoys bobbed about on the high tide about

100 yards apart, as aiming markers to represent the towers of the Moehne dam, which was one of the targets. A small dinghy on the beach had a Naval lieutenant asleep in it; it was his job to help repair the buoys if they were damaged. A slow-motion camera mounted on a tripod nearby was pointed towards the east.

Two Lancasters—one with the bomb, the other with a camera—were to fly in from that direction and drop the bomb about half a mile before the buoys so that it would bounce over the surface of the sea and go between them. The two aircraft came in low over the waves, and the bomb disappeared in a sheet of spray, re-appearing as fragments flying out of the waves—the bomb had broken. Wallis waded into the water to feel for fragments of the bomb with his feet, while men worked in a specially guarded hangar at Manston airfield in the afternoon to make the case of the second bomb stronger. The two aircraft made their second run, lower this time at 150 feet, as the sun was setting. The bomb was dropped and again re-appeared first as fragments. But the twisted body of the main bulk then came spinning out of the spray and skipped for about 100 yards before rolling under water. It was better than the first trial—but still far from good enough. Part of the casting, meanwhile, had hit the elevators on the bombing plane and jammed one of them. The pilot could only just keep his height before making a gentle turn to land at Manston.

Wallis and Gibson, together with the usual Air Ministry officials, were down at Reculver again on Thursday 22nd April to watch a new, strengthened bomb dropped. It hit the surface and rose off the water for a short while before fragments flew off again. The officials wandered back to their cars without saying a word. Wallis then said that the bomb should work if the plane made its run as low as 60 feet; Gibson said this could be done.

Wallis was down at Reculver once more on Thursday 29th April to watch another strengthened bomb dropped. Only two Air Ministry officials had turned out in the rain to watch that trial, with the Dam Busters' raid then little more than a fortnight away. 'Shorty' Longbottom, a Vickers test-pilot, flew out of the rain squalls at 250mph and only 60 feet high before dropping the bomb. It bounced once, then again and again and on and on until it slid through the marker-buoys—the bouncing bomb worked. Longbottom, banking round after the drop, could see Wallis dancing in the dunes and waving his hat in the air.

Gibson and two other pilots flew three modified Lancasters down to Manston on Saturday 8th May to have a bomb loaded in each. Their new drop-range, worked out by Wallis, was for the aircraft to come in at 60 feet, but at a slightly slower speed of 230 mph, and to drop their bombs 600 yards before the towers. Each of the three planes came in on its run, and their bombs skipped over the water and between the two larger dummy towers perfectly. One of the pilots, however, had one of his elevators torn loose by spouting water after flying a little low on his run. The bomber dipped towards the water, but the pilot managed to land safely at Manston, where a new elevator was fitted.

A bomb had hit a breakwater during one of the less successful trials at Reculver, and those watching the event from about 300 yards away had to throw themselves to the ground as the bomb whistled over their heads. It was not charged—but its weight of about five tons made it dangerous anyway. It landed in the old Roman ruins opposite the coastguard station. Some of the experimental bombs used during these trials were retrieved in May 1975 and October 1977. The final trial at Reculver took place at 7am on the day of the Dam Busters' raid.

Nineteen Lancasters took off for the Ruhr area of Germany on the night of 16th May 1943 from Scampton in Lincolnshire. Their attack breached the Moehne and Eder dams and allowed 330 million tons of water to rush into the western Ruhr valleys. The floods drowned 1,294 people, destroyed or badly damaged 125 factories, ruined nearly 3,000 hectares of arable land, killed 6,500 cattle and pigs, flooded coalmines and destroyed twenty-five bridges and badly damaged twenty-one more. Only eight of the Lancasters came back from the raid.

Gibson had spent some time at West Malling airfield; he counted his months there as among his happiest and paid repeated visits to the area until his death. He survived the Dam Busters' raid, but in the summer of 1944, when he led a bombing attack against a factory at Rheydt, near the Ruhr, he crashed into a low hill in Holland on his way home and was buried there by the Dutch.

The last and most serious fatal bombing attack ever made on Margate took place in the early afternoon of Tuesday 1st June. No air-raid warning was given, so the dozen FW 109s took the town by surprise when they carried out their bombing and machine-gun assault. They came in low over the roof-tops, and people could see clearly the black crosses on the yellow and white wings, and the bombs dropping from the planes. The raid lasted about a minute. By the time it was over, ten people had been killed, four seriously hurt and forty-six slightly

injured. One of the first casualties was one of the enemy aircraft, sho
down by anti-aircraft guns on the sea-front which peppered it
fuselage as it approached the coast; the plane roared over the tow
with smoke pouring from it, dropping its bombs and crashed nea
golf-links at the back of Margate, killing the pilot. Typhoon fighter
which swooped down on the others as they made their way hom
claimed five shot down in the sea.

Most of the damaged buildings were houses, but a cinema, church
mission hall and some shops were also hit. An infants' school was als
damaged, but the youngsters were not there because it was lunchtime
Rescue-work, helped by troops, continued without a break for mor
than twenty-four hours in a search for an elderly couple—but onl
traces of them were found. And tons of debris were moved by han
and thrown into the road in a shopping-centre before the bodies of
man and two women were found in the night. One of the bombs wer
through the upper storey of a house and came out over the front doo
before bouncing in the road and hitting some houses opposite. A ma
and his two sisters in the bombed house were unhurt, even though th
ceiling came down on them. One woman had left two parrots in th
kitchen of one of the bombed houses; she returned to find one of th
parrots saying "Oh, mother." A total of forty-one people wer
accommodated in the rest-centre in the Royal School.

Later in the month, on Sunday 27th June, a single shell fell i
Cannon Street in Dover. It hit the town at 4.26pm, three minute
before the shelling warning was sounded. The shell killed eleve
servicemen, one rating in the WRNS and a child. Ten civilians an
twenty-one service personnel were treated in hospital for injurie
some of them serious.

Towns and villages in Kent were meanwhile holding their Wing
for Victory weeks in May and June and continuing to raise way-abov
their target figures. Folkestone's target of £130,000, for example, wa
almost doubled to £248,533. Faversham and district set out to rais
£100,000 for two Sunderland flying-boats; the fund ended up a
£150,688. Eastry rural district wanted to bring in £80,000 for on
Sunderland, a Mosquito and two Typhoons—the district raised in
stead £144,044. Cranbrook rural district aimed at £100,000, th
supposed cost of twenty Typhoons, and brought in £154,352. Ton
bridge raised £95,000 in less than a week; the Medway Towns go
more than £1 million; Hythe beat its target of £50,000 with £58,33
and Ashford raised £37,481 more than its £200,000 target.

The preparations for the opening of a second front in Europe bega in Kent in August—but the invasion was a fake. A large-scale exercise known as 'Operation Starkey' was planned to take place a few days after the Allied invasion of Italy on Friday 3rd September. Its aim was to make the Germans expect an invasion in the Pas de Calais area, forcing them to keep troops in France which might otherwise be moved to Italy. It was also held to test how well troops could be moved from a concentration area, through marshalling and embarkation areas, to the selected ports and hards for a short sea-voyage; it was a test which would provide useful information for the real D-Day.

The operation began to affect people in Kent on Tuesday 17th August when a large part of the county was declared an area in which people could stay for a limited time only for certain specified purposes; this part of the operation was known as 'Harlequin'. One of two permits—for a short stay, or long stay—was needed for entry. Thousands of permits and passes were issued during the operation. Thousands of people were refused entry, and several people were prosecuted for contravening the order.

Troops were moved in a three-day exercise to marshalling areas in the south of England, and then into embarkation areas behind the ports to be used for the fake invasion—Dover, Folkestone and Deal. The 'assault force' was about to load when a last-minute change of plan replaced them on board with a force of anti-aircraft gunners and their weapons. This little armada, consisting of about a dozen blue-grey destroyers, landing-craft and light Naval vessels, sailed to within 15 miles of the French coast. Fake wireless traffic on this 'D-Day', easily monitored by the Germans across the Channel, was intended to indicate the start of an invasion. But the Germans ignored the feint—apart from firing a few shells at some destroyers which sailed even closer to the coast. The deception was so obvious, apparently, that the only reaction picked up by British radio was that of a Wehrmacht officer asking what all the fuss was about. The only other sign of enemy activity was the occasional appearance overhead of a reconnaissance plane. The bevy of ships eventually disappeared in the direction of Dungeness and went on to dock in southern England. The permit-only area of Kent was released from the restriction on Sunday 19th September.

The Italians surrendered on 8th September and declared war on Germany on 13th October, good news that was cause for optimism on the home front; three out of four people—according to official records—thought that the war in Europe would be over in less than a year.

The coastal guns opened fire in the evening of Monday 25th October at a small convoy feeling its way along the French coast. The German guns replied soon afterwards. The shell warning went in Dover at 8.25pm, and the first shell fell on the town about thirty minutes later. Most of the shells fell in the Buckland area. They started two fires and did a lot of damage in the town. Six people were killed, eight seriously injured and one slightly hurt. Fourteen people were made homeless. The last shell fell after nearly two hours at 10.45pm.

The year 1944 began badly for Deal, which suffered one of its worst days of the war on Thursday 20th January as the result of enemy shelling. The shell warning sounded at 4.48am, and the shells which caused the most damage fell at 6.10am. Eight people were killed when one shell scored a direct hit on a surface street-shelter in Robert Street, also killing two other men in the road. And another shell fell in Park Street between the Co-operative Stores and the Park Tavern, killing the landlord and his wife, who had taken refuge in a Morrison shelter. The shelling left twelve people dead, seven seriously injured and thirteen slightly hurt. Ten buildings were wrecked, twenty-three seriously damaged and sixty-five slightly damaged. These damaged buildings included the library and the gas-holder, which was pierced in four places, although gas supplies were not affected. The All Clear was sounded at about 9am.

The following day a high-explosive bomb fell on Bexley mental hospital near Dartford, wrecking two wards where patients were lying in bed and badly damaging two others. Twelve of the thirteen people killed in this raid were patients. The other victim was a male staff-nurse who had changed his night duty with another man only the day before. The bombing was preceded by a less serious incendiary attack which was dealt with by the hospital fire brigade.

Gravesend was the next town in Kent to suffer badly. A high-explosive bomb fell at the junction of Wrotham Road and Cross Lane West at 5.38am on Friday 4th February, devastating a large area round it. The larger crater caused by the bomb sucked down buildings near it; another and smaller bomb dropped about 30 yards away. At least four homes were wrecked in the raid, and thirty-eight shops and buildings within a 200-yard radius of these bombs were damaged. Rescue and demolition squads were on the scene within ten minutes, and when it was realized that some people were trapped in their shelters, neighbours helped clear the debris with their bare hands. But they were too late to save some of the people. Eight were killed in the attack, one seriously injured and three slightly hurt. The human casualties were not the only victims: incendiary bombs which fell on a farm in the area killed nine horses, thirty-six ducks and six geese; the horses had been rescued from their stables but had rushed back in again in a panic.

The worst raid ever carried out in the Rochester area made about three hundred people homeless temporarily when bombs fell on Strood at 3.30am on Tuesday 2nd March. Most of the deaths were caused when a bomb fell in a garden in the Grove Road/Station Road area and wrecked six houses in a row, burying the victims under masses of debris. Only three people in this row escaped without injury, and they were the nearest to where the bomb fell. They had taken shelter in the Anderson shelter in their garden only five minutes before the attack—apparently the only ones in the row who did. The shelter was lifted by the blast and its exit jammed by heaps of rubble, and they came out two hours later to find it on the brink of a bomb crater. The body of their lodger, who had been in the habit of staying in bed during a raid, was found in the ruins of their home many hours later. A parish priest threw a coat and trousers over his pyjamas and left home immediately after the bombing to help those in distress. The raid left eighteen people dead, eight seriously injured and thirty-eight slightly hurt. Twenty homes were wrecked, a hundred more seriously damaged and a thousand other buildings slightly damaged, including seventy-four shops. Two rest-centres were in use long before dawn, and more than 150 people made homeless reported to them before noon; by early the following morning more than a hundred people had offered accommodation to the homeless.

D-Day was little more than two months away when the security necessary for its preparation resulted in a coast-ban being implemented on 1st April. This order, mady by the Secretary of State for War 'for reasons of operational security', meant that a coastal belt 10 miles deep—from the Wash in Lincolnshire to Land's End—was out of bounds to any but those who lived there. Anyone who breached the regulations could have been fined £100 and/or sent to jail for three months.

American troops, who had begun arriving in Britain early in 1942, became a more and more common sight as the build-up for D-Day continued. These GIs, named after the words 'Government Issue' on their equipment, formed the vast majority of the 1,421,000 Allied, Dominion and Colonial troops who were in the United Kingdom by the late spring of 1944. They brought with them such rationed or unobtainable items as nylons, razor-blades and Lucky Strike cigarettes at 3d for twenty. The only contact most people had had with the USA was, of course, through what they had seen at the cinema, so the GIs had a sort of glamorous attraction for many people, which inspired anything from awe and affection to jealousy. They were, said the well-known phrase of the time "overpaid, oversexed and over here". It was to find out exactly what the British thought of them, and they of the British, that an informal meeting between six American and six British soldiers was held in the YMCA in Ashford at the beginning of May.

The Americans began by bemoaning the lack of showers in Britain, which they preferred to baths, they said. A US sergeant went on to say that the British had not made the progress they might have in this century. British girls had told him they wanted refrigerators and other things that were by then a way of life in America. He was reminded at that point that domestic production had been affected by two wars, and that the British were conservative in their habits and did not want change. Another said that US troops would find Britain more pleasant if they accepted it as it was and did not "hanker to improve" it. And a British corporal said he was quite content as long as he could earn enough for a pint of beer at the end of the day. The Americans were surprised how much Britain lagged behind their standard of automobiles, and also that the school-leaving age was still fourteen. The British soldiers then had their turn. One man said: "When you first arrived, we didn't like the blustering way you walked into the 'local', banged on the counter and demanded whisky. We had to stand aside while the landlord made a fuss of you." Another soldier said that the Americans had "cut him out with the girls"—a problem partly caused by the GIs higher pay. But a soldier from Chicago said that 'bounders' were the same the world over. Another British soldier said he had come to like the Americans within a few weeks and that those he had talked to were "grand fellows". And an American replied that they had had a "mighty fine reception" and could not have been received more kindly in Britain. The evening, it seems, ended on a note of goodwill.

A few weeks later, about thirty minutes after midnight on Monday 22nd May, a 1,000-lb bomb fell on the tented RAF camp in Coleman's Wood at Chilmington. The men in the camp were based at the nearby Ashford airfield. Eight of them were killed and sixteen seriously injured. Slight damage was also caused to Green Lane House.

But an inquest in Ashford heard of a much more serious accident involving members of the Forces, only a few days before D-Day. An instructing officer and twenty-one infantrymen were killed and several more injured when three boxes of anti-tank grenades exploded at Dymchurch. The men were on the steps of the sea-wall when a lieutenant instructor was explaining how the grenades could be ignited with a match. He lit a match and applied it—but the match burned itself out, so he lit a second. There was a 'terrific explosion' which blew him in the air and killed the men.

The account of this inquest appeared on 6th June—and would have been overshadowed immediately by news of an event in which everyone in the Allied countries had been waiting for years. By the end of the day 156,000 Allied troops had landed on the Continent. It was D-Day, and the Liberation of France had begun.

15. The Enemy is deceived

"THE HOUR OF OUR GREATEST EFFORT AND ACTION IS
APPROACHING. . . . I MUST WARN YOU THAT IN ORDER TO
DECEIVE AND BAFFLE THE ENEMY AS WELL AS TO EXERCISE
THE FORCES, THERE WILL BE MANY FALSE ALARMS, MANY
FEINTS AND MANY DRESS REHEARSALS."

Churchill, House of Commons, 26th March 1944

All day long on Monday 5th June a massive force of three thousand
landing-craft and more than five hundred warships began to gather at
a point eight miles in diameter and 25 miles south of Portsmouth and
Hayling Island. This rendezvous point was know officially as 'Area Z'
but had been nicknamed 'Piccadilly Circus' by the Navy. Shortly after
midnight on 6th June the first Allied paratroops landed in Normandy;
they were followed at 6.30am that morning by the first Allied troops
who waded ashore at Normandy from this giant armada. Both the
assault from the sea and the assault from the sky in that area had taken
the Germans by surprise. They had long expected an Allied invasion
of France but had thought it would come in the Pas de Calais area. The
deceptions carried out in Kent had helped convince the Germans that
this would be so. Operation Fortitude had been a complete success.

'Fortitude' was the name of the plan behind the plan, a giant hoax
designed to make the Germans think that any invading force would
sail from the Channel ports to the Pas de Calais area. It was, after all,
the shortest route. And it was to that end that misleading clues were
strewn all over Kent.

This deception of enemy pilots and agents had been started by the
Chief of Staff to the Supreme Allied Commander (Designate)—
known as 'COSSAC' for short—in 1943 as part of its threatened
invasion under Operation Starkey. An 'operation HQ' and the 'pump

ing-head' for a fuel-pipeline had been built at Dover, and camps, depots, roads, railway sidings and extra port facilities had been constructed in the south-east then. Good use was made of them now.

The vast but fake oil-dock and pumping-head ostentatiously set into the cliffs at Dover had been designed and built by Basil Spence, Britain's leading architect, with the help of stagehands from the film and theatre world. It was made almost entirely of old sewage-pipes, camouflaged scaffolding and boards. The dock consisted of everything that a real dock would have—pipelines, storage-tanks, anti-aircraft gun posts, guardrooms, a fire brigade, lorry-parks and jetties. The area was guarded by military police, and wind-machines blew up dust clouds to hide the fact that relatively few men were working there and to make it seem as though rapid progress was being made. The King and Montgomery both 'inspected' the dock, and Eisenhower spoke to the 'construction workers' at a dinner in the White Cliffs Hotel in Dover. The Mayor of the town even made remarks about the "opening of a new installation, the precise nature of which must remain secret until the war is over" but which would bring money into the borough as a result. The RAF flew fighter patrols overhead to 'protect' the installation, and the Royal Engineers kept it covered each night with a smokescreen. The Germans were sometimes allowed to think that they had scored a direct hit on the dock when 'hits' and resulting 'fires' were created from sodium flares. Enemy reconnaissance aircraft were allowed to fly overhead, but only if they were 33,000 feet high, where it was impossible for their cameras to spot the fakery.

All sorts of clues helped give the impression that any invasion would be launched from the Kent coast. Roads over the beach, called 'hards', were built at Greenhithe, Northfleet, Shorne marshes, Lower Upnor, Hythe, Folkestone, Dover, Deal and Walmer, and those at Gravesend, Deal and Hythe were often lit at night to make it appear that boats were being loaded in hives of activity. The corners of roads near Deal and Dover were cemented to take tanks and heavy military traffic, and additional bridges were built over the Rivers Medway and Stour. The entrances to coastal towns were heavily guarded by police, and anyone who parked in a main street might be asked to move elsewhere in case a convoy came through. Posters appeared saying "Careless talk costs lives" and "The convoy must go on." Visitors to military or naval headquarters found the maps for south-east England and the coast of northern France carefully blotted out or covered with brown paper. Kent shops were issued with special rations in sealed containers "to last over a period".

One of the deceptions involved the use of 'Bigbobs', the codename given to dummy landing-craft which were assembled in the Thames Estuary and ports in the south-east. These were made (of scaffolding canvas and wood, floating on oil-drums) at the film studios at Shepperton and then brought down by road. Smoke coiled from their funnels to make them look more realistic; they were surrounded by oil patches, and laundry hung from their rigging. They looked real from a distance, the only tell-tale sign being the flapping where the canvas touched the water. About four hundred of these craft were ranged round the coast—in creeks, harbours and river-mouths—from Lowestoft down to Dover and Folkestone. They resembled short range craft which could not possibly reach Normandy and therefore strengthened any German theory of a landing in the Pas de Calais area.

The real invasion force was meanwhile assembling in the rough triangle Gloucester-Falmouth-Brighton, getting ready to sail from the ports in southern England. The only assault force to sail from the south-east itself was the follow-up force, known as 'Force L', which consisted mainly of the 7th Armoured Division of 30th Corps, concentrated on Harwich and the Nore. The Kent coast ports were ruled out of any real embarkation largely because of the danger of shelling from the Channel guns. But the planners behind Fortitude were trying their best to make what troops there were in the county—mainly the Canadian 2nd Corps near the coast, and the British 12th Corps in North Kent—look as much like an invading force as possible. They named the American General Patton as Commander-in-Chief of the First United States Army Group, known as 'FUSAG', a group which did not actually exist, except on paper, but the Germans were allowed to glean enough to make them think that the troops in the south-east were part of this fictitious force.

Another ploy concerned Montgomery, who was the field commander of all land forces for D-Day. His headquarters were at Portsmouth, far from the Dover-Cambridge-King's Lynn triangle where FUSAG was supposed to be assembling, so, to confirm all other indications that the main troop concentrations were in this triangle signals engineers laid lines from his Portsmouth HQ to Dover Castle. His wireless traffic was then released from there and intercepted by the Germans. The ruse worked. It helped convince Field Marshal Rommel, who was responsible for strengthening the 'Atlantic Wall' of the French coast against invasion, that an attack on the Pas de Calais area was more likely than an assault on Normandy.

And still the deceptions continued. Since the summer of 1943 numerous advance-landing grounds, as these smaller airfields were called, had sprung up in Kent, including sites at Ashford, Kingsnorth, Brenzett, Egerton, High Halden, Newchurch, New Romney, Woodchurch and Headcorn. Some of these airfields were built with rubble from the bombed streets of Birmingham, carried south by freight trains. By the spring of 1944 there were enough airfields in the county for about fifty squadrons—although fewer than that number were deployed on them, so the squadrons allocated as fighter escort for the US medium-range bombers were spread round Kent; their numbers were increased physically by dummy aircraft, such as gliders, and in theory by deceptive wireless messages which the Germans would probably intercept. The plan was designed to make the Germans think that there really were fifty squadrons in Kent. The number of squadrons on the south coast was meanwhile being 'reduced' for reconnaissance aircraft by concealment and camouflage.

The security at those airfields had been tightened up after an exercise carried out by pilots from Biggin Hill in the winter. The escape drill the pilots were practising for D-Day was taken seriously, because they knew they might be forced down behind enemy lines once an invasion had started. They were dressed in civvies and driven in a covered van to 'somewhere in Kent', then dropped and told to report back to Biggin Hill without being stopped by the Home Guard or police, who were on the alert for the 'escapees'. They could get back to camp any way they wanted. Two pilots returned in a bus stolen from an army camp near Headcorn; three others simply flew back in Spitfires they found unguarded on Ashford airfield, while a Canadian took a Tiger Moth from the same place. Security was tightened up immediately.

Fake military traffic in Kent was intermingled during this period with the real thing. There were real troop camps, for example, in the areas of Wrotham, Frindsbury, Shorne, Milton Barracks, Mersham, Sandgate, Hawkinge, Betteshanger, Waldershare, River, Denton, Kingston, Broome Park, Patrixbourne, Sandling Park, Bridge, Newington, Goodnestone and Chillenden. Marshalling-areas were at St Martin's Plain, near Folkestone, Old Park at River and Downs Wood at Wrotham; and there were embarkation HQs at Wrotham and Frindsbury. Troops were often on the move to and from various camps at this time.

The county records say that "convoys were ceaseless" during this period, and abnormal loads, usually landing-craft, were requiring police attention all the time. Traffic through the main streets of

Canterbury jammed sometimes while a police officer shepherded an invasion-barge round the Westgate Towers; the main street at Strood was cleared of traffic for thirty minutes many times so that huge aircraft-wings could be taken through the town; and traffic in Ashford had to take to the side roads and lanes to give a clear route to the wingless fuselage of a bomber.

Everyone who took part in Operation Overlord, as the D-Day preparations and landings were known, agreed that every detail of the slightest importance had been taken care of—the real landing-craft were even provided with sacramental wine, while the rifle-carrying infantry were given condoms to put over the muzzles of their guns—to keep out seawater yet allow them to fire without obstruction. And there were few oversights in connection with Operation Fortitude. From April, the fields of Kent and East Anglia were often crowded with tanks, guns and half-tracks—to simulate an armoured division. But these weapons were phoney arms which were really nothing more than inflated rubber. Dozens of men kept up a shuttle-service from one part of the south-east to another, unloading their piles of folded rubber, pumping them up and leaving them camouflaged—although not too well—for enemy reconnaissance planes to spot. The equipment was packed up and moved somewhere else once one of the planes had passed overhead. Full-scale embarkation sign-posting was set up in the Dover-Folkestone area in a way which would have suggested to any enemy agents that the invasion was still six weeks off at the day it actually began. Thousands of carefully shielded truck-lights indicated large convoys. Numbers, lit at night by shielded lanterns, would appear in the streets of Dover from time to time, and scores of canvas toilets would be erected round the town. The convoy, remember, had to get through.

Another of the deceptions was the mooring of Mulberry harbour units off Dungeness. The invasion forces required a port the size of Dover which had to float up and down with the tide at Normandy, so these harbours, one of the great innovations of D-Day, consisted of a breakwater made by sunken blockships, and an outer wall made up of massive boxes of concrete, known as 'Phoenixes'. The biggest type of Phoenix weighed more than 6,000 tons and was 200 feet long and 60 feet high. Huge excavations were cut into the banks along the Thames and Medway to allow these massive units to be built in secrecy which was so effective, it is said, that even many of the twenty thousand men making them did not know what they were for. Other parts of the prefabricated Mulberries included floating roadways made of steel sections and a pier fixed to the seaward end of the roadways. Much of the equipment for the harbours was made all over the country and then assembled at depots at Southampton and Richborough in Kent, which was often covered with a smokescreen.

The Thames itself was particularly busy in this period before D-Day, and not only with the dummy craft and the follow-up troops for Operation Overlord. Thames barges converted to floating mobile kitchens were among the ships which passed down river to the assembly-point, protected by warships. Large troop-transports and other vessels carrying supplies could be seen there, their decks laden with lorries and guns, and there were also coasters loaded with ammunition, tankers, drinking-water tankers and hospital ships. Thousands of tired and shabby-looking German prisoners would be landed at Gravesend and Tilbury in the months after the invasion had begun and sent on to internment camps.

The deceptions of Fortitude continued until the last moment. At about midnight on 5th June—when the real invasion force was already under way, one of several feint attacks that night was made against beaches near Boulogne by six harbour-defence motor-launches of the Dover Command and a squadron of Bomber Command. The launches carried out radio counter-measures, towed balloons with reflectors and used special equipment and smoke; while the aircraft dropped radar-deceiving foil. These tricks were intended to emulate the echoes that would be received by radar from large ships and give the impression of an approaching convoy.

Operation Fortitude had played its part. Valuable German divisions had been kept in the Pas de Calais area for an invasion that never took place. And down in Normandy, meanwhile, the landings were relatively trouble-free.

Listeners to the BBC first heard of the invasion from the 8am news, which simply quoted German reports. Official confirmation did not come until 9.32am. "D-Day has come," announced John Snagge on the radio. The Allies were back in France.

16. The buzzbombs

About forty minutes after midnight on Tuesday 13th June 1944 reports from Folkestone told that the town was being shelled heavily. A shelling-attack also began on Maidstone an hour later. A woman in Hayle Road was killed in this bombardment, and considerable damage to property was caused in the south of the town. The shelling of those two towns at this time, particularly Maidstone, was odd, but it was later thought to be a cover-attack to draw attention from what happened next. Two members of the Royal Observer Corps were on duty in their lonely observation post near Dymchurch shortly after 4am when they heard the sound of an approaching aircraft. They had not heard anything like it before; and when it was about five miles away they identified it for what it really was. One of the men grabbed the telephone as the object came nearer and shouted the codeword "Diver, diver, diver" down the line to his HQ. The first of the flying bombs was about to fall on Britain.

This attack had long been expected. As far back as November 1939 the British Naval Attaché in Oslo had received a report which indicated that the Germans were developing 'pilotless rocket aircraft'. RAF raids on launching-sites since 1943 had postponed the start of the attack, but now the first flying bombs were on their way. The Observer Corps had been briefed about these pilotless aircraft—as they were first known, and the two men near Dymchurch were flashing the codeword through to their HQ within forty seconds of identifying it. A few minutes later, at 4.18am, the first of four flying bombs to cross the coast that night crashed at Swanscombe; the second fell two minutes later at Cuckfield in Sussex, killing several animals; the third came down at 5.07am at Crouch, near Sevenoaks; and the fourth wrecked the railway bridge at Bethnal Green in London, killing six people and injuring nine others.

The official name for the flying bomb—also known as a 'buzzbomb' or 'doodlebug'—was 'the V1'; the V stood for *Vergeltung*, meaning Revenge. It soon became obvious that they were aimed at London, even though they often fell short or overshot, many even coming down in the Channel. Their launching-sites in France meant that most of them passed over Kent. The county was in the front line once more.

The first four flying bombs had been little more than ranging shots. But the onslaught against Britain began in earnest shortly before midnight on Thursday 15th June, and the assault proper did not end until the beginning of September, by which time the launching-sites had been overrun by the Allies advancing across the Continent. By the end of the war, 1,422 V1s had been shot down in Kent and a thousand or so in the Channel from the coast; about 150 people in the county were killed by them and another 1,716 injured.

A staff conference under Churchill decided to bring a previously prepared defence plan into action on 15th June. It was thought it would take about three weeks to set the defences up, but all the weapons and barrage-balloons were deployed at the end of five days. The first line of defence consisted of daylight patrols of fighter air-craft, which flew at 12,000 feet in three broad lanes; one above the Channel between Dover and Beachy Head; another above the coast between Dover and Newhaven; and a third inland between Haywards Heath and Ashford. Other fighters were sent up to patrol the same three lines at 6,000 feet when an attack developed. Radar-controlled fighters took over at night, receiving help from the searchlight units sited every 1½ miles along the coast between South Foreland and Seaford in Sussex. Any flying bomb which got past these aircraft then had to face the 192 heavy anti-aircraft guns and 192 light anti-aircraft guns which were spaced out along the southern slope of the North Downs. The last line of defence consisted of 480 balloons anchored on the higher ground behind the guns, most of them massed along the 20-mile ridge between Cobham and Limpsfield.

Twenty-four flying bombs were shot down over Kent in the first twenty-four hours after the main attack began. The first main fatal V1 incident in the county happened on Saturday 17th June when a 'pilot-less plane' fell on a house at Benenden early in the morning and killed a couple and their married daughter. The flying bomb, which had been shot down, narrowly missed the sanatorium there, where ceilings and walls were brought down by the blast and twenty-seven beds put out of use.

It was agreed on 19th June that more guns and balloons were

needed for the defensive 'diver belt'. The balloon-barrage was organized by two Group Captains—one based at Biggin Hill and the other originally at Gravesend airfield—who were told to cover a belt of country about 20 miles long and four miles deep. Men came with their balloons and equipment from all parts of Britain—Liverpool, Manchester, Crewe, South Wales and even as far north as Scapa Flow. Most of them were given only twelve hours' notice to pack, leave their site and board a train. Their winches and equipment travelled by road, arriving in Kent in massive convoys; they could sometimes be seen stretching along the A2 for as far as the eye could see. The men and vehicles parked along the verges of the road outside the old Laughing Water near Shorne to refuel and collect their rations. The men had a hot meal and a wash there before going on to unload their balloons and inflate them. Hundreds of lorries were loaded up at Gravesend airfield with cylinders of gas—thirty of which were needed to fill one balloon. Balloon-sites on the Downs included those at Sole Street, Longfield, Cobham, Idleigh Court, Meopham Green and Fawkham Green. Local families were often willing to help the men in some way, some providing tea and coffee, some filling sandbags, and others putting rooms and sheds at their disposal. The crew at Meopham Green, for example, was supplied with cakes and pies; a woman in Snodland did all the washing for two balloon-sites (where there were usually five men to a site), while another did the cooking for two sites on several days a week.

The blackest day during the main onslaught of the flying bombs in Kent came on Saturday 24th June. A V1 shot down by a fighter aircraft hit the Newlands military camp at Charing at 6.18am. A total of forty-seven men were killed and twenty-eight seriously hurt. Four minutes later, at 6.22am, a flying bomb shot down by another fighter fell at Smarden, wrecking a bungalow at Bartley Poultry Farm and killing four people instantly. Two members of the same family were brought out of the wreckage alive but so badly injured that they died in hospital the same day. The bomb made a large crater just in front of the bungalow, and its blast stripped many of the fruit-trees opposite.

The sound of a flying bomb—which had a tail of flame—has often been compared with that of a motorcycle. The engines of the bombs cut out over their targets and were silent for about eleven seconds—a warning to those underneath—until a devastating explosion showed that they had reached the ground. They travelled at six miles a minute and could reach their target twenty-two minutes after being launched. This speed helped make them a difficult target for the defences.

But on 23rd June a fighter pilot who had run out of ammunition found an unofficial but effective way of dealing with the bombs: he flew alongside a V1 and raised his wing underneath it until a layer of air lifted the missile's wing and caused it to fly off-course and into the ground. This method prevented the bombs from reaching London, but it also caused even more suffering in Kent and Sussex, where the missiles would then come down. The Crossbow committee, which dealt with the defence against the V1, met on 24th July and decided that this tactic must be stopped.

By 29th June the defences included 680 balloons, 376 heavy anti-aircraft guns and 522 light anti-aircraft guns along the North Downs. A further 176 40-mm guns and 424 20-mm guns were expected to be in place along the coast between Hythe and Beachy Head by 1st July.

One of the most tragic flying bomb incidents occurred on Friday 30th June. Weald House at Westerham, surrounded by woods and fields, was to have been the alternative Civil Defence control-centre for the county in the event of an invasion, but it had been released from this designation by December 1943 and by the end of June had been requisitioned by the Ministry of Health as a short-stay nursery for children. The thirty youngsters staying there at the time came from a London County Council school which had been destroyed by incendiary bombs. They were all aged under five and were looked after by a female staff of eleven. At 3.37am a flying bomb—believed shot down by anti-aircraft guns—fell on Weald House. Twenty-two of the thirty children were killed, and eight of the eleven female staff also died. Many of those in the building were trapped by debris, and only a few adults had been rescued from the ruins by the afternoon. Not all the bodies were recovered until several days later on 2nd July. The final casualty toll was thirty dead, nine seriously injured and one slightly hurt.

It was the turn of the military to suffer again on Monday 3rd July. A flying bomb shot down by anti-aircraft fire fell on the Army camp in Pattenden Lane, Marden, at about 3am. Eleven people were killed, eight seriously injured and eight slightly hurt. At least six ambulances were sent to the scene, and the injured were taken to Barming Hospital. A few days after that, on 9th July, a flying bomb fell at Lynsted and damaged the parish church which had already suffered badly from bombing on 15th August 1940. Another buzzbomb came down at East Hill in Dartford at 8.49pm on that Sunday, 9th July. Eighteen homes were wrecked and fifty more made unfit to live in, while many others were slightly damaged. The A226 was blocked for a time because of damage to water mains. Seven people were killed in the incident and six others slightly hurt. By that day the number of balloons in the Diver belt had risen to 999; it went up to 1,028 by 12th July.

The greatest number of flying-bomb routes from France crossed the coast at Dungeness, so the greatest emphasis on air defence was placed near there, with the Tempest Wing flying from Newchurch on Romney Marsh and, by early July, the Mustangs of 129 Squadron and 315 (Polish) Squadron operating from Brenzett. Spitfires operated further inland from West Malling. Number 23 Squadron, stationed at Newchurch from June to September 1944 and equipped with Tempest Vs, was credited with 337¼ flying-bomb kills—far more than any other squadron.

One of the problems with the defences was the unclear demarcation between the anti-aircraft gun zones and the fighter aircraft zones; this meant, for example, that an aircraft sometimes had to stop chasing a flying bomb when it flew within range of the guns on the ground—while the guns on the ground had to hold their fire if a plane did continue to pursue a missile overhead. The relationship between the guns and the fighters grew worse. So by the middle of July it was decided to move all the guns to the coast—leaving the aircraft to patrol freely out to sea, or behind the guns and up to the balloon-belt.

All the heavy guns were in place by the early morning of 17th July, and the light guns followed after covering the movement. A total of 412 heavy guns and 572 light guns of the Royal Artillery and US Army Anti-Aircraft Artillery formations were ready to fire two days later. These coastal guns also included 168 light guns and 416 20-mm guns manned by the RAF Regiment, two hundred rocket-launchers and twenty-eight light guns of the RAC. It took only four days to move them all. Eight thousand lorries helped move 30,000 tons of stores and one million heavy anti-aircraft shells to a gun-belt which stretched from St Margaret's Bay to Cuckmere Haven. A total of 23,000 service personnel were involved, and 3,000 miles of telephone cables were laid between the gun batteries.

Warning of the flying bombs came from the radar stations at West Hythe, Swingate, Fairlight and Beachy Head, where they were plotted as soon as they left the French coast, all the way across the Channel. Radar-controlled guns fired at the V1s before they reached the English coast, and any that escaped the barrage then had to face the fighters, which were vectored onto the missiles by the radar stations. Since the radar station controlling the fighter which shot down a bomb could claim it as a 'kill', a sort of contest developed between these coastal stations: Hythe got 250 'kills', which was a hundred less than its counterpart at Beachy Head.

All the flying bombs so far sent over had been launched from the ground. But on 9th July London had been attacked by V1s fired from Heinkels based in Holland which used to cross the Belgian coast at between 300 and 600 feet and fly over as low as they could to avoid detection by the radar stations at Foreness, North Foreland and St Margaret's Bay. They would then fly up to at least 1,700 feet before releasing their load. Artillery brought in to counter this new menace included 208 heavy guns and 578 light guns arranged round the Thames Estuary and between Blackwater and Whitstable.

The second most devastating attack on Swanscombe came shortly before midnight on Sunday 30th July. When a flying bomb fell on homes in Taunton Road at 11.47am, thirteen people were killed, twenty-two seriously injured and sixty-nine slightly hurt. Two Royal Marine sergeants, home on leave after taking part in the Normandy landings, escaped with slight injuries after being blown from an upstairs window into the street below. One of the men, who lived in the house, regained consciousness to find himself lying in the street surrounded by rubble. His wife and two children, who had been in the shelter, were unhurt, the three-year-old having slept through the incident. At least fifty people had been dealt with at the first-aid post at the Northfleet paper-mills by 1.23am, and another twenty treated at the Civil Defence first-aid post in Northfleet. The seriously injured were taken to Gravesend Hospital. About eight homes were wrecked in the incident, twenty-six seriously damaged and twenty-eight slightly damaged. Rest-centres were opened at the Lawn Road School in Northfleet and the Southfleet Road Central School at Swanscombe. About thirty-nine people had already made their way to the rest-centres by 1.20am, and 132 people had made use of the Southfleet Road centre by the following afternoon.

Maidstone suffered its worst blow from the V1s on Thursday 3rd August. A flying bomb fell on the golf-course in the early hours of the morning, seriously injuring three women, slightly hurting eleven other people and damaging 450 homes. More houses in the area were damaged by a second bomb which fell at Allington an hour later. But the worst incident occurred shortly before noon, when a third flying bomb exploded in the goods yard at Maidstone West railway station. Five men were killed, five men and two women were seriously injured, and twenty men, seventeen women and three children were slightly hurt. Gas supplies and telephone lines were wrecked and 1,180 homes damaged. The last flying bomb to fall on the town came down in Hermitage Lane in the early hours of the following day.

A few days later another flying bomb did serious damage at Snodland. A V1 shot down by a fighter crashed in Malling Road at 6.58pm on Saturday 5th August, wrecking three houses and badly damaging others. Twelve people were killed, fifteen seriously injured and sixteen slightly hurt. One of the homes ruined was that of a Czech refugee doctor, who was holding his surgery inside at the time. A nine-year-old girl patient there was among the dead, and the doctor was badly cut in the face by glass splinters and bleeding heavily, but he did what he could for some of those who had been hurt before himself going to hospital for treatment. A police sergeant, his wife and two girls who were staying with the doctor were also killed in the blast, together with some of the neighbours. A couple in one of the badly damaged homes were celebrating their fifth wedding anniversary with four friends when the flying bomb fell. All six escaped with slight injuries—but the woman's father died later of injuries received in another part of the house.

The following day, at 5.10pm, another flying bomb came down in Carrington Road off East Hill at Dartford. Ten people were killed, twelve seriously injured and ninety-five slightly hurt. About eight homes were wrecked, ten seriously damaged and seven hundred others slightly damaged. Soldiers helped with the rescue-work.

It was Hythe's turn to suffer on Tuesday 15th August when a doodlebug shot down by anti-aircraft fire fell in the Earlsfield Road area of the town at 2.10pm. Five people in this area near the Royal Military Canal were killed, five seriously injured and twelve slightly hurt. Five homes were wrecked, and twenty-six people made use of the rest-centre. Another flying bomb shot down by a fighter that day destroyed the church at Little Chart. Just how heavy the onslaught was at that time is shown by the fact that the Folkestone anti-aircraft guns alone on 15th August claimed to have shot fifteen flying bombs into the sea between 8.56am and 6.45pm.

The last flying bomb to cause serious damage in Kent during this main onslaught derailed the London-to-Margate express on Wednesday 16th August. The bomb blew up the Oak Lane bridge at Newington only 20 yards in front of the speeding coast-bound train. The express ploughed into the wreckage of the bridge at 4.45pm. The engine overturned and dragged the first two coaches with it, although the driver and fireman escaped with minor injuries. More than six hundred people were on the train, many of them service people. Eight people were killed, thirty-three seriously injured and twenty-eight slightly hurt. Five Sittingbourne ambulances were first on the scene, and the casualties were taken to Medway and Maidstone hospitals. Among those killed were two Faversham servicemen returning home. One was an Able Seaman and the other a private in the Queen's Royal Regiment. They were buried at Faversham cemetery with naval and military honours respectively. Most of those hurt were civilians, but the total service casualties were four dead, nine seriously injured and two slightly hurt.

A few days later, on the night of Sunday 20th August, the *Richard Montgomery* sailed into the Thames Estuary with a load of bombs for the US air force. She anchored two miles off Sheerness to wait for a convoy while *en route* for Cherbourg. The American ship swung onto a sandbank that night, sank and split in two. Her masts can still be seen sticking out of the water, and 3,173 assorted bombs, about half her original cargo, are still inside her holds.

The experiences of the people who had to work under the flying bombs were related to Americans during the summer. Interviewer Larry Leseuer spoke to four Kent men for a programme broadcast by the Columbia Broadcasting System. One of those to speak was Mr Boulden, a shepherd. He said:

> The harvest has been a bit disturbed by these doodles. Not much, but of course the men and girls have to wear tin hats. As you know, they're not very comfortable when you're sweating. Still, it's better than catching a razor-edged chunk of metal on your head. The only casualties we've had on my farm have been the bull and one lamb; all our windows are gone, of course. You expect that, and a bit of the barn came down, too. When our windows got blasted, my wife was cut about the face, and they wanted her to lie down and rest. But she wouldn't. "I've got the men's vegetables on," she said.

This main onslaught of the flying bombs came to an end on 1st September when much of the Pas de Calais area was occupied by the Allied armies. A total of 9,017 of the V1s had been launched during that period. The defences saw 6,725 of these: of this number, 1,771 were shot down by fighters; 1,459 were shot down by guns, and 231 hit balloons. A total of 2,340 of those which got through the defences actually penetrated the Greater London area. The defences by this time included sixteen hundred balloons, eight hundred heavy guns, eighteen hundred light guns and seven hundred rocket-launchers, with 144 heavy guns in reserve. The heaviest anti-aircraft guns ever used were the six 8-inch guns of the Capel and Hougham batteries near Dover. One of the barrels alone weighed 17 tons. The coast-defence guns were sited originally to attack enemy ships in the Channel, but they could be elevated to seventy degrees to fire at any plane or flying bomb which appeared in the right area of the sky. The salvo of 256-lb shells fired up by these six giants created a massive splinter-screen in front of the V1. So many guns were trained on the Kent skies at that time, however, that it is not certain whether or not the batteries ever scored a hit.

Between 13th June and 1st September 1,378 flying bombs fell in that part of Kent outside the London area. About 592 of these had come down in July, while another 544 fell in the county in August. But only four were brought down in Kent in September. The main assault of the doodlebugs had come to an end.

Holy Trinity Church, Margate, was reduced to a shell when the town was bombed on 1st June 1943. Ten people were killed in the raid, four seriously hurt and forty-six slightly injured.

Mrs Churchill with the Mayor of Canterbury, Alderman Charles Lefevre, during a tour of the city with Mrs Roosevelt, wife of the American president, on 30th October 1942. The city was bombed the next day, and thirty-three people were killed.

This view of Canterbury, taken from the cathedral, shows the smoking ruins of the city after the devastating raid of 1st June 1942 which killed forty-three people, seriously injured forty and slightly hurt forty-one. The long building in the centre of the picture is the Longmarket.

These ruins were all that was left of The Parade and St. George's Street in Canterbury after the Baedeker raid of 1st June 1942. The tower of St. George's Church, surrounded by scaffolding, is still standing today.

This aerial view of Dover, taken shortly after the war, gives some idea of the battering the town took from the hundreds of bombs and shells which fell on it, killing 199 people.

Gunners of the 491st Battery of the 21st American Anti-Aircraft Group take a break at Headcorn in July 1944.

Women at work on the rear turrets of Stirling bombers made in the Short factory at Rochester.

This nursery at Weald House, Westerham, was filled with sleeping children when a flying bomb fell on it on 30th June 1944. Twenty-two children and eight women were killed, nine seriously injured and one slightly hurt.

Evacuees at Maidstone West railway station in 1944 wait to be taken away from the town during the main onslaught of the flying bombs.

A London-Margate express train was derailed on 16th August 1944 when a flying bomb destroyed this bridge at Newington only yards in front of it. Eight people were killed, thirty-three seriously injured and twenty-eight slightly hurt.

A barrage-balloon moored on Meopham Green. Hundreds of such balloons were anchored on the North Downs during the flying bomb attacks.

About 30 miles of pipes were wound on massive drums like this and towed across the Channel by tugs as part of the PLUTO construction. This drum broke away from its tugs and was washed ashore at Greatstone.

These innocent-looking bungalows at Dungeness really housed some of the pumping equipment for PLUTO – the fuel pipeline that ran across the Channel.

One of the three Army-manned Maunsell forts which guarded the Thames Estuary off Sheppey. Four other Navy-manned forts of a different design also formed part of the estuary defences.

The sea-defences at Deal, February 1945, with the obstacles which invading German troops would have had to overcome.

17. The shelling ends

The main battle of the flying bombs was over—but it was as though the enemy cross-Channel guns were trying to make up for the loss of these missiles. The guns began shelling the Kent coast with a new intensity early in the morning of Friday 1st September. This long-range bombardment from the German batteries at Cap Gris Nez and Calais was almost daily for the next two weeks; on one occasion the shelling lasted for twelve hours. The most serious of the attacks was also the first in this stepped-up assault on the coast.

The shelling warning in Dover went at 1.55am on 1st September, by which time the first of the shells had fallen on the town in broad moonlight. Four enemy guns carried out the attack, sending over more than a hundred shells—thirty-nine of which fell on Dover or in the harbour—in salvoes which were unbroken for more than two hours. Four people were killed when one of the first shells hit the entrance to the shelter at the Lagoon Cave in the High Street; two others died when shells fell between Anderson shelters in the Tower Hamlets area of the town. A direct hit was scored on the back of Woolworths; two small printing-works and two small building firms were seriously damaged, and fifty other small businesses and many homes were also damaged. Gas mains and a water main were fractured, and several overhead telephone wires were brought down. Several of the shells burst in the air over the town. Eight people were killed in the shelling altogether, eight seriously injured and nine slightly hurt.

Flying bombs might have almost vanished from the skies, but a new threat appeared on 8th September. The first of the V2 rockets landed in England at 6.40pm that day, killing three people at Chiswick. Another twenty-five were launched in the next ten days, and the first to come down in Kent (although in the London part of the county) fell in the Orpington area on 11th September. Between that date and 27th March 1945—when the last rocket to hit Britain also fell at Orpington

—sixty-seven of these missiles exploded in that part of the county outside London; they killed sixty-one people there, seriously injured 146 and slightly hurt another 440; most of the casualties were women and children.

All the V2s sent over between 8th and 18th September were launched from the Netherlands. Bombers of the RAF and USAAF were immediately ordered to attack the launch-sites, but these were so small and mobile that the only effective way to bomb a site was to catch a rocket being prepared for launching. It was almost the only thing the defences could do, because the rocket flew so fast that no radar or gun could track it and fire at it in time. The missiles were deadly. Each of them was 45 feet long and carried a one-ton warhead. They made no noise to warn of their approach—unlike the flying bombs—because their supersonic speed meant that the explosion as it hit the ground came first, a sort of thunderclap and white light, then followed by the sound of it coming through the air, a sound something like a distant express train. Really, there simply was not any defence against the V2. The attack of the rockets ended only when the German missile regiment was forced to withdraw by the advancing Allied forces.

Two people had also been killed at Ramsgate by shelling on 1st September, but Dover suffered most in the two-week battering from the guns. Several people in the town were killed by shells on 3rd, 5th and 11th September before the next main incident on Tuesday 12th September. The first two shells hit the town within 50 yards of each other at 5.45pm—one minute before the shell-warning went, one falling outside Christ Church in Folkestone Road and the other inside a garden in the road. Three people outside the church were killed, and a church verger who lived in the road died of his injuries later in hospital. Another of the shells killed three people when it fell among six Anderson shelters in Dickson Road. Two which were only two feet from the shell crater were wrecked; a shelter 10 feet away was not damaged at all—but one further away on higher ground was lifted out of the ground. Seven shells fell altogether on the town that night, and the All Clear did not sound until 1am the following morning. The attack left nine people dead—including a soldier and an RAF man, seven seriously injured and nine slightly hurt.

The shelling in Dover began again the following day, 13th September, when five shells burst within the first half hour after 4pm. One of the first shells fell outside the Priory Station, where the 1.15pm train from Charing Cross had just arrived. A clerk in the parcels office there was just taking parcels in when the shell fell outside the office; there was a terrific crash, and she became stone deaf and felt numbed all over. She was one of the lucky ones: five passengers were killed in the booking hall and twenty other people injured. Most people in the town stayed under cover as the rest of the twenty-three shells fell on the town during the attack. Most of them came down in the Charlton Green area, and Charlton Boys' School was wrecked. Rest-centres were opened at St Ursula's Convent and St Martin's parish hall by 4.30pm to cope with the shocked and some of the thirty people made homeless in the shelling. About two-thirds of the town was without water for a time because of fractured mains. The All Clear did not sound until 3am the following morning, by which time the casualties consisted of seven dead, seventeen seriously injured and twelve slightly hurt.

Allied troops had reached the coast at Wissant and Sandgatte on the western outskirts of Calais by the beginning of the week and were moving in on Cap Gris Nez, where the Germans had some of their most powerful cross-Channel guns. RAF Mitchells and Bostons bombed strongpoints at Boulogne on Wednesday and Thursday, 13th and 14th September, although the shelling became even worse later in the week. The shell-warning in Folkestone on Wednesday lasted eleven hours—the longest period in more than four years of suffering that form of attack. But the guns opened up again at noon on Thursday and this time shelled a wide area of Folkestone for twelve hours. Most of the salvoes were fired by two or three guns, but it is thought that six guns fired at once soon after nightfall. Bus companies ran restricted services to shopping-centres throughout that time; cinema audiences were asked to leave, and many shopkeepers found that they were serving few customers. (At one coast town, however, some holiday-makers could still be seen having picnics on the beach.)

The second phase of the flying bomb attack began on 16th September when the German air-launching squadron, by then reinforced to ninety aircraft, sent over nine missiles on the first day. Only two got through to London—but this was not thanks to the traditional Diver defences, which were too far south to be of any use. A new Diver Strip was therefore created from the Thames Estuary to Great Yarmouth, provided with guns moved from Kent and Sussex. Their move was ordered on 21st September, but because of the work involved in transferring the gun-sites—the equivalent of building two towns the size of Windsor, the deployment was not completed until 13th October. This phase continued until mid-January 1945. The defences saw 638 of the estimated twelve hundred flying bombs launched; the guns got 331½ while the fighters shot down 71½. Only sixty-six reached London, the rest coming down in the Home Counties and Norfolk. A further attempt to outflank the defences was made on Christmas Eve 1944 when about fifty V1s were launched by aircraft off the coast near Bridlington in Yorkshire. This resulted in more guns being moved from Kent to form a Diver fringe from Skegness to Whitby.

The war was going well enough in the latter part of 1944 for the government to replace the black-out in many parts of the country with the 'dim-out' on 17th September. This allowed the use of all peace-time curtains and blinds, except the flimsiest kind; frosted glass and stained-glass windows required no curtains or blinds provided that nothing inside was distinguishable from the outside. Skylights had to continue to be fully blacked-out. All these 'half-lighted' windows had to be fully blacked-out or the lights turned off if the air-raid warning sounded. The dim-out applied to most of the country, but a full black-out was still in force in the following areas: Canterbury, Deal, Dover, Faversham, Folkestone, Hythe, Lydd, Margate, New Romney, Queenborough, Ramsgate, Sandwich, Broadstairs and St Peters, Herne Bay, Sheerness, Sittingbourne, Milton, Whitstable, Bridge-Blean, East Ashford, Eastry, Elham, Romney Marsh, Sheppey, Strood and Swale.

Dover was hit again on Saturday 23rd September, when a shell fell on the Salvation Army Red Shield canteen and hostel in Snargate Street at 12.30pm. It exploded low down and buried those inside, killing five civilian helpers and two service personnel. Rescue-workers searched through the debris of the ruins for thirty-six hours. They did not give up until more than 100 tons of rubble had been turned over and much of it taken away in a procession of carts. One of the dead was Captain William Aspinall; there was a large attendance at his funeral the following Friday. Five other shells fell before the All Clear sounded at 4pm; many shops and houses were damaged but no one else died in the attack. The shelling killed seven people, seriously injured ten and slightly hurt eight others.

There were two bouts of shelling in Dover two days later, on 25th September, one shortly before noon and the other soon after 4pm. The attack caught women out doing their shopping, because in each case the shelling began before the siren sounded—a common occurrence because there was no way before hand of knowing when the attacks would begin. Three women and a child were killed when a shell fell in London Road, near Cherry Tree Avenue, and a teenager died later in hospital. Another shell which fell near the Red Cow in Folkestone Road made a massive crater. The road and mains were damaged so badly that repairs were not completed until December. A woman who was killed there was believed to have been sheltering in a doorway on her way home. The water mains were seriously damaged, and at least half the town was without a water-supply for a while. At least twelve people were made homeless, and a rest-centre was quickly opened in the Royal Hippodrome. The shelling left six people dead, eight seriously injured and nine slightly hurt. About fifty shells fell on Dover the following day—the highest number ever to fall on any town, killing four civilians and two service personnel, seriously injuring three civilians and five service personnel and slightly hurting twenty other people.

But a message containing good news was sent to the Mayor of Dover a few days later from the Brigadier of the Canadian Infantry Brigade fighting in France, and at sometime after 9am on Saturday 30th September this news was spreading throughout the Kent coast towns: the Channel guns had been silenced—the battered town of Dover had been shelled for the last time. Since the first shells had fallen on the town on 12th August 1940, more than four years of suffering the bombardment of 2,226 of these missiles had left the borough with 107 dead, two hundred seriously injured and 221 slightly injured. About two-thirds of all homes in the town, it is estimated, were damaged in some way during the shelling. A total of 158 were wrecked or had to be demolished; 1,560 were seriously damaged, 6,750 slightly damaged. Eighteen water mains were broken at various times—although Dover was never without a water-supply for more than two hours, and at one time twelve roads were closed to traffic because of craters or debris. Rescue-squads helped out at fifty-one incidents where people were trapped, bringing out twenty-three people alive and recovering thirty bodies. More than four hundred workmen had already been drafted into the town by the end of September to do repair-work on the damaged buildings.

The good news was given to people in Dover over loudspeakers which had been used previously to warn people to take cover. The *Kentish Express* said:

> The inhabitants heard the message calmly, there being very few cele-
> brations as some accounts and photographs have suggested. The people
> had too long been under strain, and they were satisfied to say just
> "Thank God it's over." Later, flags began to appear from buildings, but

many probably saved for the occasion were hidden under debris. There were thanksgiving services in some churches that night, and on Sunday references were made to the town's liberation in church sermons, but the official thanksgiving which will be held on the sea front is not to take place until Dunkirk has fallen.

The bombs and the shelling had turned Dover into a shattered and almost desolate town, but it was still home for many people—and husbands rushed to the post offices on hearing the news to let their wives and families know that it was safe to come back again. A hundred youngsters from families which had suffered most in the shelling were sent off, with some teachers, for a week's holiday at Brighton as guests of the Mayor. And the bells of St Mary's pealed out a special salute of five slow notes and two quick ones, representing the initials of the word 'Dover'.

Vans toured the streets of Folkestone shortly before 1pm on the Saturday and broadcast the following message over and over again: "A special announcement for the citizens of Folkestone. His Worship the Mayor has received official information from SHAEF that all the long-range guns on the other side of the Channel have now been captured." The news was also received quietly there, but there were cheers in some parts of the town when the announcement was made, and before long the Union Jack was run up over the Town Hall for the first time since war began. Other flags and bunting began to appear from houses, and knots of people started to assemble in the main roads to talk about the good news. Representatives of all the churches were present in the evening when a special united thanksgiving service was held in the parish church, which had itself been damaged in the shelling.

At a celebration dance held later in the evening at the Leas Cliff Hall, the manager read the following message, which he said was being sent to General Crerar, the Commander of the Canadian Forces who had captured the guns: "We desire to express sincere and grateful thanks to you and all of your command. The people living in the area on this side of the Channel have followed anxiously the great efforts of the Canadians in the hazardous job of liberating the French Channel ports. Your success is our relief, and we would be particularly pleased if you would kindly pass our thanks on to all ranks. We hope to have an early opportunity of thanking some, if not all, of the boys of your forces."

Another thanksgiving service was held the following morning and a grandsire double peal was rung on the old parish church bells for forty-five minutes in the evening; three of the ringers were men who had rung the bells for the Armistice in 1918.

The first shell had fallen on Folkestone shortly after 11am on 12th August 1940, and from that date, until the last shell fell on the town on 25th September, Folkestone had been bombarded in thirty-five attacks by 219 shells; twenty-eight people were killed by them and 189 injured; nearly six thousand buildings, mostly houses, were wrecked or damaged in these attacks. About 640 men had been drafted into the town by the beginning of October to help make damaged homes fit to live in; this work alone was expected to take months.

Children in College Road, Deal, had their long-promised treat to celebrate the end of the shelling on Monday 2nd October. The Canadians who had captured the guns were not forgotten—a cheque for £10 was handed to the Mayor to provide cigarettes for the troops. A telegram was read from the Lord Mayor of London and HMS *Dalmatia*, adopted by the town, which expressed congratulations on relief from attack and admiration for courage shown.

The first shell may have fallen on Deal at about 10am on 8th August 1940, although it is thought this may have been fired from a ship in the Channel. Eight other shells fells on the town before the first shell-warning sounded in Deal on 5th April 1943. In the ninety-eight alerts since then, 120 shells had burst in or over the town, killing twelve people and injuring fewer than fifty. Some of the daytime alerts were treated with disdain, and the police and wardens sometimes had trouble clearing people from that part of the beach open to the public. About a thousand buildings were in need of repair by the end of the shelling, and the borough surveyor said that, with only ninety men to do the work, Deal might not get back to normal for years.

Ramsgate was shelled only seven times, but the forty-two missiles which dropped on the town wrecked thirty-seven buildings and damaged 2,414 others, many of them seriously. The first bombard-ment took place on 12th February 1941 when three shells landed, although the only damage they did was to demolish the side of a bungalow. The next attack did not come until more than two years later, on 28th June 1943, when two shells fell on the town and killed a woman of seventy. Ten people died in the shelling incidents alto-gether; seven were seriously injured and thirty-six slightly hurt. The last—and worst—attack occurred on 1st September 1944, when two people were killed; three houses were wrecked; eleven had to be pulled down, and 1,223 others were damaged in some way.

About two thousand of the 2,800 or so houses in St Margaret's Bay were damaged by shells, some of them seriously. About 687 shells landed in the area, most of them in the last two weeks, but few casualties were caused. Hythe had no shells at all until the evening of 14th September 1944; several more shells fell the following day, and an elderly woman was killed.

18. In the pipeline

Lord Mountbatten, then Chief of Combined Operations, and Mr Geoffrey Lloyd, Secretary for Petroleum, had a conversation early in 1942 about a particular aspect of the Overlord invasion then being planned. Would it be much of an advantage, asked Lord Mountbatten, if fuel pipelines could be laid across the Channel soon after the invasion? It turned out that it would. And what happened in Kent and the Isle of Wight because of this led Eisenhower, the Supreme Allied Commander, to say: "This provided our main supplies of fuel during the winter and summer months." He was talking about petrol-supplies to Europe—known as 'PLUTO'.

This doggy name sprang from the initials 'Pipe Line Under The Ocean', which had its origins in the early days of the invasion preparations. After that conversation in 1942, short test-lengths of special cable were made, and a 200-yard length was tested in the Thames. These successful experiments led to a two-mile piece of cable being laid from a cable-ship in the Medway near Chatham Dockyard, followed by further trials over 30 miles between Swansea and the North Devon coast. The trials worked—and Dungeness in Kent soon became the scene of a top secret installation.

It was decided that a pumping-station should be set up in Sandown Bay on the Isle of Wight to provide 3,000 tons of petrol a day, and another at Dungeness for 3,500 tons a day. Both pumping-stations were linked to ports and oil-refineries (such as that at Grain) by a thousand-mile-long network of pipes. The logistics involved in the construction of such a network were incredible.

The pipeline from Walton-on-Thames to Lydd, for example, was 72 miles long. Most of the materials for this line were moved by the Southern Railway. Between 12th June and the end of July 1943 the railway had carried nearly 8,000 tons of pipes, each of which was about 40 feet along, weighed 8½ hundredweight and was eight inches in diameter. The 72 miles of the line were divided into six sections, each under a separate contractor and engineer. A further 459 tons of pipes, some of them lighter, were also delivered at this time to Appledore and Lydd on Romney Marsh, and another 26 miles of pipeline were being built that summer between Paddock Wood and Port Victoria. In this case, between July and August 1943, Southern Railway moved 1,357 tons of pipes, each of which was from 35 to 50 feet along and 18 inches in diameter.

The thirty reciprocating and four centrifugal pumps at Dungeness were installed at three well-dispersed sites along the coast. Some of the pumping-plant was concealed in innocent-looking 'holiday bungalows' built specially for the purpose; and great tanks of petrol, ready in case of a breakdown in the supply from the west of England, were also hidden in this way. The making of the under-water pipeline itself used 12,000 tons of lead and 5,600 tons of steel. The tubes which eventually carried the petrol were manufactured in 750-yard lengths, each weighing 15 tons. They were welded together at Littlestone railway station under a special process which allowed them to stand the terrific strain of under-water conditions. These continuous pipes, by then about 30 miles long, were wound on massive drums and towed across the Channel by two tugs.

The first PLUTO line was laid from the Isle of Wight to Cherbourg on 12th August 1944, immediately after the Cherbourg peninsula had been captured and cleared of mines. The fast advance of the Allied armies, however, soon made it important to get a petrol-supply from Dungeness to Boulogne, so the Isle of Wight link was abandoned in favour of the shorter route from the Kent coast. The pipelines from Dungeness were to have run to Ambleteuse, but it was decided to avoid having to clear the mined beach there by laying the cables to a beach inside the outer harbour at Boulogne instead. The first line was laid along that route in October and was soon joined by sixteen others; they reached a peak delivery of one million gallons a day in February 1945. They and the Sandown Bay PLUTO lines not only relieved oil-tankers for vital work in the Far East but by the end of the war had delivered a staggering 172,000,000 gallons of petrol into the hands of the Allied armies in Europe.

The war, of course, mothered many inventions. One of these, installed at Manston airfield, had another doggy name: it was called 'FIDO', from the initials of 'Fog Investigation Dispersal Operations'. It was simply a piece of equipment which could clear a gap at least 1,000 yards long and 100 feet high over a runway to allow a plane to land in fog or mist. Flying tests with FIDO had first been made in January 1943, and by the summer of 1944 this equipment had been installed at fifteen airfields in Britain, one in France and two in the USA. More than 2,500 aircraft eventually made FIDO-assisted landings in bad weather. About a thousand gallons of petrol per plane were pumped through pipes on each side of the runway and converted to controlled flames which dispelled the mist or fog. It saved many crews and their aircraft and was largely responsible for the defeat of the German offensive in the Ardennes ('the Battle of the Bulge') in December 1944 because it allowed Allied bombers to attack the enemy in foggy weather.

The Kent Channel ports were meanwhile returning to life.

In October 1944 the Ministry of War Transport chartered a fleet of coasters to carry ammunition and stores from Dover to Ostend; the Southern Ferry Service began again in November by carrying hospital trains and new locomotives; army mail was being shipped between Dover and Ostend by 8th November, and later that month the Shepperton Ferry and the Twickenham Ferry were crossing to Calais. Leave-ships brought troops home from Calais to Dover for the first time on 7th December, followed by a Calais-to-Folkestone run on 8th December. The first leave-party returned to the Continent from Dover on 4th January 1945, and four days later there was another from Folkestone. The leave-traffic increased constantly, and from the beginning of the New Year to VE Day, 1,881 leave-trains carried nearly ninety thousand men away from the ports at Folkestone, Dover, Harwich and Southampton.

This later traffic was still in the future, however, when two American soldiers appeared before a court martial in Ashford—charged with the rape and murder of a local girl of fifteen. The two men were Private Augustine Guerra, a twenty-year-old soldier, and Corporal Ernest Lee Clark, of the USAAF. They had separate trials, Guerra being the first to come before the American court martial on Friday 22nd September. Clark had his case heard on Friday 6th October. Both men were charged with the rape and murder of a girl whose body was found in the Old Cricket Ground at Black Path, Ashford, on 23rd August. The trials heard that the pair had been drinking heavily on the night of 22nd August at 'The Smith's Arms', and that when the men left, at about 10.15pm, they had stopped the girl—who had spent much of the evening at a fair—at the end of the Black Path, before going with her into the field.

Guerra said in one statement that he had held the girl down while

Clark had sex with her. He thought she had fainted, and Clark felt her pulse and heart before leaving—her heart was still beating, said Clark. The defence asked that the charge of murder in both cases be reduced to manslaughter, but the two court martials found both men guilty on all charges—and both men were sentenced to be hanged by the neck until they were dead.

By this stage of the war the threat of a German invasion of Britain had disappeared, and the Home Guard was no longer needed, so on Sunday 15th October more than three thousand officers and members of the Home Guard throughout the county attended a stand-down service in Canterbury Cathedral. The men, accompanied by their own bands of the 1st (Ashford) and 18th (Dartford) battalions, represented about sixty thousand Kent colleagues drawn from fifty battalions, three transport columns and two AA batteries. They fell in at the Chaucer Barracks and marched through the city before filling the nave for the service. The invited guests included Lord Cornwallis, making his first public appearance as Lord Lieutenant of the County since being appointed to the post on 1st September, Kent MPs and mayors, officers and commanders of all the Forces, magistrates and council chairmen.

The men reformed outside the cathedral after the service and marched back to the barracks. Lord Cornwallis took the salute outside the city walls, and the playing-fields at the barracks were crowded when the Home Guard members formed up in front of the rostrum where he made a speech.

Lord Cornwallis said:

> There is one thing of which I wish to remind you today—when we in deep anguish received into our little Kentish ports our hard-pressed Armies retreating from Dunkirk—when we saw endless train-loads being taken back to the west through our county for rest and refitting— we might have thought that there was little hope—but always remember with pride that when those tired Armies were going back west, a citizens' army was rising in the south-east, ready to fight on the beaches, in the fields and in the streets to secure the breathing-space the nations so urgently required. That citizen army was you—the Home Guard of Kent—and today I give to you all the humble and completely sincere thanks of the people of your county.

Three days later, on 18th October, the now-quiet front-line towns of Dover and Folkestone were visited by King George VI and Queen Elizabeth. Archbishop William Temple, who had been enthroned on 23rd April 1942, died at Westgate-on-Sea on 26th October.

There was little enemy action in Kent during October, the only recorded deaths occurring when two people were killed by a flying bomb which fell at Hartlip near Sittingbourne on 24th October. But November was a little busier. The first main incident took place when another flying bomb fell in the Grafton Avenue/Jackson Avenue area of Rochester, near Fort Horsted, at 8.45pm on Saturday 11th November. At least fourteen homes were wrecked and 560 others damaged in some way; windows were also smashed at Holcombe School. The casualty-detector unit was requested a few hours later to help find some of the victims, and it arrived on the scene about midnight. Eight people were killed in this attack, sixteen seriously injured and thirty slightly hurt.

It was the turn of Gravesend to suffer next when the town became the first place in Kent to be badly hit by a V2 rocket. The missile exploded in the Portland Avenue area of the town at 4.40pm on Monday 13th November. The Co-operative Society Bakery and food stores was damaged, and eleven Civil Defence staff were slightly injured when their depot at St Mary's School was hit by the blast. At least four homes were wrecked and three hundred others damaged by the explosion. The final casualty-toll was five dead, sixteen seriously injured and fifty-six slightly hurt.

The town was hit again in the last serious attack of the year when another rocket came down in the Milton Place area of the town centre at 11.45pm on Wednesday 29th November. Most of the buildings wrecked or seriously damaged were blocks of tall houses. A man in one of those buildings was spending his last evening on leave with his fiancée before returning to his camp. The couple were trapped when the rocket fell, and rescuers—including sailors—worked for hours in the glare of floodlights to reach them. A settee saved them from being crushed completely, and the girl, who was conscious all the time, gave directions to her rescuers. The injured pair were eventually released when a section of floorboards was sawn away and lifted from them. The man was found with his arms wrapped round his fiancée; he had died protecting her. At least four houses and a small engineering works were destroyed in the explosion and fifty-five buildings damaged. Eight people had been killed, fifteen seriously injured and thirty-seven slightly hurt.

The first serious incident in Kent in the last year of war was caused by an accident and not as the result of enemy action. Twenty soldiers at a lecture near an East Kent town were killed when a mine exploded, on Wednesday 10th January 1945, in a large Nissen hut while a sergeant instructor was lecturing on the mine that blew up. An inquest held a few days after the incident heard that no dummy mines were available for such lectures. The coroner, recording a verdict of death by misadventure in each case, said that he would make strong representations to the War Office regarding the absence of dummy mines for Army training purposes.

The war, meanwhile, continued to run its course towards victory. The Russians liberated Warsaw on 17th January; the Burma Road was re-opened on 22nd January, and the British and Canadian Forces reached the Rhine on 9th February.

It was about that time that an extraordinary domestic situation, created by the war, came to light in Kent. An East Kent bus-driver from Deal was reported 'missing, believed killed' while serving with the RASC at Dunkirk in 1940. His wife married a builder's foreman more than a year after he went missing, and the couple settled down to life in Dover. Her first husband was, however, not really dead: he had found himself in a prisoner-of-war camp after Dunkirk but had lost his memory and could not even remember his own name. He escaped eventually and after roaming France for months returned to England via Gibraltar, still suffering from loss of memory. His identity was established some months later after he remembered a road in Hornsey where he used to live. He was invalided from the Army in October 1942—a year after his wife had remarried—and returned to Deal a few months later to drive East Kent buses again. The man had seen his wife only once to speak to since his return to Britain. He said she appeared undecided what to do, but the woman decided that she preferred to live with her second husband.

A few days after British troops reached the Rhine, Dresden was bombed and Budapest surrendered to the Russians. But the first serious enemy action in Kent did not occur until Tuesday 27th February. A V2 rocket fell on Swanscombe in the morning of that day, killing eight people, seriously injuring twenty-seven and slightly hurting twenty-one others. About seven houses were wrecked, and almost every shop in a small shopping-centre nearby had windows blown out. Two men repairing the porch of a house, previously damaged by a flying bomb, were among those killed by the explosion. A woman in her garden at the time was badly shaken but helped search for her baby of three months, who was found in his cot beneath piles of debris and taken to hospital with head-injuries. One man, whose home was badly damaged by the blast, was in bed when he saw the ceiling collapsing on him; he held it up with his arms until he was rescued. A couple who lived close to where the rocket fell were having breakfast when their windows were blown in and the ceiling came down. The windows were also blown in at a nearby school, but the youngsters inside sheltered under their desks and were not hurt. Chickens which had escaped from a damaged chicken-house could be seen pecking about in the rubble.

Another V2 caused serious damage when it fell on a housing estate at Sevenoaks on Saturday 3rd March, killing nine people, seriously injuring thirteen and slightly hurting six others. The rocket fell only a few yards from the spot where bombs had fallen in 1940; and the estate also suffered badly when a land-mine fell there early in the war. Most of those who were killed died when two blocks of semi-detached houses were wrecked; the dead included a couple and their two children. Another couple who died had been expecting their RAF son back from Italy at the time; the woman of this couple was a Red Cross worker who had been the only person rescued alive from a trapped dug-out in one of the earlier bombing incidents. The members of one family called for help after being trapped in bedrooms and were rescued in their nightclothes. Rescue-work went on throughout the night with the help of searchlights and torches. A woman and her two small daughters who were looked after at a rest-centre opened in the town had been bombed out twice before in London and were now homeless again.

A few days later, on 6th March, the Allies took Cologne, and on 16th March Iwo Jima fell to the United States.

The last serious piece of enemy action in Kent during the war had occurred a couple of days earlier on Wednesday 14th March, when a V2 rocket fell in front of a bootmaker's shop in Sutton at Hone, near Dartford, killing ten people, seriously injuring fourteen and slightly hurting nine others. This shop and the butcher's shop next door were both wrecked by the explosion, and extensive damage was done to other homes in the area, together with the school. A couple living over the butcher's shop were killed, but their three-year-old son was found unhurt in his cot at the bottom of the garden. A man escaped with minor injuries when his wife and two sons died in another house, and an RAF pilot officer home on seven days' leave survived the attack even though his parents and a younger brother were all killed in the incident.

There were nine recorded fatal incidents in Kent in 1945 as the result of enemy activity, the last of them occurring on 16th March when a flying bomb killed four people at Dartford. All of them were the result of flying bombs or V2 rockets (sixty-seven of which fell in Kent). Ordinary bombs, according to the county War Diaries, had not caused the death of anyone in Kent since four people died in Strood in April 1944. The last V2 rocket to fall on Great Britain came down near St Mary Cray railway station at Orpington on 27th March. The last flying bomb to hit Britain—fired from a ramp bordering the Delft Canal in Holland—fell without killing anyone at Iwade near Sittingbourne on the morning of 29th March.

President Roosevelt died on 12th April and was succeeded by Truman. Belsen and Buchenwald concentration camps were taken by the British on 13th April, and shortly afterwards the Russians occupied Vienna. The Russian offensive towards Berlin began on 16th April—three days before Geoffrey Fisher was enthroned as Archbishop of Canterbury. Mussolini was killed on 28th April, and the 7th Army liberated Dachau the following day. On Sunday 30th April Hitler committed suicide in his Berlin bunker. The war was almost over.

19. This Great Deliverance

So Hitler was dead—and everyone in Britain began to wait for the declaration that war with Germany had ended. Peace, however, was putting in a hesitant appearance. The first signs of it came at 7pm on Wednesday 2nd May when the BBC interrupted a programme to report the surrender of all German forces in Italy. The programmes were broken into again at 10.30pm that night with news of the fall of Berlin. The surrender of all German forces in Denmark was announced at 8.40pm on Sunday 6th May.

People were convinced that peace would be declared at any time. But at 6pm on Monday 7th May the BBC announced that Winston Churchill would not be broadcasting that night; this was followed by another announcement at 7.40pm that the following day would be celebrated as 'Victory in Europe Day' and, like Wednesday 9th May, would be a national holiday. Churchill, broadcasting at 3pm on that historic Tuesday, told the nation that at 2.41am the previous day representatives of the German High Command had signed the act of unconditional surrender. Hostilities were to end officially at one minute after midnight that Tuesday, he continued, but a cease-fire had already begun in the interests of saving lives: "The German war is therefore at an end."

There were many wild celebrations of the type familiar from contemporary newsreels and photographs, but the news was also greeted soberly by many people—among them the families and friends of some of the 340,672 UK forces killed and missing in the war. The coastal towns of Kent, particularly quiet until the evening, were also still suffering from the black-out—continuing because it was feared that some enemy submarines might not have received the surrender instructions or would not obey them.

The last celebratory All Clear sounded on the sirens at Maidstone at 2.57pm on 8th May while planes roared overhead with food and supplies for the liberated countries. A crowd gathered outside the Town Hall at 4pm to hear the official peace announcement made by the Mayor, Lieutenant-Colonel C. Larking. Flags and bunting fluttered from shops and offices in the breeze as he talked; some people in the town were reported to have been offering up to £5 for a Union Jack. The band of the Royal West Kent Regiment was present with an armed guard in full dress uniform and about fifty standard-bearers carrying the flags of all the Allies. The Mayor paid tribute to the valour of all the fighting services and the men of the Merchant Navy. But he urged people not to relax their efforts until the barbarous 'Jap' "who knows no decency" was finally beaten. He invited every-one to visit the war memorial to pay tribute to those who had made the supreme sacrifice.

Services of thanksgiving were held in all the churches in the early evening, some of them being so full that they had to turn away people at the door. The pubs were also packed, and it was difficult to get served. Singing crowds thronged the streets, and dancing to the wire-less from open doors and windows went on until the early hours of the morning. All Saints' Church and County Hall were floodlit; search-lights flashed overhead, and buses were decorated with fairy lights.

Many of the celebrations were joined by soldiers, sailors and airmen who swarmed on buses, lorries and cars to make their way home for the fun. The clock-tower and public buildings at Gravesend were decorated with garlands of red, white and blue, made from a large amount of waxed paper left over after the coronation celebrations in 1937; the paper had been stored in vaults in the Fort Gardens and almost forgotten. The flags of Great Britain, the USA, Russia and China flew on the summit of Windmill Hill and were floodlit after dark, as were churches and other public buildings in the town. About ten thousand people flocked to Woodlands Park in the evening to watch the burning of a huge bonfire and a torchlight procession; the fire was lit thirty minutes too early by a sailor and wardens with hoses failed to put it out. An effigy of Hitler was burned on ground at Milton Place, where a V2 rocket had killed eight people on 29th November the previous year.

Crowds gathered in Elwick Road and Bank Street in Ashford at midnight to watch the burning of another effigy of Hitler, which hung from a gibbet outside the old Corn Exchange. The audience burst into 'Land of Hope and Glory' as the last remains of the effigy were beaten down with a staff. People had earlier danced in the Lower High Street to music by the Southern Railway Works Band. Ashford parish church, the Council Chamber and Willesborough Mill were floodlit; dance-halls were open until midnight, and pubs until 11.30pm, although songs such as 'Knees Up Mother Brown' and 'The Lambeth Walk' could be heard in the High Street after midnight. About a thousand people went to a special thanksgiving service conducted by the vicar in the parish church, and a collection for the relief of distress in Europe raised £22. Several street-parties were held for youngsters in the town.

Airmen from fighter squadrons appeared in the streets of Folkestone dressed in pyjamas and dressing-gowns at noon. The All Clear in the town was sounded for the last time in the afternoon. Street-parties were given for children in roads decorated with flags and bunting, and dancing at halls and in the streets continued late into the night. The black-out hampered the celebrations after dark, but grass on the Downs was somehow set alight, and a huge fire burned there for some time. Loudspeakers at Dover—previously used to warn people of shelling—relayed music for the large crowds that chose to dance, and also broadcast Churchill's announcement and the King's speech.

The official black-out at Ramsgate was waived by the council to allow the streets to be lighted until about 11pm on the Tuesday evening. The East Cliff bandstand and the Odeon cinema were floodlit, and many people danced in the streets. There was an open-air service outside the Town Hall at noon, and the square was packed as the Mayor, the Rev. H. Samuel, gave a short address. In Margate, however, the council was criticized for its poor efforts at decorating the town for the occasion; things there were described as 'flat'. Many of the visitors to the coast towns had trouble getting home again because of the packed buses and trains. Contingents of Royal Marines —who had been granted the Freedom of Deal on 14th February 1945—marched through that town with women from the WRNS, led by a Marines band. And the Free Church canteen provided everything free to all service people. A cow was spotted between Eythorne and Eastry, decorated with red, white and blue ribbon.

Bonfires were lit in all parts of Tunbridge Wells during the evening on VE Day, the biggest of them on the Common, where a shelter was razed to the ground. About six hundred people gathered round another big fire opposite the chapel at High Brooms. A piano was brought out of one house, and there was dancing and singing until the early hours of the morning. People remained in the streets throughout the night.

The Westgate Towers and St George's Church were floodlit in Canterbury, the glow illuminating the cathedral. Huge bonfires burned on various sites in the city, including the blitzed Paine Smith schools, Longport Street and several in Vauxhall Avenue. Some local dogs were decked out in patriotic colours, one of them wearing a ruffle of Union Jacks.

The Mayor of Hythe, Alderman Captain G. Few, told a big crowd outside the Town Hall: "This is The Day. Victory is ours. We knew the miracle of 1940 when we really waited for the invasion of the barbarians. That should make us thankful for this great victory. There is still another war to finish, so when you celebrate, remember your relatives, your friends and all those who are fighting the other enemy in the Far East."

Before that fighting ended, however, the country had a General Election to face. The people voted on 5th July, but the results, delayed to allow the Forces' vote to arrive from overseas, were not declared until 26th July. The result was an overwhelming victory for Labour, whose 393 seats were way ahead of the Tories' 213. The national swing was reflected in Kent, where more than seventy per cent of the electors turned out to vote. Labour gained six of the sixteen Kent constituencies to end up with eight of the seats; the Tories took the remaining eight. The most surprising Labour gain was Dover, which had been a Conservative stronghold for many years. Other gains were Chatham, Chislehurst, Faversham, Gillingham and Gravesend; Labour kept Dartford and also won the new constituency of Bexley. The Tories kept Ashford, Bromley, Canterbury, Hythe, Thanet, Maidstone, Sevenoaks and Tonbridge. Churchill was out; Clement Attlee was the new Prime Minister.

The war in the Far East continued, meanwhile. It was widely believed that war with Japan might go on for another eighteen months or two years, but that was before the Enola Gay came on the scene. This American B29 was the plane that dropped the atom bomb on Hiroshima on Monday 6th August, killing eighty thousand people. Two days later, on Wednesday 8th August, Russia declared war on Japan and began a drive into Manchuria the following day. It was on that day, Thursday 9th August, that the second atom bomb was dropped on Nagasaki. The 1pm news that day indicated that Japan had asked for an armistice, but it was not until 11.45pm on Tuesday 14th August that the BBC warned listeners to stand by for a special announcement. A few minutes later, at midnight, the voice of Attlee was heard: "Japan has today surrendered. The last of our enemies is laid low."

VJ Day was, by many accounts, something of an anticlimax after VE Day. Japan, after all, never bombed Britain in the way that Germany did, and the war in the Far East was seen by many people as a distant affair that was really the business of the Americans. Churchill, who had inspired so much patriotic fervour as a war leader, was no longer at the helm; the country was already settling down to a post-war life. The sense of relief at Japan's surrender, reported one paper, was not so acute as when Germany had collapsed in May.

But far-off war or not, it was still a cause for celebration, and when Attlee had finished talking, ships' sirens hooted across the Medway, and the bells at Gillingham parish church rang out shortly after 1am. People asleep at Folkestone were woken by a broadcast announcement from a US jeep, which was driven through the streets to an accompaniment of thunderflashes thrown from the vehicle. Ships also hooted on the Thames at Gravesend for more than two hours, and people there linked arms and danced round the clocktower. The sirens sounded in Ramsgate harbour, and soon thousands of people—many in their nightclothes—turned out on the sea-front there, where a bonfire was lit in the road. The desire just to mingle with other people was a common feeling on VE and VJ Days; and it was also a common reaction to switch on all the lights in the house, with the curtains open, in a way that had been impossible since the war began. Many youngsters were frightened by the celebration fireworks and the bright lights at night—the first they had seen since they were born.

Many people had gone to bed before the first 11.45pm announcement on the wireless, so they were not aware that Japan had surrendered until they woke on the morning of Wednesday 15th August and heard a recording of Attlee's speech at 7am. That day and the following day were declared public holidays, but because this had not been announced until late the previous night, it took many people by surprise. Some shops were open, and some were not. Some buses ran, but many did not, annoying people who were trying to catch one for work—before they realized that work had been cancelled for two days. Many people at Maidstone, for example, reported for work as usual. The town was crowded, and everywhere there were long queues of women anxious to get food, many forming before the shops were open; the biggest problem was getting bread.

The official announcement from the Town Hall in Maidstone, arranged originally for 11am, was postponed until 3pm. The band, an armed guard of honour and standard-bearers from the 13th ITC added colour to the event. The Mayor, Alderman Lieutenant-Colonel C. Larking, gave an address. The crowd sang the National Anthem and marched to the war memorial, where the Mayor laid a wreath and a short service was held, ending with the Last Post and Reveille. Wreaths were also laid at the cenotaph of the Royal West Kent Regiment. Most of the buses in the town were decorated with fairy lights. There was dancing in the widest part of the High Street and a bonfire and dancing in South Park. A man fixing bunting on the Victoria Memorial in the High Street found a pigeon's next containing three eggs. Crowds waiting for the afternoon announcement were entertained by the dancing of two bus-conductresses and a sailor, whose twenty-minute show did not even stop when someone in the crowd threw a thunderflash.

Dover Castle was floodlit for the first time since 1939, and the shell-warning loudspeakers were again used to relay dance-music and the King's speech at 9pm. The King said in this broadcast: "From the bottom of my heart, I thank my peoples for all they have done, not only for themselves but for mankind." A 60-foot high bonfire, visible from France, was lit after dark. The sleeping town of Folkestone had also been woken by fireworks fired in Shorncliffe Camp and Hawkinge airfield, where large fires were among the early-morning celebrations. A fire in the road at Cheriton was fed with wood from a big advertising hoarding. Hundreds of couples danced round and in The Leas band-stand to music from loudspeakers; and grass on the hills surrounding the town was again set on fire. Soldiers on their way back from leave to the Continent cheered loudly when they heard the news of the surrender; leave-boats sailing from Folkestone and Calais were decorated with flags. The day and evening at Faversham, however, passed quietly; some folk there, said a paper, indulged in fireworks.

Margate council anticipated VJ Day by decorating the sea-front three days before the news came. The Mayor, Mr F. Cornford, lit a big bonfire on the cliffs, where thousands of people gathered, while crowds of visitors made fires on the road along the sea-front. A massive fire on Ramsgate sands was watched by at least 22,000 people; twenty-two incendiary bombs, formerly used for ARP practice, were included in the blaze. One policeman was carried shoulder-high through the streets there. Beach-huts were tipped down the slopes at Tankerton and later put on a bonfire. Vain appeals were made by loudspeaker to the crowds, who dragged blazing embers over the grass and set fire to a large area. Another large fire and fireworks was

ᴀeld in the College Road area of Sittingbourne, together with dancing
ᴏn the recreation ground. Street-parties were held there, as they were
n many other towns.

Soldiers who marched behind a Salvation Army band at Canterbury
ᴉinging 'Roll Out The Barrel' later climbed on cars in the High Street
ᴀnd had to be stopped by police. A crowd which found a barrel-organ
ᴍarched through Westgate Towers to a bonfire on a bombed site near
ᴉhe West Station and rolled the organ onto it. Fireworks were let off at
ᴍost street-corners in the city. The High Street in Ashford, lit up and
ᴉecorated, was thronged by civilians and soldiers for community sing-
ᴉng and dancing, followed by a service conducted by the Vicar. The
ᴊarish church and Willesborough Mill were again flood-lit. Crowds
ᴀter danced and sang outside the Corn Exchange. The evening cele-
ᴊrations at Tunbridge Wells opened with a giant bonfire on the
ᴐommon, which more than a thousand people turned out to see lit
ᴊy the Mayor, Alderman C. Westbrook. Hundreds of young men and
ᴡomen danced by floodlight on the Pantiles to the music of the
ᴴotspots Dance Band.

ᴛhe civilian casualties during the war in Kent (including the then city
ᴀnd county of Canterbury and that part of Kent in the London region)
ᴡere 20,914 killed, seriously injured or slightly hurt; this figure is one-
ᴇeventh of the entire civilian casualty total for the United Kingdom,
ᴇhowing how Kent earned the nickname 'Hell's Corner'. The figures
ᴊor the present county of Kent alone (excluding those eight areas
ᴡhich have since become part of Greater London) were: 1,608 killed,
ᴉ,402 seriously injured and 5,492 slightly hurt. The unsafest place to
ᴊe during the war was undoubtedly Dover, where 199 people were
ᴋilled and 910 buildings destroyed; the battered city of Canterbury,
ᴇecond in this 'league', suffered 115 deaths and 808 wrecked build-
ᴉngs. The safest places to be, however, were Queenborough, South-
ᴊorough and Sandwich, the only three areas of Kent in which no one
ᴉied as the result of enemy action; Queenborough and Southborough
ᴡere the only two areas in which no properties were destroyed.

Other statistics prove just how much Kent had to endure during
ᴉhe war. There were more than ten thousand incidents—ranging from
ᴍinor to major—in which 29,272 high-explosive bombs fell on the
ᴄounty. Kent also suffered the bombardment of a staggering 727,784
ᴉncendiary bombs, 1,422 flying bombs, 3,513 shells and sixty-seven
ᴠ2 rockets—together with the 374 enemy aircraft which crashed in
ᴉhe county. A total of 5,209 buildings were wrecked, 16,170 severely

damaged and 181,267 slightly damaged; these included seventy oast houses damaged by flying bombs and five hundred schools damaged in some way by bombs.

But civilians were not the only ones at risk, of course. There were numerous incidents and accidents in the county which killed service personnel—the worst of which have already been mentioned; others died along with civilians in many of the bombing raids.

The contribution made by The Buffs (Royal East Kent Regiment and The Queen's Own Royal West Kent Regiment should not be forgotten: the twelve battalions raised by The Buffs served in France, Western Africa, Italy, West Europe and Burma; of the ten battalions of the West Kent Regiment, four served in the United Kingdom while the other six saw service in France, Belgium, Malta, Palestine, Western Africa, Iraq, Syria, Italy, Leros, Samos, Greece, Burma, Germany and Austria. A total of 2,990 members of the two regiments were killed in the war.

The fighting might have stopped, but its aftermath continued to be felt for a long time. Over the next few years people became used to seeing prisoners-of-war rectifying some of the damage their country had caused. The first German prisoners to start work on a housing scheme in Kent were the men who formed a working-party of twenty-five from 13th June onwards, travelling daily by bus from Ashford to prepare a site for about forty pre-fabricated houses on a site in Westgate Court at Canterbury. The prisoners were employed by the contractor to the city council. The maximum pay they would have received as laid down by the Geneva Convention would have been three shillings a week (six shillings for tradesmen), but the difference between the union rate for the job and the pay actually received by the prisoners went on food, accommodation and transport.

And so the apparatus of war was gradually disbanded in Kent. The county's Home Guard had stood down in October 1944, but the stand-down parade and service of the Civil Defence services did not take place until 3rd June 1945—and that of the Women's Land Army not until 11th August. Rationing, however, was a lingering annoyance that did not disappear finally until 1954. But what really mattered was the end of six years of hostilities, and that had come with Attlee's midnight speech on Tuesday 14th August. The new Prime Minister had told the nation then: "Peace has once again come to the world. Let us thank God for this great deliverance and his mercy. Long live the King." The war, at last, was over.

Appendices:

1. The Evacuees

The most unusual evacuees ever to have been moved from Kent must have been the 125,000 sheep and twenty thousand cattle on Romney Marsh, which were taken away in lorry after lorry in May and June 1940 when the Germans were over-running the Low Countries and it looked as though an invasion might take place at any time. The main idea was to preserve a nucleus of the Romney Marsh breed. The sheep were collected, shorn, graded and sent away at the rate of two thousand a day. Most of them went to Middlesex, Hertfordshire and Bedfordshire, although a large number also went as far west as Wiltshire and Somerset, and the King even took about a thousand of them in at Windsor Great Park. The ewes, which had just lambed, went at the bottom of the lorries, with their offspring on the top floor; a thousand lorry-loads were moved in nineteen days. This move helped thin the population of East Kent—both animal and civilian—to a fraction of what it had been in peacetime.

The first proper evacuation began on 1st September 1939—the day German troops invaded Poland. Kent was, of course, to become the most attacked county in the country during the war, a problem which seems not to have been anticipated by the planners, however, because they intended that 136,502 evacuees from London and the Medway Towns should be moved into the county in the space of a few days; most of them were children, but they also included mothers, teachers, invalids and blind people.

The evacuation from the Medway Towns of Rochester, Chatham, Gillingham and Rainham began on Friday 1st September and was spread over two days. It was planned that 39,182 people should be moved to elsewhere in the county, most of them by train but two thousand to Strood rural district by bus. The biggest single group of these, five thousand, was to be taken to Sittingbourne and Milton urban district; four thousand each were to be moved to Eastry rural district and Swale rural district, with a further 3,782 to Herne Bay and 3,500 to Bridge-Blean rural district. The Southern Railway ran twenty-seven special trains on each of the two days and also coped with the evacuation of Borstal prison on 2nd and 3rd September. It was then the turn of the evacuees from London to be moved over the three days up to 5th

September; 97,320 of them were expected. The biggest single group here, 12,999, was to go to Folkestone (subsequently to become the third most attacked town in the country), with 7,440 to Ashford urban district, 7,032 to the Malling area, 7,026 to the Dartford district, and a further 5,598 to Tunbridge Wells and 5,011 to Maidstone.

Most of the evacuees never arrived. There were tearful scenes on railway platforms as thousands of labelled children—each carrying his or her gas-mask and luggage in suitcases, kit-bags, pillowslips or even paper bags—waved farewell to their parents. But the evacuation was voluntary, and most parents refused to be parted from their children. Only 47,330 of the 136,502 evacuees turned up.

By the turn of 1940, with the country still suffering nothing worse than the Phoney War, the evacuees began returning home. Homesickness, the lack of air-raids and the demand for a parental contribution all encouraged them to do so; warning posters issued by the government and special 'Visit the Evacuee' cheap railway tickets for parents did nothing to reverse the trend. Three out of four evacuees, nationally, had gone home by January 1940—and the number of evacuees in Kent at that time had fallen to 29,653.

It became obvious to the government that parents were unlikely to let their children be evacuated until serious air-raids actually began, so in February 1940 it prepared a scheme which could be put into operation at short notice once raids started. Parents were asked to register in advance if they wished their children to be evacuated when the attacks began. The plan allowed for the evacuation of 19,200 children from Kent over four days. About fourteen thousand of these youngsters were to be billeted in twenty-nine reception-areas in Kent, while the rest would be sent to Sussex. This plan assumed that about 19,200 (sixty per cent) of the 32,500 children still in evacuable areas of the county would be allowed by their parents to be evacuated when the air-raids began. But by the end of April only 2,158 of those eligible (6·6 per cent) had registered with the scheme.

Most of this scheme had to be abandoned in May, anyway, when the Germans invaded the Low Countries, and emergency evacuation arrange-ments affecting many parts of Kent had to be made at short notice. Thousands of children and adults were moved from 19th May to 11th September to Wales, the Midlands, the West Country, Sussex, Berkshire and Oxfordshire.

The registration of children for evacuation continued in all the evacuation areas, with arrangements made between the evacuating and receiving authorities for the periodical transfer of children and mothers in organized parties. The county council was also, in the summer of 1940, making plans for the reception and billeting in the remaining Kent reception areas of 22,200 people from London and the Medway Towns. This scheme was completed in August in case of air-raids on London and nearby towns—and not, as the Battle of Britain was to prove, before time. The risk of bombing on Kent had now been realized, and more parts of the county were graded as evacuation areas. The county had consisted in September 1939 of ten evacuation areas, thirty-six reception areas and eleven neutral areas (which neither accepted evacuees nor sent them out); by November 1940 it had been reclassified to twenty-eight evacuation areas, fifteen reception areas and fourteen neutral zones.

One of the problems French troops encountered during the German invasion of their country was the disorderly fleeing of refugees. It was to prevent such a problem that in June 1940 the British government decided to prepare plans for the evacuation of all but a small part of the population in some coast towns. This scheme was to differ from all the others in that evacuation was to be compulsory. It was expected that ordinary businesses would stop and that only about three per cent of the pre-war population—those who ran essential services—would stay behind until a town was abandoned. The evacuation authorities concerned began to encourage schoolchildren, mothers with young children, the old and infirm, and those not engaged on essential work to move to neutral or reception areas if they were able to make their own arrangements.

The Kent towns included in this scheme on 20th June 1940 were Margate, Broadstairs, Ramsgate, Sandwich, Deal, Dover, Folkestone, Hythe and the parish of Minster in Eastry rural, whence evacuees were to be taken by train to Surrey. The parishes of Temple Ewell, River, St Margaret's and the Kingsdown portion of Ringwould in the Dover rural area were brought into the special scheme on 27th July. The voluntary evacuation of children from these areas to Sussex took place the following day, and a further evacuation was carried out on 29th June of children from the parishes of Minster, St Nicholas, Monkton, Acol and Sarre in the Eastry rural area. Canterbury, New Romney, Lydd and Ashford were then brought into the scheme. Plans were made immediately for voluntary evacuation, and thirty-one special trains took evacuees from Canterbury and Ashford to Berkshire and Oxfordshire over several days, beginning on 11th September.

The relatively large numbers of schoolchildren still in the special scheme areas in June 1941 was worrying the government, so the plans were changed so that children aged between five and fourteen could be evacuated before the adults—should the need arise. Such children had to be registered that month, therefore. The voluntary registration for advance evacuation was extended to mothers of registered children, children under five with their mothers and schoolchildren over the age of fourteen; and in the same month the area of the scheme was extended to include Dymchurch and St Mary's in the Romney Marsh area. A total of 23,230 women and children were registered for advance evacuation from the special scheme areas of the county from 23rd to 28th June.

Revised transport plans in August 1941 provided for 117,550 people to be moved to Surrey by train if the scheme came into operation. These were made up of the following: 13,500 from Margate; 13,800 from Broadstairs; 13,000 from Ramsgate; 11,900 from Deal, St Margaret's and Kingsdown; 14,000 from Folkestone; 18,650 from Ashford; 14,660 from Dover, Temple

Ewell and River; 3,700 from Hythe; 1,240 from Minster; 2,600 from Sandwich; 1,450 from New Romney, Dymchurch and St Mary's; 1,050 from Lydd; and 18,000 from Canterbury. The parish of Capel-le-Ferne in the Dover rural area was added to the special evacuation areas in May 1942. The plans for this special scheme were under review all the time; the invasion never took place, however, and the order for compulsory evacuation was never given.

The effect of evacuation was to turn many coast resorts into little more than ghost towns. Margate was particularly badly hit because it depended for income on its tourists—who were no longer able to visit the town because it was in a banned area. Its decline began at the start of the war. Barbed wire was put up along the sea-front in the following months; pillboxes were built to resemble kiosks and cafés, and iron posts were sunk into the sand to prevent an enemy landing. Its population shrank from forty thousand to ten thousand, and grass grew in the streets of the shopping-centre. J. B. Priestley, who visited the town in July 1940, said that the few signs of life made the place seem only more "unreal and spectral". There were 7,208 unoccupied buildings in the borough, 4,031 of which were completely empty and 3,177 of which contained nothing but furniture. Margate was broke: the rate income was negligible, and the local authority could not pay its way, so the government made monthly payments to the corporation; the town received £350,000 during the war, seventy-five per cent as a grant and the rest as an interest-free loan.

Folkestone also bore the scars of war. Concrete anti-tank blocks crossed the town from Castle Hill Avenue, through Radnor Park and on to the foot of the Downs. Barbed wire appeared on the beaches, and some sections were filled with iron scaffolding and mines. Gun-batteries appeared on The Leas and on the East Cliff, and all the roads into town had tank-traps and blockhouses. The population fell from 46,000 to six thousand, and one grocer had to be given special permission to carry on with only eight registered customers, eighteen fewer than the rationing regulations called for. The population of Dover dropped to sixteen thousand from forty thousand; Broadstairs was down to two thousand; Deal shrank from 23,100 to about seven thousand, and the population of Herne Bay fell by three thousand in a few months to thirteen–fourteen thousand.

Evacuation never did become compulsory, but by June 1941 it was the law that any child under fourteen evacuated before 23rd June was not allowed to return home; any youngster who had returned before that date was allowed to stay, however. Parents could be fined and/or jailed if they refused to send such a child back to his or her evacuation home.

Little happened on the evacuation scene after 1941 until 1944. Further evacuation plans were prepared in January that year in case of resumed enemy attacks on a big scale. These plans provided for large-scale evacuation from the London area, and the Chatham, Gillingham, Rochester, Sheerness, Gravesend, Northfleet, Swanscombe and Dartford areas. Such attacks began n June 1944 with the main onslaught of the flying bombs—and the scheme already planned came into operation on 1st July. The following areas were declared additional evacuation areas on 5th July: Sevenoaks and Dartford rural districts, Sevenoaks and Tonbridge urban districts, and parts of the Strood, Malling and Tonbridge rural districts. These were joined on 13th July by: Cranbrook rural, Tenterden borough and rural, Tunbridge Wells, Southborough and the remaining parishes in Tonbridge rural. It was later decided to evacuate generally in the broad lane travelled by the flying bombs over Kent. So on 21st August the following were declared evacuation areas: Maidstone borough, East and West Ashford, Elham, Hollingbourne, Maidstone and Romney Marsh rural districts, the rest of Malling rural and additional parishes in Strood rural. Evacuation facilities were also made available at the same time in Folkestone, Hythe, Lydd, New Romney and Ashford boroughs.

The number of people moved from evacuation areas in Kent during July and August was 22,615 unaccompanied schoolchildren and 44,665 other priority classes. The main flying bomb attack was over by September, and evacuation in Kent was suspended, except for the coastal areas shelled by the cross-Channel guns.

Many people began returning home immediately, but the Ministry of Health said on 23rd September 1944 that people evacuated from London and southern England should stay where they were. Arrangements were made at the end of October for the return in December of people whose homes were in Canterbury, Hythe, Lydd, Maidstone, New Romney, Tenterden and Tunbridge Wells boroughs, Ashford, Sevenoaks, Southborough and Tonbridge urban districts, and Cranbrook, Dartford, Dover, East Ashford, Eastry, Elham, Hollingbourne, Maidstone, Malling, Romney Marsh, Sevenoaks, Strood, Tenterden, Tonbridge and West Ashford rural districts. The position was reviewed when the V2s and the occasional flying bombs appeared, but the government decided not to reverse the decision to return the evacuees.

The official return began on 6th December when 625 passengers were brought by Southern Railways from Cardiff to Hollingbourne. The homecoming of the evacuees was in full flood within a few days. It was further decided on 9th December to make plans for the return of people to Deal, Dover, Folkestone, Margate, Ramsgate, Sandwich and Broadstairs. And on 3rd May 1945—less than a week before the war in Europe ended—the evacuees began their official return to Chatham, Dartford, Erith, Gillingham, Gravesend, Rochester, Northfleet, Sheerness and Swanscombe. This was the last in the series of major movements carried out under the evacuation scheme. By 31st December 1945, however, 1,394 evacuated people were still in the county because of damage to their homes or other reasons. For all but these the days of evacuation in Kent had come to an end.

2. Fortress Kent

Hitler called off his planned invasion of Britain after he lost the Battle of Britain in September 1940, but it could not be assumed by the military authorities in Britain that German troops had given up all ideas of such an invasion, so it was necessary to prepare a system of defence involving towns in the south-east—just in case. These defensive areas were known as 'Nodal Points' and were also sometimes called 'fortress towns' or 'anti-tank islands'. The policy was clear: an outer perimeter at each of these towns would be manned by regular troops and members of the Home Guard in the event of an enemy attack; civilian evacuation would end immediately once such an attack began; and when the fighting became fiercer, the soldiers were to fall back to an inner perimeter, sometimes known as 'a keep'. Such a town was expected to hold out for a week—giving reinforcements time to reach the scene, it was hoped, or at least delaying the enemy's advance.

The main towns in Kent were first designated as 'A Nodal Points' in the autumn of 1940 by the regional commissioner for the south-east region. Points which came under class A were expected to hold out for seven days on their own, those under class B for two days, and those under class C also for two days, although in a less vulnerable area.

The regional commissioner, together with representatives of the Military and the county council, held conferences on the spot with members of the local councils concerned over the arrangements to be brought into operation if an invasion took place. These arrangements included the supply to fuel, food and water, shelter for casualties, registration of births and deaths, air raid-precaution plans, the billeting of people who had had to leave their homes, and the provision of civilian labour. The regional commissioner and the Army decided that a small body called a 'Triumvirate' should be set up at each nodal point to maintain effective liaison between the Civil and Military authorities in an emergency. Each Triumvirate consisted of a local military commander, often an officer in the Home Guard, a police representative and a representative of the local authority, usually the Mayor or chairman of the district council, or chairman of the Emergency Committee. When these arrangements were well in hand, other areas of less strategic importance were designated 'B points', and it was decided that even small, densely populated areas of no more than one or two hundred people should also have a Triumvirate.

Category A Nodal Points in Kent, by November 1941, included Canterbury, Chatham, Deal, Dover, Faversham, Folkestone, Maidstone, Margate, Ramsgate, Sittingbourne, Tonbridge and Tunbridge Wells; Category B points at this time included Sevenoaks, Tenterden, Goudhurst and Headcorn. The most important of these points, classified at Priority 1, were Canterbury, Ashford, Maidstone, Chatham, Tunbridge Wells and Tonbridge.

The decision to make Ashford into a strongly defended garrison was made in May 1941, the month after Montgomery took over command of the 12th Army Corps in Kent and Sussex. Major-General M. Stopford, commander of the 56th Division, decided the line of the defensive perimeter on 15th May; and four days later Montgomery toured the line before confirming the perimeter. Work on it started the following day. The River Stour was deepened, and concrete and other anti-tank obstacles were built along three miles of the line. Pipes were inserted at a thirty-degree angle along 1¼ miles of the perimeter; each was filled with explosive and connected to its neighbour so that the pressing of one button could blow a tank-ditch at short notice. The first military and civil conference was held by the commander of 168th Brigade in the council chamber in the High Street five days later. Most of these defensive measures were completed by the end of July. The defences also included fifty road-blocks round the town, five rail-blocks, thirty-two machine-gun positions and anti-tank positions. Gun-emplacements and arrangements for billeting went on until September. There were thirteen hundred regular troops and seven hundred Home Guard in Ashford and, although business went on in the town as near normal as possible, exercises were held regularly until May 1942, by which time the risk of invasion was almost negligible.

Not a minute could be wasted once an attack on Ashford was imminent. When the call to action stations went out, members of the Home Guard were to collect their uniforms, arms, equipment and ration-cards from their homes and go straight to their positions—they were not even allowed to change clothes at home because of the time it would take. Mine-fields were to be laid, and all gaps and road-blocks in the defensive perimeter were to be closed. All petrol-pumps were to be sealed or destroyed, and petrol-tankers, road or rail, overturned and punctured.

The flow of food into the fortress town was to be stopped as soon as there was a threat to the town, and all those inside were to receive food from a pool under the control of the Garrison Commander, whose headquarters was at the vicarage in Vicarage Lane. Water was to be stored in an emergency—a maximum of two gallons a man to last seven days (this was the minimum amount for drinking and cooking, and it made no allowance for washing). In the event of an invasion it was hoped to evacuate all non-essential civilians under the compulsory evacuation scheme mentioned in detail in the section on evacuees. Under this scheme, all but an essential 6,500 of the 215,000 people in the coastal belt of Kent would have been moved out. But this evacuation would have come to a halt once the fortress town had sealed its perimeter— the people inside would have had to 'stay put', and they would have been prevented by force from fleeing the town if necessary.

The chief constable of Maidstone at the time was Mr Henry Vann. He wrote in a 52-page manual for the defence of his town that thousands of people were expected to try to desert their homes and head for the country-side in the event of an invasion; so he told his men that they must be ready to use force to prevent this. He said: "Unless an ordered evacuation is effected some time before invasion is imminent, and this is very unlikely, there will be no evacuation of the civil population. It is of paramount importance that when a crisis arises the public must remain where they are and any attempt at panic evacuation must be stopped, if necessary by force, regrettable though this course may be." Maidstone, like Ashford and all the fortress towns, had an outer perimeter and an inner circle which would have been the last line of defence. This latter area in the town—which contained the Town Hall—was bounded by the High Street, Mill Street and Palace Avenue.

The line of the outer perimeter at Canterbury was drawn from Barton Mill to the Pilgrims' Way, on to the East railway station and Westgate gardens before continuing the circle to join again at Barton Mill. This line was fortified strongly with tank-traps. The city, like all other anti-tank islands, was divided into sectors; its headquarters was in Hawkes Lane, and the nine sectors included some well-known places such as the Cavalry Barracks, West-gate Gardens and St Martin's Priory. The inner perimeter contained all the city within the city wall; within this last line of defence there were two sectors, one based in Marlowe Avenue and the other in the Mint Yard at King's School. The crypt at the cathedral and the Simon Langton Schools were to be used as hospitals. Both the inner and the outer lines were to be manned by the Home Guard, with additions of regular troops; there were also seven liaison officers from the Civil Defence to co-ordinate the services. There were exact instructions about which buildings were to be demolished on the edge of these perimeters; and people from a 500-yard belt adjoining the outer perimeter would have been evacuated and billeted in the city centre.

The risk of invasion lessened as the war developed. In October 1944 the government decided that it was time to disband the work of the Triumvirates and the Invasion Committees. The Allied forces were pressing on towards Germany—and the fortress towns were never needed. But these nodal points were, of course, only part of the defences which Kent had to protect itself from an enemy invasion.

The most crude of these were probably the makeshift barriers erected across all main roads by the Home Guard in 1940, with the help of the military. These included tree trunks from the saw-mills at Chilham; a plough and steam-tractors at Farningham Hill; a plough, water-tank, boiler, carts and overturned car at Westenhanger, and tar-barrels from the distillery at Tonbridge. It was hoped at Margate to check the German advance by using bathing-machines filled with sand. Many of these lighter barricades eventually gave way to concrete anti-tank blocks. These were laid so quickly at Maidstone that those doing the job forgot to leave room for normal traffic to cross the bridge—a mistake which was soon rectified.

Another form of defence was the Ironside line, built quickly between June and August 1940 in case of invasion after Dunkirk. It was one of five lines of pillboxes, gun-emplacements and anti-tank obstacles built across the more vulnerable areas of England. Most of the Kent remnants of this line can be found in Maidstone, Tonbridge, Tunbridge Wells and Sevenoaks areas. It was named after General Sir Edmund Ironside, who planned to use the Rivers Medway and Eden in the line as anti-tank ditches. The line was manned in places by the then LDV, but it was never much used because General Alanbrooke, who succeeded Ironside, discontinued the building of fixed defences in September 1940 and adopted a system using mobile groups of mechanized infantry.

The Thames, a clearly visible highway for planes to follow to London, created a gaping hole in the defences with its wide-open estuary, so the Admiralty got Mr Guy Maunsell, a civil engineer, to design offshore forts which would close this gap. Seven were eventually built at Northfleet, on a site next to Bowater's paper-mill, and towed into position in 1941/42. The three manned by the Army were in the shallower water off Sheppey at Nore, Red Sands and Shivering Sands. Each of these forts consisted of seven towers 90 feet high, six of them circling the seventh and linked by catwalks. One of those in the circle had a searchlight, while the others had guns. The other four forts, manned by Naval and Marine personnel, were sited at Tongue Sands, Roughs, Knock John and Sunk Head. Each of them consisted of a four-deck steel platform resting on two concrete towers 60 feet high and 24 feet in diameter. They were equipped with guns, radar and searchlights.

The lower estuary was also closed by boom-defences consisting of two massive concrete fences which jutted from each bank to leave a 'gate' in the centre of the river which was the only entrance and exit for ships on the Thames. About three thousand convoys passed through this gate before the boom was dismantled.

Part of the coastal defences included twenty-seven guns of various sizes round Dover. One of the most famous of these—a 14-inch gun with a range of about 27 miles—was installed above St Margaret's Bay and fired its first aggressive round on 22nd August 1940. This gun was soon nicknamed 'Winnie', after the Prime Minister. Its 14-inch partner, 'Pooh', was installed nearby in February 1941. They were joined by three 13·5-inch railway-mounted guns called 'Scene-Shifter', 'Peace-Maker' and 'Gladiator'. The fourth railway mounting, called 'Boche-Buster', and travelling on the Elham Valley line, had been altered to fire 18-inch shells, each weighing 1¼ tons and standing 6 feet 7 inches high. It first fired on 13th February 1941. It was

Europe's biggest railway gun; the barrel itself weighed 90 tons and the whole gun and wagon 250 tons. Its range was only 22,300 yards, so it was retained for counter-invasion purposes. 'Winnie' wore out its barrel after it had fired only fifty rounds, and, because so few barrels were allotted for these big guns, they were used less and less. Two 15-inch guns were installed near St Margaret's-at-Cliffe and were ready by the end of May 1942. About twenty-six ships had been sunk by the Dover guns by the end of 1944. The four 14-inch and 15-inch guns, known as 'the Big Four', opened fire on the German batteries across the Channel on 17th September 1944 in the first cross-Channel battery duel in the history of artillery. This battle was in support of a land operation carried out by the 2nd Canadian Corps against German positions in the Pas de Calais.

3. Home Guard and Civil Defence

When the German invasion of the Low Countries began on 10th May 1940, it looked like the first step in a course which would lead to the invasion of Britain. So four days later, on Tuesday 14th May, the new Secretary of State for war, Anthony Eden, broadcast a radio appeal for men to join a new force of Local Defence Volunteers. Men at Gillingham and Cranbrook were signing on while he was talking, and eager volunteers at Folkestone were still queueing to sign on at midnight. Boys at King's School in Canterbury put their names down for this force, and one of the first to enlist at Ashford was Mr Edward Albery, the prospective Labour candidate for the town. About 250,000 men had enrolled nationally within twenty-four hours, and this number had risen to more than a million by mid-July.

The official age limit was seventeen to sixty-five, but the ages of recruits varied in fact from fifteen-years-old to those in their eighties; one man at Canterbury, who was eighty-five gave his age as sixty-five in order to join. Churchill referred to the LDV in a speech on 23rd July as 'the Home Guard'; the name was adopted officially shortly afterwards.

The spirit of improvisation in those early days can be illustrated by taking a look at what happened in Maidstone. Brigadier-General H. Franklin, who had been appointed zone commander for Kent, contacted Colonel W. Baker on 15th May to ask him to help form a local group of volunteers. Two hundred rifles arrived for him the following morning; Colonel Baker had nowhere to put them, so half were stored at Maidstone police station and the other half sent to Leeds Castle. Eight men volunteers turned up at the police station at 5.30pm on 17th May to form the first patrol of Maidstone LDV. They collected their rifles and ammunition and set out on patrol each with a white handkerchief tied round his arm as the only sign of their official standing. A second patrol of employees and neighbours had meanwhile been formed by Sir Adrian Baillie MP at Leeds Castle. By 10.30pm on 17th May more than a thousand LDV members were on duty in the Kent coastal and nearby areas. They and their colleagues had become known at this time as 'Parashots', because their main duty was expected to be tackling invading enemy parachutists. Proper weapons were scarce in those early days. The volunteers on patrol in Kent during the second half of May, for example, had about one rifle between ten men—which meant that they were far better equipped than volunteers in other parts of the country.

By Sunday 26th May there were up to four hundred volunteers in this Maidstone people's army. Patrols of twenty men were sent out with five rifles and twenty rounds of ammunition between them—and little training for their job. The force had grown to be a thousand-strong by the end of June, but it was still poorly equipped and without uniforms. Its members received no pay and, at first, no money to cover expenses. The only 'uniform' issued at first was an armband with the letters 'LDV' on it. But uniforms of denim overalls arrived for the men at Maidstone on 8th July; eight hundred applied for the four hundred which had been delivered. The volunteers in the town had no headquarters at first, so the men patrolled their areas continuously from 9.30pm to 5am the following day. Their first HQ was set up when they were loaned a hall in June.

The Home Guard units, as they were known by this time, were formally affiliated to their county regiments on 3rd August 1940 and allowed to wear their badges.

Home Guard service became compulsory on 17th February 1942, and anyone who failed to attend for up to forty-eight hours of training a month faced prosecution in the civil courts, where a month in jail or a sizeable fine might be imposed. By the summer of 1943 the Home Guard nationally consisted of 1,750,000 members in eleven hundred battalions. Many Great War veterans and middle-aged businessmen made up the bulk of the original LDV, but by 1943 many youngsters in their teens had brought the average age of members down to under thirty—only seven per cent were ex-servicemen.

When the Home Guard was stood down in 1944, it had become well-armed, well-disciplined and capable of taking over all sorts of duties which left the professional soldiers free to get on with the business of fighting. More than three thousand officers and members of the Kent HG attended the official stand-down service at Canterbury Cathedral on Sunday 15th October. The county Guard by this time consisted of sixty thousand men from fifty-two battalions, three transport columns and two AA batteries.

The Civil Defence set-up consisted of a wardens' service, report and control-centre service, rescue service, casualty and decontamination service. Each local authority maintained its own Civil Defence force, and most authorities in Kent were part of the South-Eastern CD Region, which had its headquarters in Tunbridge Wells and which also covered that part of Surrey outside the London region, East and West Sussex, and the county boroughs of Canterbury, Brighton, Eastbourne and Hastings. The local authorities in Kent closest to London became part of the London Civil Defence Region and formed a separate group, called 'Group 8' which consisted of the then Kent boroughs of Beckenham, Bexley, Bromley and Erith, and the urban districts of Chislehurst and Sidcup, Crayford, Orpington and Penge.

In March 1939 the government considered that there were certain areas round Naval and home ports where special arrangements for the control of Civil Defence would be necessary. The military authorities gave permission in September 1939 for county divisional offices and a control centre to be set up in Fort Amherst, part of the defences built on high ground overlooking the Medway to repel an anticipated Napoleonic invasion. Local authorities in this area were told on 3rd November 1939 that they would combine in the new Medway Group to make the best possible use of the naval and military units in the area as well as air-raid precautions services of the county districts. The group consisted at this time of Dartford borough and rural district, Swanscombe, Northfleet, Gravesend, Strood rural district, Chatham, Gillingham, Sittingbourne and Milton, Faversham and Swale rural district, Sheerness, Queenborough and the Sheppey rural district. This group was under the control of the Commander-in-Chief of The Nore for operational purposes, although the county council was responsible for all administration through its Civil Defence committee. This 'Naval co-ordinated area' was later reduced in size to cover only the Medway Towns, part of Strood rural district and the Island of Sheppey; the rest of the Medway Group reverted to the control of the county headquarters.

The county produced a national first in 1940 when it brought about the birth of the country's first mobile reserve—a sort of flying-squad of helpers which could be sent in quickly to a bombed area. It was proposed in May that year that the Mobile Reserve should consist ultimately of three companies of about two hundred people each; each company would consist of a number of first-aid parties, ambulance and combined rescue and decontamination squads. This reserve actually totalled 420 men at the end.

The stand-down parade and service of the Civil Defence in Kent was held in Maidstone on Sunday 3rd June 1945. The parade of eleven hundred representatives from every local authority in the county—representing 25,000 CD workers—assembled at Maidstone Barracks and marched to All Saints' Church. The service was held with Canon A. Standen officiating. Lord Cornwallis, the Lord Lieutenant of Kent, and Sir Garrard Tyrwhitt Drake, then Mayor of Maidstone, were both present. The parade marched past the saluting-base at County Hall after the service; the salute was taken by Lord Cornwallis, accompanied by the Civil Defence Inspector General, Wing Commander Sir John Hodsoll, and the County Controller.

Lord Cornwallis said: "Let it be your proudest memory that you were fully trained, always ready, and never failed to meet or deal with those emergencies."

4. Kent War Figures

Local Authority (as WWII)	Civilian only			Property Wrecked	Property Severely Damaged	Property Slightly Damaged	HE Bombs	Incendiary Bombs (Approx.)	Flying
	Killed	Seriously Injured	Slightly Injured						
Ashford area	103	162	245	184	393	11,357	974	12,645	
Bridge-Blean	29	35	84	81	151	1,705	1,364	18,300	
Broadstairs	7	6	48	18	163	3,916	278	300	
Canterbury	115	140	240	808	1,047	5,691	445	10,000	
Chatham	47	47	225	297	454	4,024	267	1,535	
Dartford MB	92	72	205	174	357	9,741	553	11,982	
Dartford RD	50	80	280	120	894	9,154	5,359	200,000	
Deal	64	55	198	172	718	3,216	173	118	
Dover MB	199	307	420	910	2,998	7,135	464	1,500	
Dover RD	5	10	8	36	141	1,942	389	2,380	
Eastry RD	20	32	57	27	65	1,421	667	1,700	
Elham RD	15	15	57	27	203	3,043	930	6,500	
Faversham	17	26	60	12	29	2,075	442	1,283	
Folkestone	85	181	484	290	1,486	10,499	378	1,113	
Gillingham	57	68	184	168	359	5,200	275	3,885	
Gravesend	38	81	202	45	212	7,799	292	300,000	
Herne Bay	9	21	39	12	45	1,023	104	1,090	
Hollingbourne	10	20	38	11	170	1,536	946	1,720	
Hythe	24	36	106	96	385	1,939	79	Nil	
Maidstone MB	60	105	182	127	210	6,384	264	1,000	
Maidstone RD	9	16	59	22	198	1,624	689	7,000	
Malling RD	46	62	164	36	287	3,664	1,979	11,332	
Margate	35	40	201	268	592	11,487	584	2,489	
New Romney area	12	32	52	61	218	2,047	718	3,823	
Northfleet	40	47	39	35	104	2,849	362	11,000	
Queenborough	Nil	Nil	5	Nil	1	124	52	1,000	
Ramsgate	84	89	139	393	418	8,100	860	283	
Rochester	75	86	360	276	1,221	8,614	238	14	
Sandwich	Nil	2	8	7	107	661	52	1,000	
Sevenoaks UD	22	59	111	42	133	4,480	98	4,000	
Sevenoaks RD	62	70	188	86	169	4,694	3,259	53,500	
Sheppey RD	8	13	8	12	39	791	633	680	
Sheerness	2	Nil	18	8	4	1,230	23	150	
Sittingbourne	31	47	109	64	153	4,875	828	17,000	
Southborough	Nil	1	18	Nil	45	2,169	23	15	
Strood RD	8	32	74	29	162	1,059	1,983	22,987	
Swanscombe	62	105	141	93	367	3,308	211	5,000	
Tenterden area	21	64	151	34	235	4,432	704	3,500	
Tonbridge UD	9	27	101	17	232	3,402	142	1,200	
Tonbridge RD	11	45	30	14	157	2,824	673	3,400	
Tunbridge Wells	15	31	36	13	113	5,488	186	660	
Whitstable	10	35	118	84	735	4,545	232	700	
Total	1,608	2,402	5,492	5,209	16,170	181,267	29,272	727,784	1,

All the Swale Rural District statistics, with the exception of casualty figures, are divided in
above list as follows: those for East Swale are given under Faversham and those for West Sw
under Sittingbourne. All the Swale casualties—which were ten killed, seventeen seriously inju
and thirty slightly hurt—are included in the Faversham total.

5. Hell's Corner

Kent earned the nickname Hell's Corner during the war because of the heavy bombardment it suffered as the result of enemy action, especially during the Battle of Britain. So many people were killed or injured in Kent alone from 1940–45 that the civilian casualties for the county represent one-seventh of the entire civilian casualty total for the United Kingdom.

The civilian casualties during the war in Kent (including the then City and County of Canterbury and that part of Kent in the London region) were 2,974 killed, 6,072 seriously injured and 11,868 slightly hurt—a total of 20,914. The total UK casualty figures were 60,595 killed and 86,182 injured—a total of 146,777.

We can see how heavily Kent suffered if we compare its figures to those from neighbouring counties. The figures available to us here are only for the number of people killed and seriously injured, however, which in Kent's case was a total of 9,046. This is the number to bear in mind for the following comparisons.

Surrey escaped relatively lightly with only 332 deaths and 581 injuries (a total of 913); Essex suffered 855 deaths and 1,767 injuries (a total of 2,622); while 1,008 people were killed in Sussex and 1,783 people injured (a total of 2,791). When the figures from all three counties are added together they are still 2,720 behind the casualty total for Kent.

The counties of Lancashire (which contained Manchester and Liverpool) and Warwickshire (containing Birmingham and Coventry) might have been expected to suffer badly because of these large centres of industry and population. In fact, their casualty totals are little higher than that for Kent. And those for Yorkshire (containing Sheffield) and Hampshire (containing Portsmouth) are even lower than Kent's.

Lancashire suffered 4,800 deaths and 4,615 injuries (a total of 9,415); Warwickshire suffered 3,881 deaths and 5,189 injuries (a total of 9,070); Hampshire suffered 2,176 deaths and 2,638 injuries (a total of 4,814); while 2,358 people were killed in Yorkshire and 2,328 injured (a total of 4,686).

These figures would suggest that these counties suffered a battering comparable to that of Kent. But it is worth examining the totals a little more closely. For instance, 3,881 people were killed in Warwickshire during the war. However, 2,241 of these were killed in Birmingham alone and a further 554 died in just one night in November 1940 in the serious raid on Coventry. Again, 2,176 people were killed in Hampshire but 930 of these died in Portsmouth only. Both lots of figures suggest that although certain individual towns and cities in other counties suffered badly no other county received such a general overall battering as Kent. The highest single death total from a bombing raid in Kent was 50 at Ashford in 1943. The fact that this is a small fraction of the total death toll in the county indicates how numerous and widespread the other raids on the county must have been.

Kent was split into two parts during the war for Civil Defence purposes. The Kent boroughs of Beckenham, Bexley, Bromley and Erith, and the urban districts of Chislehurst and Sidcup, Crayford, Orpington and Penge formed part of the London Civil Defence Region (all eight local authorities becoming part of Greater London in 1965). The casualty figures for this area alone during the war were 1,366 killed, 3,670 seriously injured and 6,376 slightly hurt (a total of 11,412).

The rest of the county (what is now present-day Kent) formed part of the South East Civil Defence Region. The casualty figures for this area were 1,608 killed, 2,402 seriously injured and 5,492 slightly hurt (a total of 9,502).

Of the total 146,777 total UK casualties: 51,509 were killed and 61,423 seriously injured by conventional bombing; 6,184 killed and 17,981 seriously injured by flying bombs; 2,754 killed and 6,523 seriously injured by V2 rockets; and 148 killed and 255 seriously injured by shelling. Of these casualties, 80,397 (including nine-tenths of the flying bomb total) occurred in the London Civil Defence region and 66,380 in other parts of the country. These figures show, to no-one's surprise, that London fared worse than anywhere else in the country.

(I am indebted to the Imperial War Museum and the Public Records Office for much of the above information).

6. Casualty Figures

This list consists of all known civilian fatal incidents in Kent during the war. Almost all these casualty figures are taken from the Civil Defence War Diaries held by the County Archives at Maidstone. Anyone who adds up the fatal casualties for a particular area may sometimes find a discrepancy between that total and the number listed in the general Kent War Figures given earlier. There were 103 deaths in the Ashford area, for example, and ninety-eight of these are accounted for in the list which follows. The difference in this case, and others, is invariably because some of the casualties listed as seriously injured later died of their injuries after the War Diary entry was made. These later deaths have been taken into account where known. Three figures are given for each incident, each separated by a stroke: the fatal casualties are given on the left; those seriously injured in the centre, and those slightly hurt on the right. So in the Gillingham incident of 18th July 1940, for example, the figure of 5/4/22 shows that five people were killed, four seriously injured and twenty-two slightly hurt. The initial in brackets after each incident shows the type of enemy action responsible: B means Bombing (including incendiary bombs and parachute mines); S means cross-Channel Shelling; PC means a Plane Crash, usually where a damaged aircraft crashed into buildings; MG means Machine Gun bullets from an aircraft; AAS means Anti-Aircraft Shell; FB means Flying Bomb; and R means V2 Rocket.

1940

July:

3rd Bekesbourne 1/2/1 (B)
17th Ashford 3/1/10 (B)
18th Gillingham 5/4/22 (B)
19th Oare 1/0/2 (B)

August:

10th Malling 1/15/0 (B)
12th Ramsgate 1/2/3 (B)
12th Sarre 2/1/9 (B)
12th Worth 1/0/0 (B)

12th Dover 2/3/9 (S)
12th Bekesbourne 6/1/1 (B)
13th Whitstable 2/3/7 (B)
13th Sheppey 2/0/2 (B)
16th Northfleet 29/18/9 (B)
18th Sevenoaks 3/0/6 (B)
18th Kemsley 1/4/1 (B)
21st Canterbury 5/1/5 (B)
22nd Dover 2/4/7 (S)
24th Ramsgate 31/11/47 (B)
24th New Romney 2/1/0 (B)
24th Dover 1/2/0 (S)

25th Dover 3/0/2 (PC)
26th Folkestone 3/3/19 (B)
27th Gillingham 20/22/18 (B)
28th Tenterden 2/0/0 (B)
30th Lympne 5/0/0 (B)
31st Whitstable 1/1/3 (B)
31st Hollingbourne 1/1/1 (B)
31st Deal 2/1/2 (B)
31st Sheppey 1/0/2 (B)

September:
1st Gravesend 2/0/0 (B)
1st Elham 1/0/0 (PC)
2nd Maidstone 2/8/5 (B)
2nd Eastchurch 2/0/1 (B)
4th Bapchild 2/0/3 (B)
6th Dartford 24/0/15 (B)
6th Hollingbourne 1/0/0 Shrapnel
7th Elham 6/0/0 (B)
8th Dartford RD 4/0/0 (B)
8th Malling 1/0/0 (B)
8th Dover 1/0/0 (B)
9th Dover 4/3/2 (S)
9th Canterbury 9/6/7 (B)
10th Whitstable 3/0/11 (B)
10th Sevenoaks 4/0/2 (B)
11th Tunbridge Wells 2/0/2 (B)
11th Dover 7/13/36 (B&S)
12th Tunbridge Wells 12/2/14 (B)
13th Maidstone 4/7/0 (B)
14th Swanscombe 5/0/0 (B)
15th Bilsington 1/1/1 (PC)
16th Ashford 2/9/0 (B)
18th Gillingham 5/22/31 (B)
18th Rochester 3/2/3 (B)
18th Maidstone 1/0/2 (B)
22nd Dartford 1/5/0 (B)
25th Bridge-Blean 1/3/2 (B)
26th Dover 2/4/13 (S)
26th Ashford 7/0/2 (B)
27th Maidstone 22/44/45 (B)
29th Sittingbourne 8/0/5 (B)
29th Dartford 4/0/1 (B)
30th Maidstone 1/2/8 (B)
30th Dover 1/4/7 (S)

October:
2nd Sittingbourne 7/0/0 (B)
3rd Bridge-Blean 1/0/0 (B)

4th Hythe 3/0/22 (B)
4th Deal 8/4/1 (B)
4th East Swale 4/7/5 (B)
5th Lydd 2/5/9 (B)
5th Ash (Dartford) 1/6/0 (B)
5th Gillingham 2/0/1 (B)
5th Chatham 8/3/20 (B)
5th Herne Bay 1/5/3 (B)
5th Folkestone 4/0/1 (B)
6th Northfleet 3/3/0 (B)
6th Folkestone 9/7/22 (B)
6th Deal 1/0/1 (B)
8th Stone 4/0/1 (B)
8th Medway 2/0/1 (B)
8th Hythe 1/3/3 (B)
8th Dover 2/6/1 (B)
8th Beltring 6/11/0 (B)
10th Maidstone 9/1/1 (PC)
11th Faversham 1/2/9 (B)
11th Folkestone 1/5/5 (B)
11th Canterbury 9/2/6 (B)
12th St Michaels 2/2/2 (B)
12th Headcorn 4/1/3 (B)
14th Canterbury 2/1/25 (B)
15th Sittingbourne 1/2/4 (B)
15th Wrotham Heath 9/6/2 (B)
15th Deal 1/3/3 (B)
16th Penshurst 1/0/1 (B)
17th Hildenborough 1/1/1 (B)
17th Sevenoaks 1/0/9 (B)
17th Rochester 7/2/8 (B)
18th Dover 1/1/1 (S)
18th Dartford 1/0/1 (B)
18th Tunbridge Wells 1/0/1 (B)
19th Margate 3/0/2 (B)
20th Whitstable 1/1/2 (B)
20th Dover 3/3/0 (S)
21st Tonbridge 1/0/2 (PC)
22nd New Romney 3/0/0 (B)
22nd Hythe 1/1/0 (B)
22nd Deal 1/3/10 (B)
23rd Chalk 2/1/3 (B)
24th Langdon 2/1/0 (B)
25th Maidstone 7/8/0 (B)
25th Dover 2/5/3 (S)
26th Allhallows 3/1/4 (B)
26th Folkestone 1/3/1 (B)
27th Penshurst 6/1/4 (B)
29th East Peckham 1/0/1 (B)

30th Kilndown 1/1/0 (B)
31st Sandhurst Cross 1/1/0 (B)
31st Maidstone 3/14/19 (B)

November:
1st Hadlow 2/0/0 (B)
1st Riverhead 2/1/1 (B)
1st Gillingham 1/0/0 (B)
1st Dover 1/0/2 (S)
2nd Ramsgate 8/5/18 (B)
2nd Deal 1/0/5 (B)
5th Swanscombe 1/3/12 (B)
5th Sittingbourne 5/4/5 (B)
6th Gravesend 1/0/4 (B)
8th Sevenoaks 1/1/0 (B)
8th Chatham 1/0/3 (B)
9th Kingsdown 1/2/3 (B)
10th Swanscombe 27/6/5 (B)
10th Farningham 4/0/0 (B)
10th Gravesend 1/0/5 (B)
11th Strood 2/3/0 (B)
11th Malling 8/3/0 (B)
11th St Margaret's Bay 1/0/3 (B)
11th Ramsgate 1/0/8 (B)
12th Dartford 5/6/0 (B)
13th Folkestone 1/1/1 (B)
13th Dover 6/12/12 (B)
14th Margate 1/5/13 (B)
14th Dover 1/1/1 (B)
16th Gillingham 3/4/15 (B)
16th Margate 2/0/3 (B)
17th Goudhurst 1/0/4 (B)
18th Folkestone 14/14/46 (B)
21st Buckland 2/0/0 (PC)
23rd Nonington 3/7/3 (B)

December:
3rd Chatham 7/0/42 (B)
5th Sittingbourne 4/1/3 (B)
8th Chevening 1/2/0 (B)
8th Northfleet 3/0/3 (B)
9th Kemsing 1/0/3 (B)
9th Stone 9/0/0 (B)
9th Gravesend 1/0/1 (B)
12th Sheppey 1/1/2 (B)
12th Ashford 2/5/8 (B)
14th Chatham 15/20/103 (B)

1941
January:
4th Ramsgate 4/13/9 (B)
7th Folkestone 1/0/1 (B)
10th Chatham 3/6/0 (B)
11th Ramsgate 2/0/0 (B)
12th Dartford 2/6/0 (B)
12th Stone 1/4/0 (B)
12th Gravesend 1/3/0 (B)

February:
3rd Ramsgate 3/0/4 (B)
4th Marden 5/3/4 (B)
21st Gillingham 1/0/0 (B)

March:
3rd Ramsgate 3/0/2 (B)
9th Northfleet 1/0/0 (AAS)
10th Sheerness 2/3/3 (AAS&B)
11th Crockenhill 5/2/5 (B)
11th Longfield 1/0/0 (B)
15th Gravesend 2/2/3 (B)
19th Meopham 1/6/1 (B)
19th Folkestone 3/7/1 (B)
19th Stone 4/6/17 (B)
19th Sutton at Hone 1/0/1 (B)
20th Ramsgate 3/2/7 (B)
20th Hythe 1/1/2 (MG)
24th Hythe 3/2/0 (B)
31st Dover 1/0/5 (S)

April:
8th Rochester 11/28/66 (B)
9th Ramsgate 2/0/0 (B)
17th Margate 4/2/25 (B)
19th Gillingham 2/0/0 (B)
19th Gravesend 1/2/4 (B)
19th Rochester 4/1/4 (B)
19th Sutton at Hone 4/6/18 (B)
20th Dartford 13/6/15 (B)
20th Hollingbourne 1/2/3 (B)
20th Canterbury 1/0/5 (B)

May:
5th Minster (Sheppey) 2/0/0 (B)
6th Eastry 9/2/3 (B)
7th Dover 3/8/8 (S)
10th Deal 1/1/1 (MG)
11th Gillingham 4/4/10 (B)

11th Upchurch 3/0/0 (PC)
29th Folkestone 13/4/32 (B)

June:
12th Dover 15/20/23 (B)
14th Ramsgate 4/1/11 (B)
14th Sittingbourne 2/7/10 (B)
14th Milton (Sitt) 1/4/11 (B)
14th Snodland 2/1/2 (B)
23rd Aylesford 1/1/1 (B)

July:
8th Margate 3/3/9 (B)
31st Dartford 2/1/0 (PC)

August:
3rd Broadstairs 1/0/19 (B)
16th Broadstairs 5/1/10 (B)

September:
7th Ramsgate 8/5/9 (B)
7th Dover 3/0/2 (B)
8th Margate 3/2/7 (B)
17th Dover 3/6/22 (S)

October:
1st Dover 1/0/0 (B)
2nd Dover 8/13/32 (B)
11th Whitstable 2/6/36 (B)
21st Dover 2/5/0 (B)

November:
1st Dover 1/3/1 (S)
9th Margate 3/1/2 (B)
9th Ramsgate 1/0/5 (B)
18th Sturry 15/11/0 (B)

December:
23rd Herne Bay 1/6/8 (B)

1942
March:
23rd Dover 16/6/5 (B)

April:
3rd Dover 16/18/4 (B)
24th Folkestone 1/15/14 (B)

May:
5th Folkestone 1/9/10 (B)
6th Deal 7/3/7 (B)
8th Deal 3/10/15 (B)
10th St Mary's Bay 1/0/0 (B)
10th Hythe 2/2/10 (B)
17th Folkestone 3/1/1 (B)
18th Deal 2/0/2 (B)

June:
1st Canterbury 43/40/41 (B)
3rd Canterbury 5/5/18 (B)
7th Canterbury 1/0/2 (B)

August:
11th Deal 8/6/55 (B)
15th Folkestone 1/0/5 (B)
21st Hythe 3/10/28 (B)

September:
1st Lydd 2/3/0 (B)
5th Dover 2/5/12 (B)
29th Betteshanger 2/1/22 (B)

October:
5th Dover 4/8/6 (S)
22nd Deal 15/7/15 (B)
24th Cliffe 1/0/0 (PC)
26th Ashford 11/0/16 (B&MG)
31st Herne Bay 2/1/4 (B)
31st Sturry 1/5/0 (B)
31st Barham 1/1/1 (MG)
31st Canterbury 33/54/56 (B)

November:
5th Deal 3/1/6 (B)
9th Folkestone 2/3/12 (S)
27th Ashford 1/2/2 (MG)

December:
10th Folkestone 1/5/4 (S)
10th Dover 1/2/1 (S)
16th Tonbridge 3/13/21 (B)
22nd Ashford 2/2/1

1943
January:
18th Margate 2/0/0 (B)
26th Ramsgate 2/3/1 (B)

26th Broadstairs 1/0/2 (B)
30th Margate 4/3/11 (B)

February:
3rd Ashford 6/11/15 (B)

March:
4th Chatham 5/1/5 (B)
4th Gravesend 1/12/11 (B)
24th Ashford 50/77/79 (B)

April:
5th Folkestone 2/0/4 (S)
9th Folkestone 3/7/13 (B)

May:
9th Dover 1/0/1 (S)
22nd Dover 4/1/11 (B)

June:
1st Margate 10/4/46 (B)
27th Dover 1/7/3 (S)
28th Ramsgate 1/1/0 (S)
29th Dover 4/3/4 (S)

July:
4th Strood RD 1/7/2 (PC)
5th Ramsgate 2/3/0 (S)

August:
16th Ramsgate 1/2/3 (B)
24th Dover 1/2/0 (S)

September:
25th Folkestone 2/2/3 (S)

October:
4th Ramsgate 3/4/10 (S)
7th Greenhithe 1/0/1 (B)
18th Northfleet 3/6/12 (B)
22nd Hoo 1/0/1 (B)
25th Dover 6/8/1 (S)

November:
2nd Gravesend 1/4/10 (B)
3rd Ramsgate 2/1/0 (S)
18th Sevenoaks 1/6/9 (B)

December:
21st Northfleet 1/7/4 (B)

1944
January:
20th Deal 12/7/13 (S)
21st Dartford 13/13/1 (B)
22nd Crockham Hill 3/6/1 (B)
22nd Gravesend 1/5/2 (B)
22nd Dover 2/2/6 (B)
29th Sittingbourne 1/1/3 (B)
29th Sevenoaks 1/0/0 (B)
29th Northfleet 1/0/0 (AAS)
29th Gillingham 3/0/19 (B)
29th Swingate 2/11/0 (S)
29th Dartford 2/3/2 (B)

February:
4th Gravesend 8/1/3 (B)
13th Halstead 4/0/2 (B)
19th Strood 3/7/26 (B)
24th Wingham 1/0/1 (AAS)

March:
2nd Strood 18/8/38 (B)
2nd Sutton at Hone 1/1/5 (B)
3rd Maidstone 1/0/1 (B)
14th Hollingbourne 2/3/1 (B)
20th Dover 2/1/1 (S)
22nd Dartford 1/0/1 (B)

April:
19th Strood 4/10/53 (B)

May:
24th Folkestone 2/5/1 (S)

June:
6th Gillingham 4/1/0 (PC)
7th Dover 1/4/3 (S)
13th Maidstone 1/0/0 (S)
17th Benenden 3/1/5 (FB)
17th Ruckinge/Kingsnorth 2/2/3 (FB)
19th Tonbridge 1/2/5 (FB)
19th Benenden 1/5/1 (FB)
24th Smarden 6/0/0 (FB)
30th Westerham 30/9/1 (FB)

July:
3rd Folkestone 3/8/47 (FB)
4th East Peckham 1/0/0 Shrapnel
6th Maidstone 1/0/1 (MG)
7th Ruckinge 1/2/0 (FB)
9th Higham 1/1/9 (FB)
9th Dartford 7/0/6 (FB)
11th Biddenden 1/1/0 (FB)
12th Benenden 1/1/0 (FB)
15th Bredgar 2/0/2 (FB)
19th Rolvenden 2/1/2 (FB)
20th Offham 1/0/0 (FB)
27th Capel 1/1/2 (FB)
28th Brabourne 1/3/1 (FB)
30th Swanscombe 13/22/69 (FB)

August:
3rd Maidstone 5/7/40 (FB)
4th Horsmonden 1/0/1 (MG)
4th Littlebourne 1/3/25 (FB)
5th Snodland 12/15/16 (FB)
6th Tunbridge Wells 1/0/8 (FB)
6th Dartford 10/12/95 (FB)
7th Swanscombe 2/18/29 (FB)
7th Boughton Monchelsea 1/0/3 (FB)
8th Benenden 1/13/20 (FB)
9th Ightam 2/7/14 (FB)
10th Hythe 1/0/8 (FB)
15th Dymchurch 1/3/1 (FB)
15th Hythe 5/5/12 (FB)
16th Appledore 1/0/0 (MG)
16th Newington 4/24/26 (FB)
16th Strood 4/1/21 (FB)
29th Otford 2/1/0 (FB)
29th Dover 1/3/3 (S)
29th Smarden 4/2/2 (FB)

September:
1st Ramsgate 2/2/17 (S)
1st Dover 8/8/2 (S)

3rd Dover 1/4/2 (S)
5th Dover 1/0/0 (S)
10th Folkestone 2/4/8 (S)
11th Dover 1/1/2 (S)
12th Dover 7/7/9 (S)
13th Folkestone 1/9/6 (S)
13th Dover 7/17/12 (S)
14th Folkestone 6/10/25 (S)
15th Hythe 1/1/8 (S)
15th Folkestone 1/2/6 (S)
23rd Folkestone 1/2/4 (S)
23rd Dover 5/10/8 (S)
25th Dover 6/8/9 (S)
26th Dover 4/5/20 (S)

October:
24th Hartlip 2/0/1 (FB)

November:
8th Swanscombe 1/8/22 (FB)
8th Rochester 8/16/30 (FB)
13th Gravesend 5/16/56 (R)
13th Chatham 1/0/0 (Mortar)
29th Gravesend 8/15/37 (R)

1945
January:
15th Whitstable 1/6/45 (R)

February:
18th Rochester 2/4/18 (R)
19th Stoke 1/0/12 (R)
23rd Sevenoaks 1/1/4 (R)
27th Swanscombe 8/27/21 (R)

March:
3rd Sevenoaks 9/13/6 (R)
11th Westerham 1/7/49 (R)
14th Sutton at Hone 10/14/9 (R)
16th Dartford 4/4/23 (FB)

Sources

The Flying Bomb, Richard Anthony Young (Ian Allan Ltd)
Fight for the Sky, Douglas Bader (Fontana)
Battle Over Britain, Francis K. Mason (McWhirter Twins Ltd)
RAF Biggin Hill, Graham Wallace (Putnam)
The Last Ditch, David Lampe (Cassell)
Though the Streets Burn, Catherine Williamson (Headley Bros)
Kent: The County Administration in War, W.L. Platts (KCC)
Fighter, Len Deighton (Cape)
The People's War, Angus Calder (Cape)
War on the Line, Bernard Darwin (Southern Railways)
Instruments of Darkness, A. Price (Kimber)
Operation Sealion, Peter Fleming (Pan)
The Nine Days of Dunkirk, David Divine (Pan)
Kentish Fire, Hubert S. Banner (Hurst and Blackett)
Strike from the Sky, Alexander McKee (New English Library)
Operation Sealion, Richard Cox (Thornton Cox)
How We Lived Then, Norman Longmate (Arrow)
The War Years in Faversham, Herbert Dane (Austin and Sons)
Historic Haven: the story of Sandwich, Dorothy Gardiner (The Pilgrim Press)
Maidstone 1549–1949, Raymond Hewett
Midst Bands and Bombs, A.B.C. Kempe (*Kent Messenger*)
Deal and the Downs in the War of Liberation, E.C. Pain
The Invasion of Europe, Alan A. Michie (Allen and Unwin)
Civil Engineer in War, volumes one and three (Clowes and Son Ltd)
Fighter Squadrons of the RAF, John Rawlings (Macdonald)
Some Were Spies, The Earl Jowitt (Hodder and Stoughton)
After the Battle; number 11 (Battle of Britain Prints Ltd)
The Cavalry Journal; Nov/Dec 1944
The Defence of the UK, B. Collier (HMSO)
Victory in the West, L.F. Ellis (HMSO)
Purnell's History of the Second World War; volumes five and eight
Sturry—The Changing Scene, K.M. McIntosh

Blitz on Britain, Alfred Price (Ian Allan Ltd)
Enemy Coast Ahead, Guy Gibson VC (Michael Joseph Ltd)
Epics of Aviation Archæology, Bruce Robertson (Patrick Stephens)
About the Romney Marsh (M.F. Bird)
The Dam Busters, Paul Brickhill (Pan)
Dunkirk, Robert Jackson (Granada)
D-Day, Warren Tute (Sidgwick and Jackson)
The Home Front, Arthur Marwick (Thames and Hudson)
Keep Smiling Through, Susan Briggs (Fontana)
Anti-Aircraft, Ian V. Hogg (MacDonald and Jane's)
Roof Over Britain (HMSO)
A Handbook on Kent's Defences, D. Bennett (Kent Defence Research Group)
The Struggle for Europe, Chester Wilmot (Collins)
The Secrets of D-Day, Gilles Perrault (Corgi)
Battle Over Kent (Kent Battle of Britain Museum)
The Spirit of Kent; Lord Cornwallis, H. R. Pratt Boorman (*Kent Messenger*)
Military Archæology, Terry Gander (Patrick Stephens)
Public Records Office documents in the WO199 group
The following publications: *Kent Messenger, Kentish Express, Kentish Gazette, Isle of Thanet Gazette, East Kent Mercury, Dover Express, Folkestone Herald, Gravesend and Dartford Reporter, Chatham Observer, Chatham, Rochester and Gillingham News, Tonbridge Free Press, Kent and Sussex Courier, Kent Life* and *The East Kent Gazette*
The Civil Defence War Diaries for Kent in the County Archives

Index